CLAIMS RESERVING
IN NON-LIFE INSURANCE

INSURANCE SERIES
Volume 1

Series Editors:

F. DE VYLDER
Catholic University of Leuven
Leuven, Belgium

M.J. GOOVAERTS
Catholic University of Louvain
Louvain-la-Neuve, Belgium

J. HAEZENDONCK
University of Antwerp
Antwerp, Belgium

NORTH-HOLLAND
AMSTERDAM · NEW YORK · OXFORD

CLAIMS RESERVING IN NON-LIFE INSURANCE

G. C. TAYLOR

E. S. Knight & Co.
Consulting Actuaries
Sydney, Australia

1986

NORTH-HOLLAND
AMSTERDAM · NEW YORK · OXFORD

ISBN: 0 444 87846 7

Publishers:
ELSEVIER SCIENCE PUBLISHERS B.V.
P.O. Box 1991
1000 BZ Amsterdam
The Netherlands

Sole distributors for the U.S.A. and Canada:
ELSEVIER SCIENCE PUBLISHING COMPANY, INC.
52 Vanderbilt Avenue
New York, N.Y. 10017
U.S.A.

Library of Congress Cataloging-in-Publication Data

Taylor, G. C. (Gregory Clive), 1945-
    Claims reserving in non-life insurance.

    (Insurance series ; v. 1)
    Bibliography: p.
    1. Insurance--Reserves.   2. Insurance--Adjustment
of claims.   I. Title.   II. Series.
HG8076.T39 1985   368'.014   85-16238
ISBN 0-444-87846-7 (U.S.)

to Rhonda

— a small repayment towards a very large debt

PREFACE

Despite its date of publication this book was in fact conceived in late 1981. Some of the editors of the journal **Insurance: Mathematics and Economics**, then in its commencement stages, asked me to write a survey article on Claims Reserving. This was thought to be a topical subject, even a hot seller, for the first issue of the new journal.

I agreed to provide this required article, but the date of publication of this book is an indication of the extent to which I let my co-editors down. Little did I realise, in acceding to their request, the exact magnitude of the task on which I was embarking. They, as I, realised that such a survey paper would be rather longer than the typical paper appearing in such a journal. I recall giving a solemn admonition that it might run to 40 or 50 printed pages. Clearly, I was just as surprised as they to find, once the task was commenced, how much needed to be said to provide anything even approaching a complete treatment of the subject. Finally, as is now apparent, the volume of material transcended that appropriate for publication as a paper and hence fills this volume.

Having appealed to volume of material as excusing the protracted period of gestation of this text, I should nevertheless hasten to point to those areas not covered by it. It is to be emphasised that only questions concerned with modelling of claim payment experience, and the implication of such models for projection of this experience, are pursued here. In particular, such issues as:

(i) the legal and financial propirety of discounting reserves for outstanding claims in anticipation of future investment income;

(ii) the legal and financial propriety of including in such reserves a loading for the associated expenses of claims administration;

and various topical subjects of debate are not discussed at all. Also not discussed are the practical considerations involved in the choice of parameters leading from the model of claims experience to the projection of future claim payments, e.g. future rates of claims escalation, investment return and claims administration expenses.

The omission of these subjects is not intended to minimize their practical importance. Indeed, small changes in these areas, made virtually with the stroke of a pen, can wreak devastating effects on an insurer's annual profit. However, despite their importance, these issues can be separated from the theoretical treatment of the modelling problem, and this has been done in order to circumscribe the subject of the book rather more compactly than would otherwise be the case.

Very little prior knowledge is assumed. The book is adressed essentially to those actuaries or statisticians with some interest in the area of determining reserves for outstanding claims for the purpose of placement in a balance sheet (either published or notional). It is assumed, therefore, that the reader has at least an understanding of the nature of such a reserve, and accordingly valuable text has not been spent in defining it and discussing its effect on accounts. It follows then, that the reader probably requires a rudimentary acquaintance with general insurance accounting.

The subject is treated quantitatively, and so some mathematics is required. However, for the great bulk of the analysis, very elementary algebra, calculus and statistics suffice. The major exception to this statement, found in the more sophisticated methodology of Chapters 8 to 10, is the requirement of reasonable facility in matrix manipulation, especially manipulation of quadratic forms associated with second moments of random variables.

As to the scope of material covered in the book, it is intended to include the majority of methodology developed over the last decade or so.

This volume is an attempt to survey methods of analysis of non-life insurance claims data and projection of outstanding claims. The scope of the survey is intended to include the majority of methodology developed over the last decade or so. No pretence is made that only the mathematical detail of the various methods is reported. Opinion on them is freely given.

The book can be divided into three main parts.

The first part, which includes Chapters 1 to 6, discusses the state of the art at present, various generalities of the background to claims reserving, and in particular argues the case for stochastic models.

The second part, which includes Chapters 7 to 10, provides details of the various claims reserving techniques. A uniform format is adopted in dealing with each separate technique. Its discussion is divided into four sections:

 (i) the model;

 (ii) estimation of the model parameters;

(iii) projection of outstanding claims;

(iv) comment.

Apart from (iv) (and occasionally (i)), the discussion here tends to be quantitative and detailed. Some readers may prefer to skip these sections and treat them as a reference.

The third part, consisting of Chapters 11 to 16, reverts to more descriptive and occasionally dialectic material. It deals with a number of matters which, while not specific to any particular method of estimating outstanding claims, nevertheless form part of the backdrop against which decisions as to the estimates of outstandings to be adopted must be made.

At some point in the compilation of this work, I became aware of what might be seen as an "Australian bias". The attentive reader might well detect that the material dealt with in the text, and the references given at the end of it, are weighted in what seems to be an unduly heavy manner towards Australian developments. I am anxious to assure him that this is not a manifestation of any form of jingoism on my part. Indeed, after adequate reflection, I do not consider the "bias" to be anything other than a proper reflection of the developments which have taken place during the past decade or so. It is a fact that the subject of Claims Reserving has been an extremely topical one in Australia during this period. Over the same period Australian insurers have passed through an era of quite straitened circumstances as a result of which they have been hard put to maintain margins of conservatism in their accounts. This, in turn, has rendered the "heavy-handed" actuarial approach to reserving quite impractical, and made the issue of Claims Reserving for these insurers a much more finely poised one. The resulting research effort has been commensurate and is reflected in this volume.

As with most books, it is virtually impossible for the author to acknowledge all his sources properly. The discussion and debate of the methodology set out in this volume has proceeded for some years amongst my colleagues both within Australia and overseas. I have benefited from these discussion which have involved very many individuals. In this respect, I am in the debt of virtually all contributors to the subject of Claims Reserving. And not least to those with whom I most vehemently disagree, for my attempts to refute their arguments have undoubtedly sharpened my appreciation of some of the issues involved.

A few individuals were, however, prominent in their assistance in my compilation of this volume. Firstly, I should record my thanks to F.R. Ashe. Many of the points considered in this survey were also discussed with him. In all cases he was able to add substance to what had already been included.

Although he has not taken part actively in the writing of the survey, he has influenced several parts of it substantially.

I have had many discussions with my business partner, J.R. Cumpston, and have benefited from those. My thanks are due to R.A. Buchanan who proof-read the manuscript and alerted me to many errors.

It always seems to me unnecessary for an author to point out that errors in his work are his own. They obviously are. However, rather than buck convention, I confess to responsibility for the blunders which undoubtedly remain in this text despite all efforts to the contrary.

Sydney

Australia

June 1984.

TABLE OF CONTENTS

1. INTRODUCTION

Assumptions, hasty, crude, and vain,

Full oft to use will Science deign;

The corks the novice plies today

The swimmer soon shall cast away.

A.H. Clough, Poem (1840)

1.1   State of the art

In May 1981 the first monograph (van Eeghen, 1981) on claims analysis of which I am aware appeared. It contained a bibliography consisting of 52 items. The fact that only one of these pre-dated 1970 is indicative of the rapidity with which the subject has grown.

Such growth, while healthy, generates confusion. Even as I write, I have just received a copy of the 1981 Presidential Address (Kimber, 1981) of the Institute of Actuaries of Australia, which states:

> "To many insurance managers, and possibly also to some
> statutory authorities, we are still in a phase of pursu-
> ing a number of different theoretical approaches which can
> produce a variety of answers to the same practical prob-
> lems. While the general insurance industry is crying out
> for some authoritative guidance, actuaries appear to be en-
> gaged in little more than "ivory tower" activities, for ex-
> ample, increasing the number of alternative methods of es-
> timating outstanding claims reserves without deciding on
> which method might be generally accepted."

While this is the most opportune example of these sentiments they are not by any means peculiar to Kimber. The same sentiments have been expressed many times in the last few years in various English and Australian forums.

To some of those engaged in research in this field, the process of development which has been taking place is seen as a gradual pushing forward of the frontiers of understanding; with new methods supplanting, or possibly supplementing, old. To others, and to many of the interested spectators, those who have a need for claims analysis but are not active in its development, the process is a frustrating one. It appears to them that the growth of subject towards adulthood has become directionless and delinquent; that more and more methodology is developed purely for its own sake; that debate on the subject grows ever more esoteric, academic and irrelevant as actuaries pursue nice points of theory while practitioners lose millions of dollars in their business; in short, that actuaries stand fiddling while Rome burns.

One can, of course, understand the howl of anguish vented by an insurance executive who, on consulting an actuary for "the answer" to his claims reserving problem, not only is given a variety of answers but is simultaneously informed that consultation with another "expert" is likely to produce a different variety of answers.

Ignoring the possibility that this situation is born out of pure incompetence, on the part of the insurer for failure to produce accurate information or on the part of the actuary for failure to analyse it properly, one can identify several reasons for its existence. This is done in the next few subsections.

1.2   Claims analysis as a pre-science

As is to be expected of any discipline in its infancy, the majority of models introduced at various stages of its development are rather crude representations of reality. As each shortcoming of such a model is recognised and the appropriate refinement made, what appears to some as an unruly plethora of models is enlarged further. Such a situation is reminiscent of what the scientific philosopher Thomas Kuhn (1970) called a **pre-science**. According to Kuhn's view, as expressed by Chalmers (1976, p.88):

> *"It is the lack of disagreement over fundamentals that dis-*
> *tinguishes mature, normal science from the relatively dis-*
> *organized activity of immature* **pre-science** *. According*
> *to Kuhn, the latter is characterized by total disagreement*
> *and constant debate over fundamentals, so much so that*
> *it is impossible to get down to detailed, esoteric work."*

If this sounds an accurate description of the current state of non-life insurance claims analysis, then the very next part of the same passage is even more apposite. Chalmers continues:

> *"There will be almost as many theories as there are workers*
> *in the field and each theoretician will be obliged to start*
> *afresh and justify his own particular approach."*

Seen from this vantage point, the current state of "confusion" of claims analysis appears as an integral part of the procession from ignorance to understanding, and not as a form of degeneration as seems to be implied above by Kimber.

1.3 The stochastic nature of the claims process

With a few notable exceptions which will be identified later, it is probably fair to say that actuaries have simply not faced up to the stochastic nature of the claims reserving problem. This is probably traceable to the fact that the traditional problems adressed by actuaries (at least those of the English-speaking variety), e.g. life insurance, retirement funding, have been of such a type that stochastic considerations have been either elementary or of rather minor importance.

However that may be, the fact is that the great majority of claims analysis models are really only models of first moments. Second an higher moments are rarely mentioned. The model formulation is often such that, to the uninitiated, it might not be apparent that the problem has stochastic features at all.

Statements such as *"It is pointless to concern oneself with second moments until the problem of first moments has been solved"* are, in my opinion, as uninformed as they are unprofitable. Because, of course, "the problem of first moments" will never be solved except perhaps in the sense of producing estimators of outstanding claims which resemble minimum-variance estimators. In other words, even with data problems, inflation uncertainty and so on set aside, the inherently stochastic nature of the claims process will prevent the actuary from stating the amount of outstanding claims with certainty. All that can be done is to construct an estimate and indicate the margin of uncertainty. Models which provide a truer representation of the actual process will tend to reduce the margin of uncertainty associated with the estimate.

Thus one arrives at the conclusion that it is only in terms of second moments (or some similar distributional characteristics) that "the solution" of the problem of first moments can be adjudged to be indeed the solution. On this reasoning, the statement, *"It is pointless to concern oneself with second moments until the problem of first moments has been solved"*, becomes a logical absurdity.

The common practice of actuaries currently in providing estimates of outstanding claims is to quote:

> (i) a single ("best" or "central") estimate;

> OR (ii) a range, determined in a subjective and undefined manner, in which the amount of outstanding claims is "likely" (but with unspecified probablitity) to lie;

> OR (iii) both (i) and (ii).

If several actuaries choose alternative (i), then of course there is a reasonable chance that in the presentation of their results, their voices will mingle in the cacophony of which Kimber complains (Section 1.1).

If alternative (ii) is chosen, its nebulous nature is likely to render it futile. In particular, what meaning is to be attached to the concept of "likely". Does it mean "with 95% probability"? "With 50% probability"? Or what? There may be a temptation for the actuary to adopt **tacitly** a high probability, thus expanding his likely range to the point where it is too wide to be of practical use. On the other hand, if a low probability is adopted tacitly, with the concomitant narrowing of the likely range, the term "likely" may be misleading to the recipient of estimates.

Alternative (iii) suffers equally from the dubious value of (ii).

Now consider a situation in which several actuaries estimate outstanding claims for the same portfolio and on the basis of the same data. But suppose that, contrary to common practice, each actuary considers total outstanding claims as a random variable and provides:

 (i) an estimate of the mean;

(ii) an estimate of the variance of (i).

In such circumstances the recipient of the advice can:

 (i) form some idea of the significance or otherwise of differences between the several estimates of the mean;

(ii) form an opinion of the quality of the estimates of mean by reference to the associated variances.

Hence the collection of estimates of mean which, in the absence of second moment estimates, might seem inconsistent, may well be seen to be consistent in the light of the second moments.

1.4   The complex nature of the claims process

My final comment on the ideas exemplified by the passage quoted in Section 1.1 is just that the claims processes in the liability classes of business are complex ones. Years of persistent effort by actuaries do not seem to have exhausted the subtleties involved. It is hardly surprising, therefore, that new methods continue to replace old.

Indeed, each actuary involved in the estimation of outstanding claims is under a professional obligation to provide his client with the best quality estimate of which he is capable. It is this obligation, just as much as personal research motivations, which will provide the stimulus for further refinements of claims analysis techniques in the future. And no amount of querulous appeal for unity of actuarial thought nor rhetoric directed against the failure to reach such unity will change this simple fact.

1.5   Taking stock of the situation

Sections 1.2 to 1.4 attempt to explain why the "confusion" endemic in claims analysis (Section 1.1) exists and, to some extent, why its existence is inevitable.

However, as well as understanding the existence of this confusion, it is necessary to form some strategy to alleviate it as far as possible. The best such strategy appears to me to reside in a taxonomy of the various models in use. With these models characterized and classified, the world of claims reserving should at least be transformed from a featureless landscape into one in which the passing traveller can identify those areas which warrant his inspection; and can even note the paths followed by early pioneers, the factors which motivated their navigation, and the yawning crevasses which lay in wait for them.

For this reason this volume will place rather heavy emphasis on taxonomic considerations.

Although Section 1.3 has deprecated nonstochastic models (for a few of which the author is responsible) almost to the point of condemnation, such models will be examined in subsequent sections. The reasons for this are several.

Firstly, this volume, as a survey, must consider the world as it is, and not as it might have been.

Secondly, despite the inadequacies of nonstochastic models, much has been learnt from them over the years. In many cases, most of the properties of a nonstochastic model can be carried over to a parallel stochastic version.

Thirdly, although I feel sure that the hypothetical scenario described in the last paragraph of Section 1.2 is the one towards which actuaries will gravitate, progress is likely to be slow and painful, and in the immediate future a thorough understanding of nonstochastic models and their shortcomings will prove valuable.

2   PROCEDURAL COMPONENTS
OF ESTIMATING OUTSTANDING CLAIMS.

A disciplined approach to claims analysis, in common with all forms of prediction based on mathematical modelling, consists of three quite distinct phases:

  (i) construction of a model;

 (ii) calibration of the model;

(iii) prediction by the model.

The process may be interactive, with repetitions of some or all of the steps. For example, the calibration stage may elicit evidence of specific shortcomings of the model, so that the whole process might be recommenced at step (i). A slightly more elaborate view of mathematical modelling, but one consistent with the above, is presented by McLone (1976).

2.1   Construction of a model

The claims process must be represented by a parametric structure, such as (to use a very crude example):

amount of claims paid in the j-th year following the year of origin

$$=$$

number of claims incurred in the year of origin

$$\times$$

a factor dependent on j but nothing else.

In Kuhn's (1970) therminology, a **paradigm** of the claims process must be hypothesised.

This step is, without doubt, the most difficult and offers greatest scope for ingenuity. Reasonably standard procedures are available at steps (ii) and (iii), but step (i) may require some clever inductive inference.

One must beware of permitting the difficulty of this step to discourage one from considering it in proper depth. For, as a general rule, poor models produce poor estimates – poor estimates possibly in the sense of intolerable bias, and certainly in the sense of large variance relative to that achievable with alternative models.

2.2   Calibration of the model

Whereas Section 2.1 chooses a parametric **structure** to represent the claims process, but with parameters unspecified, step (ii) consists of associating specific values with these parameters. Step (ii) might equally well be called "fitting the model".

If carried out properly, the calibration stage will consist not only of mere estimation of parameter values, but also of some form of check on the quality of fit of model to data. For example, cross-validation, i.e. comparison of one part, C say, of the data set with the values fitted to C by the model calibrated on the basis of only data not included in C (Mosteller and Tukey, 1977). Some examples of checking quality of fit are given by Taylor (1981a, 1982a, 1983) and Zehnwirth (1981).

Diagnostic checking might reveal stochastic irregularities (e.g. Zehnwirth , 1981) and features of the data which do not accord with the model. This might lead to a return to step (i) and refinement of the model adopted (e.g. Taylor, 1983, Section 9).

The extent to which the process of modelling, calibration, prediction, is interactive with the investigator is very much dependent on the vigour with which the quality of model fit is pursued. It is not exaggerating, I think, to say that the absence of this sort of checking from the bulk of actuarial papers on claims analysis has been a major factor contributing to the slowness with which progress has been made.

2.3   Prediction by the model

The expected value, variance, etc. of outstanding claims are functions of the parameters included in the model structure discussed in Section 2.1. Therefore, just as calibration consisted of estimation of the parameters, prediction consists of estimation of the relevant functions of those parameters.

To be more specific, suppose that ω denotes the vector of parameters included in the model. Let $\hat{\omega}$ be the vector of estimates obtained at calibration. Let the function $f(\omega)$ denote the expected value of outstanding claims. It may not be linear in ω. As is well-known as a general statistical proposition, the estimator of $f(\omega)$ with the best properties may not be simply $f(\hat{\omega})$.

Prediction will therefore consist of selection of a function $\hat{f}$ such that $\hat{f}(\hat{\omega})$ provides an estimate of $f(\omega)$ with desirable properties.

Once the function $\hat{f}$ has been selected, prediction becomes merely a matter of plugging in estimated parameter values and reading out the response.

2.4   Maintaining separation of the procedural components

Clarity of thought will be enhanced if the three components in the estimation of outstanding claims are kept strictly separate. Failure to appreciate the distinction between the components will lead to wrong decisions.

For example, Cumpston (1977) criticised the separation method on the ground that:

> "The major defect of the separation method at present was that it used cumulative payment ratios to project outstanding claims."

This statement represents a failure to distinguish between the stages of calibration and prediction — a failure probably induced by a similar failure on the part of the authors of the paper (Taylor and Matthews, 1977) on which Cumpston was commenting. For whatever one may be inclined to say for or against the separation method, its properties as a method of **analysis**, i.e. calibration, have nothing at all to do with the prediction formulas set down in the original paper (Taylor, 1977).

Although pains have been taken above to point out the conceptual distinction between construction and calibration of model, the actual method of calibration will often be very much geared to the parametric structure of the model. The reasons for this are examined in Section 5.3. Because of such cases, in what follows a statement of model and the method used for its calibration will be given in consecutive subsections.

In a number of cases, the available options as to prediction methods will depend to only a minor extent on the form of model and the method used for its calibration. In such cases it is convenient to consider these options as a separate issue. Section 5.4 does this.

3.   CLAIMS DATA

3.1   General

We begin by considering the data likely to be recorded within the insurer's system and therefore potentially available to the actuary. This will, of course, represent a mass of information part of which will be irrelevant to the claims analysis problem and which will certainly require some condensation before the commencement of analysis.

The fact that specific forms of condensation have become enshrined in government regulation engenders a risk that they will come to be regarded as God-given or at least scientifically preferred. There is a more insidious risk of an intensely practical nature. There is a tendency for supervisory authorities to become locked into the existing system. A Catch 22 situation arises from the fact that individual insurers will be disinclined to embark on elaborate and expensive modifications to statistical systems as long as they are not strictly required by regulation; and the fact that supervisory authorities may be apprehensive about pressing for compulsory elaborations of statistical reporting when virtually no member of the industry is already using the proposed techniques. Thus, after an initial flurry of activity on the introduction of new supervisory legislation, the situation is likely to settle into one of ever-increasing inertia against change.

Naturally, the extent to which supervisory authorities feel comfortable or otherwise in pressing for statistical reform will be heavily dependent on the degree of Ministerial support that can be reasonably expected — and so dependent ultimately on the political philosophy of the powers of the day.

On the other hand it may be fair to say that insurers, taken as a group, have been rather slow to recognise the benefits of accurate and comprehensive statistical systems.

Although particular formats, motivated by statutory requirements, are widely adopted in summarizing claims statistics, we prefer at this stage to take a rather more catholic view of data potentialities. It is noted, therefore, that, in respect of each claim, the insurer's system is likely to record at least the following:

 (i) date of occurrence of the event generating the claim;

 (ii) date of notification of the claim;

(iii) the amount and date of each payment;

(iv) The physical estimate of outstanding amount at each review date (e.g. each quarter-end) during the currency of the claim;

 (v) date of finalization of claim (if finalized);

(vi) the values assumed by the insured in respect of a number of risk factors (e.g. in motor vehicle insurance, type of vehicle, age of driver, etc.).

    It will be convenient at this point to establish a notation for these items. Let

$$\begin{aligned}
a_z &= \text{a vector of values identifying the risk factors} \\
&\quad \text{associated with the } z\text{-th claim;} \\
i_z &= \text{date of occurrence of the } z\text{-th claim;} \\
k_z &= \text{date of notification of the } z\text{-th claim;} \\
j_{zm} &= \text{date of } m\text{-th payment in respect of } z\text{-th claim} \\
&\quad (j_{zm} = \infty \text{ if } m\text{-th payment does not exist});\\
c_{zm} &= \text{amount of } m\text{-th payment in respect of } z\text{-th claim;} \\
d_{zh} &= h\text{-th review date of physical estimate of amount} \\
&\quad \text{outstanding in respect of } z\text{-th claim;} \\
o_{zh} &= \text{amount of that estimate;} \\
g_z &= \text{date of finalization of } z\text{-th claim } (g_z = \infty \text{ for a claim still} \\
&\quad \text{open at the date of analysis of claims).}
\end{aligned}$$

    Let the above data set be denoted by I.

    To ease symbolic manipulation, it will prove useful to extend the system of notation somewhat. Let

$c_{zaikjmg}$ = amount of claims paid in respect of claims which:

are numbered z;

are associated with risk factors a;

occurred on date i;

etc;

o_{zaikdg} be similarly defined.

Clearly, there is a great deal of redundancy in this notational system. For example, if the z-th claim did not occur on date i, then immediately $c_{zaikjmg} = 0$. The system does have the advantage, however, that summation over values of a given suffix may be represented by replacement of that suffix by a dot. For example, the total of claim payments in respect of accident date i is $c_{..i....}$; of this amount the total paid on date j is $c_{..i.j..}$.

Now let

n_{zaikg} = number of claims with characteristics z, a, i, k, g.

Note that j, m do not appear in this subscript as a single claim may have many payments or it may have none .

In this notation it is to be understood that the dates j_{zm}, d_{zh}, g_z may be recorded to any specific accuracy. They are not necessarily expressed in the day/month/year form. For example, it may be that only the month of a claim payment is recorded.

Although the next subsection will consider the question of condensation of this mass of data, it should be remembered, particularly in theoretical development, that the above will usually represent the aggregate of information available. No part of it should be discarded without due consideration.

3.2   Condensation of the available information

Supervisory authorities will not normally have access to the entire body of this information. Even the actuary employed by, or consulting to, an insurer, is unlikely, through constraints of time or cost in the production of statistics, to have full access. Certainly, all of the methods of analysis in this volume involve some condensation of I.

We give a couple of practical examples of ways in which I is collapsed to more tractable proportions in practice.

Consider Reid's (1978) method of analysis (see Section 8.3). The values of a_z, k_z, d_{zh}, o_{zh} are not required at all. The values of i_z, j_{zm} are usually recorded only according to year. The values of c_{zm} are summarized as follows. The symbol $c_{z.i...g}$ represents the total amount paid in respect to claim z provided that it occurred at date i and was finalized at date g. The total amount of claims which occurred at date i and were finalized at date g is $c_{..i...g}$. Let

$$n^+_{..i...g} = \text{number of values of } z \text{ for which } c_{z.i...g} > 0, \text{ i.e. number of}$$
$$\text{non-zero claims making up } c_{..i...g};$$

$$n^e_{..i...g} = \text{number of values of } z \text{ for which } c_{z.i...g} \in (v_e, \infty], \text{ i.e. number}$$
$$\text{of claims included in } n^+_{..i...g} \text{ which fall in cost-band } (v_e, \infty].$$

Reid's method is based on values of $n^e_{..i...g}$. To take a much simpler example, the chain ladder method discards a_z, k_z, d_{zh}, o_{zh}, g_z. It summarizes the c_{zm} by requiring only the values of $c_{..i.j..}$.

It is realised, of course, that the notation used in this section is cumbersome. In later sections oriented towards particular methods of analysis steps will be taken to simplify the notation (at the cost of generality). The more general and laborious notation has been retained in this section in order to emphasise the wide range of options available for collapsing the (potentially) available data to a working data set.

3.3   Australian and British statutory information

Despite the range of options mentioned at the end of the preceding subsection, it is inevitable, partly for the reasons given in Section 3.1, that a number of methods of claims analysis be geared to the use of data in the form required by statute. It is therefore useful at this early stage to review such statutory forms in the cases with which the author is familiar.

The Australian statutory returns require i_z, k_z, j_{zm}, g_z to be recorded only to the year. Further k_z, j_{zm}, g_z need only be recorded as the appropriate one of the values i_z, i_z+1, ..., i_z+6, $\geq i_z+7$. The returns require 4 categories of information:

$n_{..ik.}$ = number of claims which occurred in year i and were notified in year k;

$n_{..i.(g+)} = \sum_{\alpha=g+1}^{\infty} n_{..i.\alpha}$ = number of claims which occurred in year i and were still outstanding at the end of year g;

$c_{..i.j..}$ = amount of claim payments in year j in respect of claims which occurred in year i;

$o_{..i.j.}$ = physical estimate of amount outstanding in respect of claims which occurred in year i and were reported by the end of year j.

The British statutory returns require rather more information than this (Abbott, Clarke, Hey and Treen, 1974). They require in addition that $c_{..i.j..}$ be subdivided into:

$c_{..i.j.j}$ = amount paid in respect of claims finalized in the year in question;

$c_{..i.j..} - c_{..i.j.j}$ = amount paid on account of claims still outstanding at the end of the year in question.

Estimates are also required of number and amount of IBNR claims. However, these figures are estimates, not observations, and so are excluded from our discussion of data.

4   GENERAL MODELS

4.1   Notation

A certain amount of notation was introduced in Chapter 3. However all such notation related to **observations** on the claims process. Following the remarks made in Section 1.3 on the desirability of recognising the stochastic nature of the claims process, we shall need to develop a notation which allows this.

Almost always the convention will be adopted that upper case Latin letters denote random variables; lower case Latin letters realizations (or observations) of those random variables; Greek letters parameters underlying the random variables. This convention will be followed unless it conflicts in particular cases with widely accepted alternative notation. In many cases, as in Chapter 3, lower case Latin letters are used as subscripts, where they represent indexes, rather than realizations of random variables. This meaning will usually be obvious.

Following the convention outlined above, let

a_z = a vector of values identifying the risk factors associated with the z-th claim (as in Section 3.1);

I_z = date of occurrence of the z-th claim;

K_z = date of notification of the z-th claim;

J_{zm} = date of m-th payment in respect of z-th claim ($= \infty$ if never paid);

C_{zm} = amount of m-th payment in respect of z-th claim ($= 0$ if $J_{zm} = \infty$);

d_{zh} = h-th review date of physically estimated amount outstanding in respect of z-th claim (as in Section 3.1);

O_{zh} = amount of that estimate;

$$G_z = \text{date of finalization of } z\text{-th claim.}$$

Of course, i_z, k_z, j_{zm}, c_{zm}, o_{zh}, g_z denote realizations of the random variables I_z, K_z, J_{zm}, C_{zm}, O_{zh}, G_z. This was the meaning ascribed to them in Section 3.1.

In addition, the number of claims N falling within the scope of the claims analysis will be a random variable.

This notation is extended to $C_{zaikjmg}$, O_{zaikdg}, N_{zaikg} in the same way as in Section 3.1.

The summation convention of using dots, introduced in Section 3.1, is also extended to the above random variables.

Statistical operators are denoted by curly characters:

$\mathcal{E}[X] = \text{expected value of } X;$

$\mathcal{V}[X] = \text{variance of } X;$

$\mathcal{C}[X, Y] = \text{covariance of } X \text{ and } Y.$

Where possible, the expected value of a random variable (denoted by an upper case Latin letter) is denoted by the corresponding lower case Greek letter, e.g.

$$\mathcal{E}[C_{..i.j..}] = \gamma_{..i.j..}.$$

Finally, as remarked in Section 3.2, the above notation will be contracted in various ways adapted to specific methods of analysis. For example, the chain ladder method requires only the observations $c_{..i.j..}$, as noted in Section 3.2. It is natural, then, to contract this symbolism to simply c_{ij} **in that case.** Clearly, such contractions will need to be dealt with in connection with the particular models to which they relate.

4.2   Definition of the outstanding claims problem

Consider the actuary faced with the task of evaluating outstanding claims at date b. It is supposed, as is commonly the case, that information is available up to but not beyond b. The amount of information potentially available is I, as discussed in Section 3.1. Through time- or cost-constraints, or perhaps merely the actuary's preferences, this body of data will have been reduced to a set I_{red} of summary statistics in the manner described in Section 3.2.

It is necessary to estimate outstanding claims (either with or without discounting for the effect of future investment return), as at date b, in respect of each accident date i up to and including b. This total of outstanding claims is :

$$P_{..(b-).b.} = \sum_{i=-\infty}^{b} P_{..i.b.}, \qquad (4.2.1)$$

where the subscripts are the same as for the random variable O_{zaikdg} (see Section 4.1), and

$P_{..i.b.}$ = amount outstanding at date b in respect of claims
which occurred at date i.

$$= C_{..i.(b+)..}$$

$$= \sum_{j=b+1}^{\infty} C_{..i.j..} \qquad (4.2.2)$$

By (4.2.1) and (4.2.2),

$$P_{..(b-).b.} = \sum_{i=-\infty}^{b} \sum_{j=b+1}^{\infty} C_{..i.j..} \qquad (4.2.3)$$

Now $P_{..(b-).b.}$ is a random variable. It has mean value

$$\mathcal{E}[P_{..(b-).b.}] = \Pi_{..(-b).b.}$$

$$= \sum_{i=-\infty}^{b} \sum_{j=b+1}^{\infty} \gamma_{..i.j..}, \qquad (4.2.4)$$

by (4.2.3). The problem of estimation of outstanding claims consists of computing an estimate $\hat{\Pi}_{..(b-).b.}$ of $\Pi_{..(b-).b.}$.

Such estimate will be based wholly or partly on I_{red}. It will be obtained by the three steps discussed in Chapter 2. Thus a model is chosen which establishes $\Pi_{..(b-).b.}$ as a function $\Pi_{..(b-).b.}(\Omega)$ of some set Ω of parameters.

An estimate $\hat{\Omega}$ of this set must be obtained. This is where the model of Section 2.1 becomes relevant. Let $\mathcal{R}_{red}$ denote the set of random variables whose realization is I_{red}. Consider $\mathcal{R}_{red}$, I_{red} as vectors. Then

$$I_{red} = \mathcal{E}[\mathcal{R}_{red}] + u$$

$$= E(\Omega) + u, \qquad (4.2.5)$$

where $E(\Omega)$ is some function of the set Ω of parameters underlying the claims process, and u is a vector of random variables with zero mean.

As pointed out in Section 2.3, $\Pi_{..(b-).b.}(\hat{\Omega})$ will not necessarily be a satisfactory estimator of $\Pi_{..(b-).b.}(\Omega)$, though very often lack of knowledge of distributional characteristics may force one to make this simple approach. But, if possible, one should consider what estimators $\hat{\Pi}_{..(b-).b.}(\hat{\Omega})$ might be adopted.

4.3   General models proposed in the literature

Probably the most important step in the procedure outlined in Section 4.2 is that represented in (4.2.5). This equation expresses the expected values of the observations as some particular algebraic structure of (unknown) parameters. Note the generality of (4.2.5).

It is useful at this stage to review a couple of the specific versions of (4.2.5) proposed in the literature. There are, of course, many to choose from, but attention will be confined here to some which claim reasonable, or even total, generality.

Consider, for example, the general model proposed by Finger (1976). The data assumed available by Finger constitute an array of observations O_{ij} (using his notation) in respect of exposure period i and development period j. The proposed "generalized loss reserve development model" is then (still in Finger's notation):

$$O_{ij} = C_{ij}F_jS_iK_{i+j} + e_{ij}, \qquad (4.3.1)$$

where the C_{ij} are known parameters, the F_j, S_i, K_{i+j} unknown parameters and the e_{ij} random errors.

This can be related to (4.2.5) by taking I_{red} to be the array of O_{ij}, the parameter set Ω to consist of the F_j, S_i, K_{i+j}, and the model structure:

$$E(\Omega) = C_{ij}F_jS_iK_{i+j}. \qquad (4.3.2)$$

Consider, as a second example, Johnson (1980). He writes (in his own notation);

$$P_i(T) = \sum_{t=T+1}^{\infty} N(i)B(i)R_i(t)L_i(t), \qquad (4.3.3)$$

where the total portfolio of claims is regarded as consisting of subportfolios labelled by i;

$P_i(T)$ denotes total claim payments made after time T;

$N(i)$ denotes number of claims (in the subportfolio);

$B(i)$ denotes average claim size in real terms;

$R_i(t)$ describes the distribution of claim payments, in real terms, over time;

$L_i(t)$ denotes an inflation index.

Equation (4.3.3) (more precisely, a slightly different form) is described by Johnson as "a simple yet generalised and complete description of the claims runoff process for a defined portfolio of claims".

Consider the generality of (4.3.1) and (4.3.3) respectively. If, in (4.3.3), one sets:

$$R_i(t)L_i(t) = C_{i,t-i}F_{t-i}K_t; \qquad (4.3.4)$$

$$N(i)B(i) = S_i; \qquad (4.3.5)$$

then (4.3.3) becomes:

$$P_i(T) = \sum_{t=T+1}^{\infty} C_{i,t-i}F_{t-i}S_iK_t$$

$$= \sum_{j=T-i+1}^{\infty} C_{ij}F_jS_iK_{i+j}.$$

Apart from the absence of the error term, this is identical to (4.3.1). Thus, in terms of expected values, (4.3.1) is a special case of (4.3.3).

It is easy to see that (4.3.3) is, in fact, more general than (4.3.1). Suppose, for example, that the (unknown) claims escalation in year $(i+j)$, which is envisaged as embraced by the K_{i+j} factor, varies according to the extent of development of the exposure period (as indeed is assumed in Reid's method (Section 8.3)). Then a model of the following form is required:

$$O_{ij} = C_{ij}F_jS_iK_{i+j,i} + e_{ij}, \qquad (4.3.6)$$

which is not within the compass of (4.3.1). Remember that C_{ij} includes only known parameters, and so does not deal with the problem of unknown claims escalation.

Thus (4.3.1) cannot be seen as possessing total generality.

Now consider (4.3.3). If (4.3.4) is replaced by:

$$R_i(t)L_i(t) = C_{i,t-i}F_{t-i}K_{t,i},$$

and (4.3.5) is retained, then (4.3.3) produces (once again apart from the absence of an error term) the required model (4.3.6).

There are, however, two points on which Johnson's generalized statement (4.3.3) scores unfavourably.

Firstly, it may be noted that it includes no stochastic structure.To this extent it seems less than "a complete description of the claims runoff process".

Secondly, and perhaps paradoxically, the very generality of (4.3.3) is, from one point of view, a detraction from its merit. Since $P_i(T)$ consists of a sum of terms, each indexed by i and t, it is obvious that the summand of (4.3.3), which includes a factor $R_i(T)$ indexed by i and t, is a sufficiently general representation. In a strictly abstract sense, (4.3.3) is a mere tautology.

Note that the building of a model of any process consists of algebraic formulation which is to some extent specific. Presence of complete generality amounts to complete absence of a model. Conversely, model-building consists of reduction of the admissible set of possiblities from structureless generality to a structured, smaller but more specific set.

Johnson's generalized statement, and the remarks of the preceding paragraph on it, bring a realization of the alternative purposes which relations such as (4.3.3) may be called upon to fulfil. I call these alternative purposes **descriptive and prescriptive**.

Because of its complete generality , apart from stochastic considerations ,(4.3.3) provides a suitable framework for **description** of the apportionment of the claims (actual claims paid or projected to be paid) relating to subportfolio i over its years of development. It also provides for inclusion of operationally useful information such as average claim size in real terms.

Thus Johnson's generalized statement can be viewed as **descriptive**. In its complete generality, it provides **no structure** to the claims process. It carries no methodological implications.

Finger's representation on the other hand is **prescriptive**. Once particular meanings have been assigned to the parameters and variables appearing in the equation, it provides an algebraic structure relating those parameters and variables. This structure may then be exploited in the estimation of the unknown parameters.

The descriptive approach to claims data may be of use in comparison of portfolios. Where two separate portfolios are under consideration, there may be good reason to adopt quite different models in the two cases. Algebraically, this means that the parameter set Ω and the function $E(.)$ in (4.2.5) differ as between the portfolios. With differing parameter sets, comparison of the two claims runoff processes is likely to be extremely difficult.

The descriptive approaches may ease comparison. Essentially, Johnson's generalized statement eliminates from an experience the effects of exposure volume $N(i)$ and claims escalation $L_i(t)$; it then allows comparison of:

(i) average claims cost in constant dollar values;

(ii) length or brevity of the tail of claim payment delay distribution.

But the descriptive approaches will provide only a partial answer to the problems of comparison. For the very absence from them of any element of model-building implies that they will be able to **describe** differences between portfolios but without an ability to attribute those differences to causes, e.g. different speeds of finalization, changing speeds of finalization, different proportions of zero claims, different orders of settling claims with respect to size, etc.

4.4   Summary

The literature contains two types of approach to the problem of claims modelling . In Section 4.3 these have been called **descriptive and prescriptive**.

The uses of descriptive approaches are limited. In particular, what they do **not** do is to provide any guide to the model-building required in specific cases.

The prescriptive approaches do provide an algebraic structure. However, in doing so they are necessarily less general than the descriptive approaches.Note that Finger's formulation (4.3.1) is inadequate for some methods of analysis e.g. Reid's (1978), Taylor's see-saw (1981a, 1982a, 1983). The danger with prescriptions such as (4.3.1) is that they may become dogma, and accordingly inhibit further enquiry.

All things considered, it seems to the author that, if generality is being sought, it is unlikely that a more specific prescriptive statement of the claims process can be made than (4.2.5).

5   TAXONOMY OF METHODS

5.1   Taxonomy of methods of claims analysis generally

Section 2.4 strongly recommended distinction between the construction, calibration and prediction phases of claims modelling. It follows that any taxonomy of methods of claims analysis ought to consist of separate taxonomies of model structures, methods of model-fitting, and methods of projection. This system is followed in this chapter.

As in most taxonomic systems, classification of methods of claims analysis can proceed at various levels. The top levels establish the fundamentally distinct classes of model. The bottom levels deal much more with points of detail. This corresponds for example to the family/genus/species/etc. classification scheme of zoology.

5.2   Taxonomy of models

5.2.1 *The higher levels of classification*

It follows perhaps from the remarks made in Section 1.3 that we see the primary division between models according to whether or not they contain explicit recognition of the stochastic nature of the claims process. Thus models are divided into

STOCHASTIC;

NONSTOCHASTIC.

This is a deep division in principle. Its implications deserve some consideration.

The nonstochastic models can usually be characterized by an equation of the type (4.2.5) with the stochastic error term omitted, thus:

$$I_{red} = E(\Omega); \qquad (5.2.1.1)$$

or, verbally;

$$\text{data} = \text{algebraic combination of parameters.} \qquad (5.2.1.2)$$

Although it may appear pedantic to labour the difference between (4.2.5) and (5.2.1.1), there are in fact a number of serious disadvantages associated with the latter.

Firstly, (5.2.1.1) is self-contradictory. For, when the parameter set Ω has been estimated by $\hat{\Omega}$ it will be found that

$$I_{red} \neq E(\hat{\Omega}),$$

contradicting (5.2.1.1). Indeed, unless the number of parameters in Ω is as large as the number of data items in I_{red}, it will not be possible in general to satisfy (5.2.1.1). A self-contradictory model can scarcely be regarded as an aid to clear thinking.

Secondly, reasoning about the nonstochastic model tends to become logically sloppy. For example, one is likely to hear such statements as: *"The data set under consideration is too small to permit meaningful statistical treatment"*. Such statements are clearly wrong. A statistical analysis can be made of any data set, no matter how small.

The point is, however, that small samples lead to large uncertainty. Thus, while statistical analysis of a small data set can be performed and estimates of outstanding claims calculated, these results will have large margins of uncertainty associated with them.

Of course, the antagonists of stochastic models are likely to respond that this last situation does not represent "meaningful statistical treatment". This seems to the author also wrong. Provided that the model has been chosen carefully, the results of its analysis represent the maximum information which can be gleaned from the data. Anyone who wishes to claim that the derivation of maximum information from data is not meaningful needs to explain himself a little further.

Thirdly, the non stochastic models contain little or no machinery for the investigation of the factors which tend to bedevil statistical analyses, e.g.:

(i) quality of data;

(ii) quality of model;

(iii) the effect of large claims.

Any or all of these difficulties may go undetected in an analysis by a nonstochastic model. If detected, they are likely to lead to qualifications of the results which are couched in vague terms. On the other hand, a stochastic model will automatically "detect" all of these difficulties in the sense that:

(i) erroneous data will increase the appearance of statistical instability, and so lead to a larger margin of uncertainty being associated with the results of the analysis;

(ii) large claims may, in a proper statistical treatment, appear as obvious outliers, and can be weighted appropriately less by standard robust procedures (see e.g. Huber, 1977);

and so on.

A little further comment about erroneous data. It is often claimed that refinement of statistical methods of claims analysis is futile in view of the doubts which almost always seem to surround the quality of data. This view is probably made most explicit by Truckle (1978);

> *"What I have sought to do is to expose the dubiety of apply- ing sophisticated statistical techniques to rough-hewn ma- terial the ruggedness of which implies an inherent variabil- ity which swamps the refinements of the models. Viewed in abstraction there is a seductive quality about claims statistics which lures the unwary into supposing that they have a natural purity which warrants the parading of math- ematical elegance. But the statistics are only the outward manifestation of an earthly commercial process which calls for worldly-wise and utilitarian solutions".*

Such sentiments overlook the fact that only by means of the "sophis- ticated statistical techniques" will it be possible to distinguish between the " inherent variability" and unnecessary variability in results due to poor modelling or poor parameter estimation.

The next major classification of models which might be made is between:

MACRO-MODELS;

MICRO-MODELS.

By MICRO-models is meant those models which work at the individual claim level. Examples are provided by Bühlmann, Schnieper and Straub (1980) and Hachemeister (1980). The structures of such models deal with the development of individual claims throughout their lifetimes.

MACRO-models, on the other hand, deal with claims **en masse**. Most claims analysis models fall into this category. The model is described in terms of aggregates of claims, each claim within a given aggregate possessing particular attributes common to that aggregate. For example, the separation method (Taylor, 1977a) deals with aggregates of claim payments characterized by year of origin and year of development of the claim.

There does not appear much to be said at present on the merits and demerits of these two classes of model. Certainly, the bulk of research has been concentrated on macro-models. This reflects the fact that, in practice, claims information is usually available in some aggregated form, rather than any belief in the inherent superiority of macro- over micro-models. But at this stage virtually no evidence is available on the comparative performances of the two classes of model. We must content ourselves with merely observing the distinction between them.

One further point may be noted. It is that there is no such thing as a nonstochastic micro-model. This is not to say that such a model could not possibly exist. It is open to any one to produce one. However, once one descends to the level of treating individual claims, to ignore the stochastic nature of the process being treated would make rather a nonsense of the investigation. It is probably reasonable, therefore, to regard the nonstochastic micro-model class as null. Subject to this, the upper orders of our taxonomy of models produce the following schematic cross-classification.

	Macro	**Micro**
Stochastic	Stochastic Macro-models	Stochastic Micro-models
Nonstochastic	Nonstochastic Macro-models	

Fig.1 *Higher orders of taxonomy of models*

5.2.2 *The middle levels of classification*

At this level models are probably best classified according to their dependent variables. Since the object of the exercise will usually be estimation of outstanding claims, or equivalently estimation of the amount of claims incurred in respect of a particular group of claims (e.g. a particular set of years of origin), it follows almost inevitably that the dependent variables of the claims model will include either claim payments or amounts of claims incurred.

Macro-models may or may not include claim numbers as dependent variables. Thus, two further levels of classification can be discerned, the first of which distinguishes between models:

(i) WITH CLAIM NUMBERS AS DEPENDENT VARIABLES;

(ii) WITHOUT CLAIM NUMBERS AS DEPENDENT VARIABLES;

and the second of which distinguishes between models having:

(i) CLAIM PAYMENTS;

(ii) AMOUNTS OF CLAIMS INCURRED;

as dependent variables.

Since micro-models specifically model the development of individual claims, there is not much sense in speaking of their including claim numbers as dependent variables. Thus, it is not meaningful to attempt to subdivide the "stochastic micro-model" cell of Fig. 1 according to the presence or absence of numbers of claims among the dependent variables.

For example, the separation method (Taylor,1977a) provides an example of a method which does not model claim numbers but does model the claim payments associated with each combination of year of origin and development year. On the other hand, Reid's (1978) method is one which models both numbers of claims (finalized for each combination of claim size and operational time-interval) and also the amounts of payments associated with these groups of claims.

Thus, at the middle level of taxonomy, **each of the three cells** in Fig.1 yields the following further cross-classification.

	Claim payments modelled	**Amounts of claims incurred modelled**
Claim numbers modelled	Model: claim numbers, and claim payments	Model: claim numbers, and claims incurred
Claim numbers not modelled	Model: claim payments	Model: claims incurred

Fig.2. *Middle orders of taxonomy of models*

5.2.3 *The lower levels of classification*

The lowest level of classification of models might be according to the explanatory variables included. A comprehensive list of these, as far as the better-known models are concerned, is as follows (roughly in order of importance):

 (i) volume of exposure, by year of origin;

 (ii) development time, e.g. development year as an explanatory variable of claim payments;

(iii) claims escalation (or inflation), which may be either estimated independently of the claims data or inferred from those data;

(iv) variables, labelled by year of origin, other than exposure (see(i) above), e.g. average claim size;

 (v) speed of finalization of claims;

(vi) individual claim size, e.g. as in Reid's (1978) method;

(vii) the division of each tabulated amount of claim payments between payments in finalization and partial payments;

(viii) other variables (we do not insist that the list of (i) to (vii) is exhaustive).

In an abstract sense, it would be possible to aggregate (i) and (iv) since both deal with variables labelled by accident year. The two have been separated to reflect the practical preeminence of (i). Virtually all models allow for (i), though sometimes implicitly (e.g.the payment ratio method (see Sawkins, 1975)), whereas many do not allow for (iv). Indeed, the effects of (iv) can be subtle and difficult to detect (see e.g. Taylor, 1983).

We draw attention to the use in (iii) of the term "claims escalation". The term, as opposed to "claims inflation", was suggested by Matthews (1979) in order to emphasize the distinction between the escalation to which claims are subject and the standard measures of price and wage inflation within the community. The term "claims escalation" will continue to be used in subsequent sections.

5.2.4 *Summary of the classification*

The various levels of classification dealt with in Sections 5.2.1 to 5.2.3 may be summarized as in the following diagram. The whole taxonomy consists of a 5-way cross-classification according to the attributes displayed in **Fig.** 3, though some of the cells in the cross-classification will be null, e.g. all nonstochastic micro-models as mentioned in Section 5.2.1.

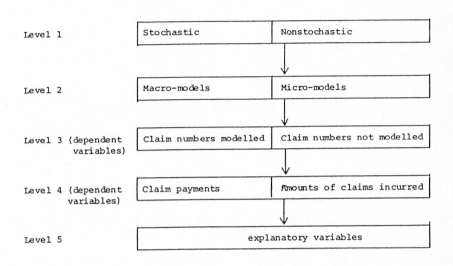

Level 1	Stochastic	Nonstochastic
Level 2	Macro-models	Micro-models
Level 3 (dependent variables)	Claim numbers modelled	Claim numbers not modelled
Level 4 (dependent variables)	Claim payments	Amounts of claims incurred
Level 5	explanatory variables	

Fig.3. *Summary of levels of taxonomy of claims models*

5.3   Taxonomy of fitting techniques

As was foreshadowed in Section 2.4, there will often be a degree of dependency between the model adopted and the method of calibration of the model. Expressed another way, the classification of models and methods of calibration together will not be the simple cross-classification of models and methods of calibration taken separately. It will be a subset of that cross-classification. We consider the reasons for this.

It is recalled from **Fig. 3** that the most basic level of classification of models is as between those of stochastic and nonstochastic natures respectively. The fact is that the cleavage between those two classes of model is so deep as virtually to imply different approaches to calibration.

The essential feature of the stochastic models is that the distributional hypotheses which they advance provide a framework within which calibration of the model may be carried out according to a procedure which is in some sense "optimal", e.g. least squares, maximum likelihood, etc.

After all, the fitting of a model to claims data is, in common with a great many other model-fitting exercises, an exercise aimed at identification of the factors generating that experience and quantification of those factors as opposed to the superimposed random errors. It stands to reason therefore that an explicit formulation of those errors and their properties is likely to equip one better for the task of eliminating them, i.e. estimating the parameters of the model effectively. With an explicit formulation of the random errors of the claims process, estimation of the parameters underlying that process can be pursued with rigour.

Contrast this with the nonstochastic models. With random errors unrecognised, estimation of the model parameters lapses into an ad hoc mode. Since random errors are not (formally) admitted to exist, it is clearly impossible to follow such strategies as minimization of their mean square. Often some "obvious" method of estimation will be used. The usual version would be based on (4.2.5) with the random vector u omitted. If the set Ω consists of n parameters, then one chooses n independent functions f_i of the data, to obtain from (4.2.5):

$$f_i(I_{red}) = f_i(E(\Omega)), \qquad i = 1, \ldots, n. \tag{5.3.1}$$

The system (5.3.1) provides n equations relating n unknowns deterministically, and is solved as a purely algebraic, rather than stochastic, system.

Now, for large samples, in which the random component of (4.2.5) becomes insignificant, such an approach will lead to reasonable estimates of Ω unless the particular functions f_i or E introduce singularity problems. However, in the field of claims analysis, sample sizes seem to be virtually never of sufficient size to justify this cavalier treatment of the problem. The approach outlined above provides no guidance at all as to the efficiency (i.e. in the statistical sense of stability of estimates) of the various possible choices of the f_i.

Once again, the separation method (Taylor, 1977a) can be cited as providing an example of the points under discussion. In this method, the set Ω consists of the parameters r and λ. The functions f_i represent the formation of column and diagonal sums, one column for each r parameter and one diagonal for each λ parameter. Full details are given in the original paper on the subject.

In summary then, methods of estimation of parameters in nonstochastic models tend to suffer from the following defects:

(i) In neglecting a non-negligible component of the problem (the random vector u of (4.2.5)) they represent a fuddled and unscientific means of operation;

(ii) The lack of rigour and discipline resulting from (i) leads to a free-for-all in the selection of a method of parameter estimation which pays little heed to, and indeed is poorly equipped to attempt to heed, the statistical efficiency properties of the resulting estimates.

5.4   Taxonomy of projection methods

Sawkins (1979, Section 4) has identified three methods of projection. In his nomenclature, they are:

(i) ratio method;

(ii) direct future payments method;

(iii) total payments method.

Methods (i) and (ii) are more commonly applied in practice than (iii). Indeed, method (iii) has come under attack by Cumpston (1980). Nonetheless, questions of its practical appropriateness aside, it is properly identified by Sawkins as a separate method of projection.

Brief descriptions of these methods of projection are given by Sawkins (1979) on p.479. All three methods are applied after a model of some sort has been fitted to the data. Working directly from this model and the estimates of its parameters, one can calculate directly estimates of future claim payments. These estimates constitute **the direct future payments method**.

In general, because of the stochastic nature of the claims process and perhaps inappropriateness of the model fitted, past claim payments will differ from those fitted by the model. Note that the direct future payments method of projection effectively ignores such deviations of experience from model, treating them as purely random and without consequences as to the future. The other two methods of projection take a diferent view of these deviations.

The **total payments method** assumes effectively that any deviation of past experience from the model will be compensated in future experience.Therefore, for each accident year, outstanding claims are first calculated on the basis of the direct future payments method, and then reduced by any excess of actual over model past payments.

The **ratio method** makes an assumption essentially opposite to that made by the total payments method. In particular, the ratio method assumes that if past experience has exceeded the model by a certain percentage, then the same percentage excess will occur in the future. Thus, for each accident year, outstanding claims are first calculated on the basis of the direct future payments method, and are then adjusted by the ratio of actual to model past payments.

The above three methods of projection can be described algebraically as follows.

Consistently with Section 4.2, let $\hat{\Pi}_{..i.b.}$ denote the estimate of outstanding claims at balance date b in respect of date of occurence i, where this estimate has been formed directly from the estimated parameters underlying the claims model, i.e. **the direct future payments method of projection**.

Then according to the total payments method,

$$\text{estimated outstanding claims} = \hat{\Pi}_{..i.b.} - \sum_{j=i}^{b}(C_{..i.j..} - \hat{C}_{..i.j..}), \qquad (5.4.1)$$

where $\hat{C}_{..i.j..}$ denotes the value of $C_{..i.j..}$ fitted by the model.

According to **the ratio method**,

$$\text{estimated outstanding claims} = \hat{\Pi}_{..i.b.} \sum_{j=i}^{b} C_{..i.j..} / \sum_{j=i}^{b} \hat{C}_{..i.j..} . \qquad (5.4.2)$$

We comment only very briefly on the above methods of projection.

The direct future payments method, since based directly on the model fitted to claims experience, seems straightforward in concept and requires no comment.

On the other hand, one might be forgiven for entertaining some reservations about the other two methods of projection. Briefly, the structure of the sequence of calculation (both model-fitting and projection) which they imply is as follows:

(i) construct a model of the claims process;

(ii) calibrate the model by reference to claims experience;

(iii) compare the calibrated model with the experience, essentially to examine goodness-of-fit;

(iv) to the extent that goodness-of-fit is poor, make adjustments to the estimates of outstanding claims produced by the model.

Step (iv) is the one in doubt. Substantial action is required at this step only in the case of poor goodness-of-fit. This would normally imply an unsatisfactory model. In such circumstances it would seem logical to return to Step (i) and adjust the model to accord with reality. The practice, envisaged by Step (iv), of adjusting the outstanding claims estimated by an inadequate model seems unsatisfactory since, as long as the model remains inadequate, one cannot be certain of the meaning of its estimates. And it is these which are adjusted to produce final estimates of outstanding claims.

There can be occasions on which the ratio method of projection can be justified logically. For example, we shall see (Section 7.1.1.1) that the **chain ladder model** might or might not include parameters which allow for changes in average claim size from one accident year to another. The inclusion or exclusion of these parameters does not affect the estimation of the remaining parameters. It is easy to show that the following two procedures are equivalent:

(i) exclude the average claim size parameters from the chain ladder model and adopt the ratio method of projection;

(ii) include the average claim size parameters in the chain ladder model, estimate them on the basis of ratios of the type occuring in (5.4.2), and then use the direct future payments method of projection of outstanding claims.

Note, however, that, although Steps (i) to (iv) above have been justified in this case, the justification rests on the fact that Step (iv) is equivalent to a revision of the basic model and estimation of the additional parameters.

To summarize, Steps (i) to (iv) above appear logically objectionable, and the methods based on them, ratio method and total payments method, should at least be treated with caution. For ourselves, we have a very strong affinity for the direct future payments method as the only one of the three which appears logically acceptable.

5.5   Other taxonomies

The literature does not appear to contain any comprehensive attempt at taxonomy of methods of estimation of outstanding claims.

Matthews (1980) distinguishes between "first generation" and "second generation" analyses. It seems that Matthews has in mind, as first generation analyses, those which are based on no more information than, for each past accident year:

(i) numbers of claims notified, subdivided by year of notification;

(ii) past claim payments, subdivided by year of payment;

and perhaps

(iii) the total amount of physical estimates of outstanding claims on each past balance date.

Second generation methods would appear to encompass all other (more elaborate) methods, bringing "further factors into the analysis such as size of claim and delay to settlement".

While Matthew's division of methods is useful for some purposes, it is not, and presumably was not intended to be, a complete classification.

A different classification is given by Sawkins (1979). Again, two main classes of method are distinguished;

(i) **ratios of payments methods;**

(ii) **normalised payments methods.**

Ratios of payments methods are defined (page 445) as those which assume constancy of the ratio:

$$\frac{\text{payments in development year } t+1}{\text{payments in development year } t,}$$

or some slight variant of this.

Normalised payments methods, as the term is used by Sawkins, embrace those methods which explicitly introduce into the calculations a measure of the exposures in various accident years.

Sawkins finally concludes (p.454) that "Normalised Methods are more stable than Ratio of Payment Methods".

Thus, Sawkins' taxonomy compromises a dichotomy of methods, and enables a conclusion about the comparative efficiencies of the two parts of the dichotomy. It would seem, however, that there are some problems associated with both the taxonomy itself and the conclusion on efficiency to which it leads.

Firstly, nowhere does Sawkins give a formal definition of normalised payments methods. The definition which I have adopted is mere inference from a lengthy passage (Sawkins, 1979,448-50). As Sawkins himself points out, "Ratio methods eliminate automatically the need to adjust data for changes in the amount of risk from one Year of Origin to another". In other words, ratio methods can be thought of as

either (i) involving models which contain no factor measuring the exposures in different years of origin;

or (ii) involving models which do contain such exposures but use methods of estimation which cause the cancellation of these exposures in calculation.

As regards (ii), it is easy to see how the exposures can cancel when a ratio of payments of the type displayed above is taken.

Given the above two ways of viewing ratios of payments methods, one may feel entitled to ask exactly what property they possess which excludes them from the class of normalised payments methods. Or is it that, whatever normalised payments methods are, they are defined specifically to exclude ratios of payments methods? Clear answers to these questions do not seem to have been provided.

Secondly, it may be noted that Sawkins does not distinguish between construction of a model on the one hand and calibration of the model on the other, as is done in Chapter 2 of this volume. It is clear that the taking of ratios of payments represents merely a technique of fitting whatever model is being used to the data. It has nothing to do with the construction of the model itself. However, on pages 445-70 of his paper, Sawkins deals with "methods", which take into account numbers of claims finalized, numbers of claims outstanding or numbers of claims handled. In terms of the distinctions made in Chapter 2 of this volume, these clearly represent different models from the models underlying, for example, the ratios of payments methods. On the other hand, the ratios of payments methods and normalised payments methods may be no more than different estimation procedures applied to the same model. However, in Sawkins' paper the use of ratios of payments, normalised payments and numbers of claims finalized are just regarded as different "methods". Consequently, when he asserts superiority of one method over another, it is not clear whether the superiority is being asserted in respect of model or method of fitting the model to data. One suspects the latter.

Thirdly, Sawkins' conclusion about the superiority of normalised payments methods does not pretend to be more than an empirical statement. As such, it cannot be taken as an established fact. Moreover, in view of the difficulties alluded to above as regards the definition of his terms, an analytic justification of his assertion would not be easy.

Finally, without wishing to suggest that it creates any particular problem, we point out that Sawkins' taxonomy deals only with a relatively small subset of the available claims models. In particular he does not differentiate claims models at higher levels (in the terminology of Section 5.2.4) than Level 3. His attention is confined to nonstochastic macro-models.

5.6   Nomenclature for the taxonomy of models

Since Section 5.2.4 introduces five different levels of differentiation of claims models, it is useful in the interest of brevity to introduce a nomenclature.

Each model may be described as lying within the class denoted by:

$$X_1/X_2/X_3/X_4/X_5,$$

where X_i is a descriptor of the type of model adopted at Level i of our taxonomy.

The descriptors X_i can assume the following values:

$$X_1 = S(\text{stochastic});$$
$$= NS(\text{nonstochastic});$$

$$X_2 = MAC(\text{macro-model});$$
$$= MIC(\text{micro-model});$$

$$X_3 = N(\text{claim numbers modelled});$$
$$= NN(\text{claim numbers not modelled});$$

$$X_4 = P(\text{claim payments as dependent variables});$$
$$= I(\text{amounts of claims incurred as dependent variables });$$

$X_5 = E(\text{exposures});$

$\quad = A(\text{average claim sizes});$

$\quad = F(\text{numbers of claims finalized});$

$\quad = I(\text{claims escalation (or inflation)});$

$\quad = T(\text{time (real or operational — see Section 7.3.3.1) elapsed since date of occurrence of claim});$

$\quad = S(\text{speed of finalization of claims});$

$\quad = C(\text{total amount of claims in respect of a year of origin});$

$\quad = Y(\text{year of origin});$

$\quad = D(\text{size of individual claim});$

$\quad = P(\text{total partial payments to date in respect of a year of origin});$

$\quad = N(\text{number of payments in respect of an individual claim});$

$\quad = Z(\text{seasonality effect.}).$

The final descriptor might consist of several of the available values, e.g. E, I, T.

As an example of the use of this nomenclature, the separation model can be seen to belong to the class $NS/MAC/NN/P/E, I, T$.

A dot in place of any descriptor means that the value of that descriptor is left unspecified, e.g. $NS/MAC/NN/\cdot/E, I, T$ indicates the same class of models as in the preceding paragraph except that whether the model includes claim payments or amounts of claims incurred as a dependent variable is not specified.

6.   MODELS AND METHODS —
PRELIMINARY COMMENTS

6.1   General approach

The subsequent sections survey most of the claims models appearing in the literature. The order in which they are dealt with is not that which follows most naturally from the taxonomic schema set out in Section 5.2.4, but rather follows the progression from simplest to most complex.

Each subsection dealing with a particular model is divided into four further subsections. The first of these describes the model, the second the method of fitting that model to the data, the third the method of projecting outstanding claims, and the fourth gives brief comments. In this third case, outstanding claims will usually be projected only on the basis of the **direct future payments method** (Section 5.4), the reader needing to bear in mind the available modifications to this method (again, see Section 5.4).

As has been remarked earlier in this volume, there is no necessary dependency between the form of model and the fitting technique. The following sections present models in conjunction with the fitting techniques actually associated with them in literature. It is clear, however, from what has been said before this that there is in fact a range of fitting techniques available.

Certain general points can be made regarding the fourth subsection, containing comments, on each model or method. Different models involve different dependent and independent variables. The strengths and weaknesses of a model will depend on which of those variables are included. For example, models of the $\cdot / \cdot / NN / \cdot / \cdot$ type, which do not include claim numbers as explanatory variables, will be vulnerable to changes in the speed of finalization of claims. Likewise, a method such as the basic chain ladder method (Section 7.1.1), which assumes a constant rate of claims escalation from year to year will be suspect when this assumption is violated by the facts.

In general, any method will be suspect when observation reveals fluctuation in some variable which has been excluded from the relevant model. In the following subsections, this fact is taken for granted. Comment is made only when there is something further than this to be said.

For the sake of definiteness, each method is presented algebraically as if its application is quite mechanical. In fact, there is no reason why this must be the case. Blind pursuit of the formulas presented is poor actuarial practice. It is open to the user of any particular method, at any point, to pause, reflect and perhaps make adjustment to the rigid procedure presented here.

For example, there might appear to be a distinct discontinuity between say the last 5 years' experience and prior experience. It may then be justifiable to discard all, or at least a good part, of the prior experience.

The distinction between macro- and micro-models is rather a blurred one. In Section 5.2.1 the distinction was suggested to be that between models which are based on individual claim information (micro) and those which are based on bulk claim information (macro).

Such a distinction is a little naive. Certainly, many of the models dealt with in the following sections never have recourse to individual claims data, and there is no doubt that such cases fall within the ambit of macro-models. Certainty that a particular model is within the scope of definition of micro-model is, however, more difficult to come by. For most methods of claims analysis will, for reasons of manageability, need to form accumulations of individual claims data at some stage. To take an example, consider the model of Hachemeister (1980) (see Section 9.3). It requires tracking of the development of estimated amounts incurred in respect of individual claims from period to period and observation of the manner in which these amounts move up and down. Clearly, this requires rather more detailed observation of individual claims than is normally assumed by most claims analysis models discussed in the preceding sections. On the other hand, as will be seen in Section 9.3, application of the model does not require retention of all this information. All that is required is a tabulation, for each year of experience, of the number of claims which both:

(i) commence the year with an estimate of a particular size,

(ii) complete the year with an estimate of a particular size (not necessarily the same as in (i)).

Once data have been compiled in this form, it might be said that they constitute "bulk claims data", the criterion mentioned above for inclusion of the model in the class of macro-models.

Thus, our decisions as to which models to include in Chapter 8 (stochastic macro-models) and which in Chapter 9 (stochastic micro-models) are not without a certain degree of arbitrariness. The allocation of models to these two chapters has been made mainly on the basis of the degree of detail required in individual claims data before aggregation into bulk data takes place. We freely admit that the allocation is debatable.

Probably the model which would attract most dispute on this score is Reid's (Section 8.3), which is a detailed model but has been classified as of the macro-type.

One final comment may be in order at this point on the course to follow in reading the remainder of the volume. The next few chapters deal with various claims models in some detail. Each section dealing with a particular model is divided into four subsections:

 (i) description of the model;

 (ii) method of estimation of the parameters in the model;

(iii) method of projection of outstanding claims on the basis of the fitted model;

(iv) comment on (i), (ii) and (iii).

Subsections (ii) and (iii) tend to be restricted largely to technicalities. Subsection (iv), on the other hand, obviously consists of more general commentary. In addition, subsection (i) will often contain comment of a historical nature, or of a type providing a motivation of the model or relating it to other models.

It follows, therefore, that the reader concerned more with a general appreciation of the subject than with mastering the finer detail may do well to concentrate on subsections (i) and (iv) in the next few chapters, at least at a first reading.

6.2.   Notation

Basic notation was introduced in Section 3.1. That notation was designed to be very general, but is correspondingly unwieldy. It was promised in Section 3.2 that, for treatment of individual models, the notation would be simplified. In the following sections, various simplifications have been adopted, in each case oriented to the needs of the model of the moment.

While this does lead to a more mnemonic presentation of the models, it also requires the introduction of further notation. The additional notation required by a model is introduced in the section dealing with that model in order that its genesis from the generalized notation be clear. However, for reference purposes, it may be useful to have a summary of all such additional notation. This is given below.

As was pointed out in Sections 3.2 and 3.3, practical applications of data usually require that dates such as i_z = date of occurrence of the z-th claim, k_z = date of notification of the z-th claim, etc. be recorded only in groups such as according to calendar year, calendar month, etc. In the notation presented below it is assumed that this practice is followed, though we shall not be specific about the length of the time-intervals over which these groupings are carried out. Thus i_z, becomes the "period of occurrence of the z-th claim", k_z the "period of notification of the z-th claim", and so on.

6.3   Additional notation

The notation of Sections 3.2 to 4.1 is abbreviated as follows. Realizations of random variables are abbreviated in the same way as are the corresponding random variables.

I_j = set of periods of origin for which development period j is tabulated;

$I_{(j)} = \cap_{k=0}^{j} I_k$ = set of periods of origin for which all development periods up to j are tabulated;

$I_{j,j+1}$ = set of periods of origin for which an operational time period including $(t_j, t_{j+1}]$ (see below) is tabulated;

E_i = measure of exposure in period of origin i;

$N_i = N_{..i..}$ = number of claims incurred in period of origin i;

$N_{ij} = N_{...i.j.} =$ number of claims finalized in development period j of period of origin i ;

$M_{ij} = \sum_{k=0}^{j} N_{ik} =$ number of claims finalized up to the end of development period j of period of origin i ;

$F_{ij} = N_{ij}/N_i =$ speed of finalization of claims in development period j of period of origin i ;

$M_i(j) =$ number of claims finalized by real development time j, i.e. j (not necessarily integral) development periods after the beginning of the period of origin, in respect of period of origin i;

$t_i(j) = m_i(j)/n_i =$ operational time for period of origin i, corresponding to real development time j

$=$ proportion of claims incurred in period of origin i which have been finalized by real development time j;

$\bar{t}_{ij} = \frac{1}{2}[t_i(j) + t_i(j+1)] =$ average operational time passed through during development period j of period of origin i;

$\bar{t}_{ij}^{(k)} = \bar{t}_{ij} \wedge u_k = \min(\bar{t}_{ij}, u_k)$ for some partition $\{u_0, \ldots, u_n\}$ of the operational time-interval $[0, 1]$

$=$ **confined operational time** associated with the point u_k;

$f_i(j) = \partial t_i(j)/\partial j = [\partial m_i(j)/\partial j]/n_i$

$=$ instantaneous speed of finalization at real development time j of period of origin i;

$C_{ij}^* = C_{..i.j..} =$ claim payments in development period j of period of origin i;

$A_{ij}^* = \sum_{k=0}^{j} C_{ik}^* =$ claim payments up to end of development period j of period of origin i;

$B_{ij}^* = C_{ij}^*/E_i =$ claim payments in development period j of period of origin i, per unit of exposure in period of origin i;

$O_{ij}^* = O_{..i.j.} =$ physical estimates of claims outstanding (possibly plus IBNR allowance) at end of development period j of period of origin i;

$I_{ij}^* = A_{ij}^* + O_{ij}^* = $ insurer's estimate, as at end of development period j, of claims incurred in period of origin i;

$P_{ij}^* = P_{..i.(i+j).} = $ outstanding claims at end of development period j of period of origin i;

$S_{ij}^* = C_{ij}^*/N_{ij} = $ claim payments in development period j of period of origin i per claim finalized in development period j; on occasion, we also use S_{ij}^* to denote claim payments per claim handled;

$A_{ij}^*/M_{ij} = $ claim payments up to the end of development period j of period of origin i per claim finalized (or handled) up to the end of development period j;

$A_{ij}^{f^*} = $ claim payments up to the end of development period j of period of origin i in respect of claims finalized by the end of development period j;

$A_{ij}^{p^*} = A_{ij}^* - A_{ij}^{f^*} = $ claim payments up to the end of development period j of period of origin i in respect of claims unfinalized at the end of development period j;

$S_{ij}^{f^*} = A_{ij}^{f^*}/M_{ij} = $ average size of claims finalized up to the end of development period j of year of origin i;

$C_{ij}^{(z)^*} = $ has the same meaning as C_{ij}^* but in respect of just the claim numbered z;

$H_{ij}^{(z)} = $ the number of payments making up the total $C_{ij}^{(z)^*}$;

$\mu_i = $ average claim cost, expressed in the money values of the base period, incurred in period of origin i;

$\lambda_k = $ claims escalation index in period k;

$\alpha_i^* = $ total amount of claim payments in respect of period of origin i;

$\rho_j^* =$ proportion of claim payments in respect of a period of origin payable in development period j (applies only to models in which this proportion is assumed the same for all periods of origin);

$\xi_j^* =$ proportion of amount incurred in a given period of origin recognised by the change of physical estimates between the ends of development periods $j-1$ and j.

$\eta_j^* =$ proportion of amount incurred in a given period of origin recognised by the change of physical estimates between the ends of development periods $j-1$ and j, expressed as a proportion of opening physical estimates for development period j.

$g_j^* =$ proportion of opening physical estimates (inflated) represented by claim payments in development period j.

$$C_{ij}, A_{ij}, B_{ij}, O_{ij}, I_{ij}, P_{ij}, S_{ij}, A_{ij}^f, A_{ij}^p, S_{ij}^f, \alpha_i, \rho_j, \xi_j, \eta_j, g_j$$

have the same meanings as

$$C_{ij}^*, A_{ij}^*, B_{ij}^*, O_{ij}^*, I_{ij}^*, P_{ij}^*, S_{ij}^*, A_{ij}^{f^*}, A_{ij}^{p^*}, S_{ij}^{f^*}, \alpha_i^*, \rho_j^*, \xi_j^*, \eta_j^*, g_j^*$$

but with all money amounts converted to the values of some particular base period;

$C_i(t_j, t_{j+1}), S_i(t_j, t_{j+1})$ have the same meanings as C_{ij}, S_{ij} respectively except that they refer to operational time interval $(t_j, t_{j+1}]$ instead of development period j;

$C_i(0, t_j), S_i(0, t_j)$ are abbreviated to $C_i(t_j)$, $S_i(t_j)$ respectively;

$C_i^f(t_j), S_i^f(t_j)$ have the same meanings as $C_i(t_j), S_i(t_j)$ except that the former are based on only claims finalized by operational time t_j;

$P_i(t)$ has the same meaning as P_{ij} except that it refers to operational time t instead of the end of development period j;

Q_j = payments per claim incurred (inflation-adjusted) in development period j.

$r_{st}(j, k : i)$ = probability that a claim from period of origin i with status s at development epoch (real or operational) j will have status t at development epoch k $(> j)$;

$G_{st}(x : j, k : i)$ = the d.f. of claim size in respect of a claim from period of origin i which has status t at development epoch k, having had status s at development epoch j.

$G(x : t)$ = d.f. of x, the amount of claim payments in respect of a particular year of origin (conceptually infinite in number of claims incurred), between successive finalizations (counting in these claim payments the amount paid in finalization of the first but not the second of the finalizations) within an infinitesimal operational time interval containing t;

$G(x, t)$ = the joint d.f. of x and t where these two variables have the same meaning as in the definition of $G(x : t)$;

$G_{nz}(x, t)$ = the part of $G(x, t)$ relating to non-zero claims, i.e.

$$G_{nz}(x, t) = \begin{cases} G(x, t)/[1 - G(0, \infty)], & x > 0; \\ 0, & x = 0 \end{cases}$$

assuming $G(0-, \infty) = 0$);

$G_z(t)$ = that part of $G(x, t)$ relating to zero claims; i.e.

$$G_z(t) = G(0, t)/G(0, \infty)$$

(assuming $G(0-, \infty) = 0$);

$H(x, t)$ = the decumulative d.f. associated with $G(x, t)$;

$$H(x, t) = 1 - G(x, \infty) - G(\infty, t) + G(x, t);$$

7   NONSTOCHASTIC (MACRO) MODELS

7.1   Models of the $NS/MAC/NN/P/\cdot$ type

7.1.1 *The basic chain ladder method —*
$NS/MAC/NN/P/T,Y$ type

7.1.1.1   Model

The investigation of various methods of analysis of claims run-off data gained substantial momentum in the U.K. and Australia in the early 1970's. This resulted essentially from the failure of a large general insurer, the Vehicle and General, in the U.K., the subsequent inquiry into that company's affairs, and the introduction of legislation establishing wider supervisory powers over general insurance operations. Similar legislation was enacted in Australia in 1973.

The basic chain ladder method, to be dealt with in this section, was (to the knowledge of the author) the first method to be applied widely to run-off data. Its antiquity is reflected in the fact that it is one of the crudest methods to be reviewed in this volume.

Given its position as the grandfather of claims analysis techniques in the U.K. and Australia, its origins are fascinatingly difficult to trace.

The use of the chain ladder method, or some variant of it, was championed in the early 1970's by Prof. R.E.Beard during his days as a consultant to the U.K. Departement of Trade. I believe that the rather whimsical name of the method is due to him. It appears that the method had achieved a quite firm entrenchment in practice by 1973 or 1974.

One can find the ideas inherent in the chain ladder method emerging in the actuarial literature around this time. The English authors, Clarke and Harland (1974, pp.30-33), describe a model which includes all the ingredients of the chain ladder model, and in fact their method of estimation of its parameters is the same as is presented in Section 7.1.1.2 below. The authors give no references to earlier work in this area, apparently believing their method to be original.

About the same time one can find essentially the same model appearing in an application of Credibility Theory to claims reserving (Kramreiter and Straub, 1973, pp.180-183). In that paper the chain ladder method is presented merely as an example to which the theory developed earlier is applied. Consequently, even if the authors had been able to provide a reference, it would not have been altogether unnatural in the circumstances for them to have omitted it.

Van Eeghen (1981, p.30) provides a much earlier reference (Homewood, 1968). However, while this paper does deal with the general philosophy of liability estimation by means of run-off data, it gives no treatment of the chain ladder method in particular.

A personal communication from Prof R.E.Beard states that the chain ladder method is of about this vintage, but once again no specific reference is given.

The origins of the method remain slightly obscure. It appears that it probably originated in the accounting literature and was subsequently absorbed into, or rediscovered in, the actuarial. For example, Skurnick (1973,24-26) describes a method, referred to by him as the "projection method", which is virtually identical to the chain ladder method. He provides an earlier reference (Harnek, 1966) from the insurance accounting literature.

Of course, one must bear in mind that both chain ladder model and estimation method are fairly obvious and might have been derived several times over in past literature. It is possible that such derivations, if they exist, could extend a considerable period into the past.

The method uses an array of claim payments subdivided by period of origin and development period, i.e. an array of observations on the random variables $C_{..i.j...}$.

The notation for these random variables is reduced to just C_{ij}^*. We find it convenient to use the star to signify that the effect of inflation has not been removed, reserving C_{ij} for inflation-adjusted claim payments.

In its simplest form, the model is:

$$c_{ij}^* = \alpha_i^* \rho_{j'}^* \qquad (7.1.1.1.1)$$

where α_i^* is some constant dependent on period of origin and ρ_j^* is some constant dependent on development period j.

Note that, since the model is nonstochastic, it is expressed by giving a parametric form for the realization c_{ij}, as in (5.2.1.1) and (5.2.1.2).

Without loss of generality, the ρ_j^* factors may all be rescaled so that:

$$\sum_{j=0}^{\infty} \rho_j^* = 1, \qquad (7.1.1.1.2)$$

the rescaling constant being absorbed into the α_i^* factors. Then α_i^* may be thought of as the total amount of claim payments payable in respect of period of origin i, and ρ_j^* as the proportion of this total (for any i) payable in development period j.

As has been pointed out on previous occasions (Taylor and Matthews, 1977; Taylor, 1981a), the basic chain ladder model may be viewed as rather more elaborate than (7.1.1.1.1). The method may in fact be considered of the $NS/MAC/NN/P/C, I, T$ type.

For, in the event of a constant rate ϕ of claims escalation from period to period, (7.1.1.1.1) may be written:

$$c_{ij}^* = \alpha_i^* (\rho_j^* / \lambda^{i+j-u}) \lambda^{i+j-u} \quad (\text{u arbitrary}, \lambda = 1 + \phi)$$
$$= \alpha_i \rho_j \lambda^{i+j-u}, \qquad (7.1.1.1.3)$$

where ρ_j is proportional to $\rho_j^* / \lambda^{i+j-u}$ but has been rescaled to satisfy:

$$\sum_{j=0}^{\infty} \rho_j = 1, $$

and the rescaling factor has been absorbed into α_i. Then

$$c_{ij}^* = n_i \mu_i \rho_j \lambda^{i+j-u}. \qquad (7.1.1.1.4)$$

The interpretation of this formula is as follows. The factor λ^{i+j-u} adjusts claim payments, for claims escalation, from the common money values of period u to the values of the period of payment $i + j$. Therefore, α_i is the total amount of claim payments, expressed in the values of period u, in respect of period of origin i. Similarly, ρ_j is the proportion of this total (for any i) payable in development period j. The amount α_i can be decomposed into the two factors n_i, the number of claims incurred in period of origin i, and μ_i, the average claim cost (in period u values) incurred in period i.

The fact that either (7.1.1.1.1) or (7.1.1.1.4) can be adopted as the basic chain ladder model is demonstrated in the next subsection.

7.1.1.2   Estimation

Consider the model (7.1.1.1.4). Define
$$a^*_{ij} = \sum_{k=0}^{j} c^*_{ik} = \text{claim payments made up to the end of the } j\text{-th}$$
development period of period of origin i. By (7.1.1.1.4),

$$a^*_{ij} = n_i \mu_i \lambda^{i-u} \sum_{k=0}^{j} \rho_k \lambda^k.$$

Thus

$$a^*_{i,j+1} / a^*_{i,j} = \sum_{k=0}^{j+1} \rho_k \lambda^k / \sum_{k=0}^{j} \rho_k \lambda^k. \tag{7.1.1.2.1}$$

Now let

I_j = set of periods of origin for which development period j is tabulated,

J_i = set of development periods for which period of origin i is tabulated;

$$I_{(j)} = \cap_{k=0}^{j} I_k.$$

Since (7.1.1.2.1) applies for each value of i for which $a^*_{i,j}$ and $a^*_{i,j+1}$ are both available, the right side can be estimated by a combination of these various estimates. Thus

$$\sum_{i \in I_{(j+1)}} a^*_{i,j+1} / \sum_{i \in I_{(j+1)}} a^*_{ij} = \sum_{k=0}^{j+1} \rho_k \lambda^k / \sum_{k=0}^{j} \rho_k \lambda^k, \tag{7.1.1.2.2}$$

Since the above development has been made for the model (7.1.1.1.4), it clearly covers the simpler model (7.1.1.1.1) (just set $\lambda = 1$).

There is in fact no reason why the basic equation (7.1.1.2.1) should not be replaced by an alternative involving $c^*_{i,j+1}$ and c^*_{ij} on the left. However, the version given above is the one which appears to be used.

7.1.1.3   *Projection of outstanding claims*

For this section only, write β^*_j for the right side of (7.1.1.2.2). Outstanding claims in respect of period of origin i, at the end of development period j are:

$$p^*_{ij} = a^*_{i\infty} - a^*_{ij}$$
$$= a^*_{ij}(\beta^*_j \beta^*_{j+1} \beta^*_{j+2} \cdots - 1)$$

provided that the continued applicability of the claims escalation factor λ is assumed for the future.

If the difference between β^*_k and unity is negligible for $k > K$, this reduces to:

$$p^*_{ij} = a^*_{ij}(\prod_{k=j}^{K} \beta^*_k - 1). \qquad (7.1.1.3.1)$$

Note that the estimate of outstanding claims has been obtained by the ratio method of projection, which is the usual one used in connection with the basic chain ladder method.

7.1.1.4   *Comment*

In the terminology of Sawkins(1979) (see Section 5.5 of this volume), the basic chain ladder method involves an estimation procedure (Section 7.1.1.2) of the ratios of payments type.

It is intuitive, and to some extent empirically supported, that a method which proceeds by calculation of ratios (7.1.1.2.2) and the subsequent chained multiplication of those ratios is likely to produce highly variable results.

Perhaps the greatest drawback of the basic chain ladder method is that it projects the average (in some sense) past claims escalation rate into the future. This suffers two disadvantages. Firstly, because the loading for future inflation is implicit, its magnitude is not clear. Secondly, because the loading for future inflation is essentially an average of past inflation rates, it may be inappropriate to the future.

Berquist and Sherman (1977) present a number of variations of the chain ladder method. These are concerned with the fact that the ratios $a^*_{i,j+1}/a^*_{ij}$

may display trends, contrary to the assumption implicit in (7.1.1.2.1.). The methods are directed toward identification and projection of such trends. They are summarized by van Eeghen, (1981, pp.33-46).

Kremer (1982) has examined the chain ladder method in the framework of the ANOVA model, in much the same way as was done by Taylor (1979) in respect of the separation method. Kremer exhibits the connection between his estimators so obtained and those developed in Section 7.1.1.2. Once again the development is parallel to Taylor's.

As an incidental matter, it is interesting to consider the results of Hachemeister and Stanard (1975). They deal with the rather different problem of projecting numbers of Incurred But Not Reported claims. For them, our C_{ij}^* denotes the number of claims from period of origin i reported in development period j. The object of the exercise is to estimate values of P_{ik}^*, the number of claims of period of origin i which are still unreported at the end of development period k. Hachemeister and Stanard show that, if the claims of a given period of origin are multinomially distributed over development periods, then the basic chain ladder method described above is maximum likelihood. This justifies the method already in existence before the paper by Hachemeister and Stanard (see Skurnick, 1973, p.42).

7.1.2 *Inflation-adjusted chain ladder method —*

   NS/MAC/NN/P/T, Y, I, type

7.1.2.1   Model

The inflation-adjusted chain ladder operates in exactly the same manner as the basic chain ladder, but uses claim payments from which the effect of claims escalation has been removed by conversion to common money values.

The basic equation is (7.1.1.1.4) but modified to allow for claims escalation which is not necessarily equal from year to year. Let λ^{i+j-u} in (7.1.1.1.4) be replaced by λ_{i+j}/λ_u where λ_{i+j} is the value of an appropriate claims escalation index in period $(i + j)$. Define

$$c_{ij} = c_{ij}^* \lambda_u / \lambda_{i+j}$$

= claim payments in development period
j of period of origin i, converted to the
money values of base period u.   (7.1.2.1.1)

Then (7.1.1.1.4) and (7.1.2.1.1) yield:

$$c_{ij} = n_i \mu_i \rho_j.$$ (7.1.2.1.2)

Comparison of (7.1.1.1.4) and (7.1.2.1.2) shows that, structurally, the inflation-adjusted chain ladder model is the special case of the basic chain ladder model, $\lambda = 1$ (zero claims escalation).

7.1.2.2   *Estimation*

The reasoning is as in Section 7.1.1.2 with stars removed and $\lambda = 1$. Thus, by (7.1.1.2.2)

$$\sum_{i \in I_{(j+1)}} a_{i,j+1} \Big/ \sum_{i \in I_{(j+1)}} a_{ij} = \sum_{k=0}^{j+1} \rho_k \Big/ \sum_{k=0}^{j} \rho_k.$$ (7.1.2.2.1)

7.1.2.3   *Projection of outstanding claims*

The reasoning is as in Section 7.1.1.3 with stars removed and $\lambda = 1$. Write β_j for the right side of (7.1.2.2.1). Then (7.1.1.3.1) is replaced by:

$$p_{ij} = a_{ij} \left(\prod_{k=j}^{K} \beta_k - 1 \right)$$ (7.1.2.3.1)

This gives outstanding claims in values of the base period. If the inflated version is required, p_{ij} must be apportioned to individual periods.

Note that

$$c_{ik} = a_{i,k+1} - a_{ik}$$
$$= a_{ij}\beta_j\beta_{j+1}\ldots\beta_{k-1}(\beta_k - 1) \qquad \text{for } k > j.$$

Then

$$p_{ij}^* = \sum_{k=j+1}^{\infty} c_{ik}^*$$

$$= \sum_{k=j+1}^{\infty} c_{ik}\lambda_{i+k}/\lambda_u.$$ (7.1.2.3.2)

where λ_{i+k} is the value of **the claims escalation index** projected for payment period $(i + k)$.

7.1.2.4   *Comment*

The first criticism of the basic chain ladder method made in Section 7.1.1.4 applies equally to the inflation-adjusted chain ladder method.

Clearly the use of the explicit inflation index introduced into (7.1.2.1.1) overcomes the other objections raised against the basic chain ladder method. For this reason the inflation-adjusted chain ladder method will usually be preferable to the basic chain ladder.   This will be particularly so when substantial changes in inflation rates have occurred in the recent past or are expected in the near future, for in these circumstances the basic chain ladder's implicit assumption of a constant rate of claims escalation breaks down.

Nevertheless, one difficulty which cannot be dismissed is that of selecting an appropriate claims escalation index.   Different indexes will apply to different classes of business, and even to different segments of the one class of business. This problem is discussed at some length by Sawkins (1979, pp.470-478).   A particular problem is **superimposed inflation,** a term used by Benktander (1979) to cover the differential (apparently persistently positive) between rates of claims escalation and standard measures of inflation. Cumpston and Mack (1978) and Cumpston (1979) give data which suggest that superimposed inflation in Australian liability insurance may be substantial.

It has been pointed out by Taylor and Matthews (1977) that certain methods of analysis of data contain a self-correction mechanism which will deal with superimposed inflation. More particularly, if claims escalation is understated by a constant margin (e.g. superimposed inflation) in both past and future, the result derived will be the same as if accurate measures of claims escalation had been used. The inflation-adjusted chain ladder is one such method.

Understatement of past claims escalation leads to overestimation of the average delay from occurrence to payment of claim.   This overestimation, when fed back into the projection of the future, compensates for underestimation of future claims escalation.

As remarked in Section 7.1.1.2, there is no reason why the estimation carried out in (7.1.2.2.1) should not be based on $c_{i,j+1}$ and c_{ij} instead of $a_{i,j+1}$ and a_{ij}. Again, however, the form presented in Section 7.1.2.2 appears to be the one in use.

7.1.3 *The payment ratio method —*

   $NS/MAC/NN/P/T, Y, I,$ *type*

7.1.3.1   *Model*

The method appears to have been introduced by Sawkins (1975, pp.358-365). The model is exactly as for the inflation-adjusted chain ladder method (Section 7.1.2).

7.1.3.2   *Estimation*

Estimation is similar to that used under the inflation-adjusted chain ladder method, but with one important difference on which comment will be made in Section 7.1.3.4.

After adjustment for inflation has been made to claim payments, equation (7.1.1.2.1) applies once again with $\lambda = 1$. In the inflation-adjusted chain ladder method, this leads to (7.1.2.2.1). But the payment ratio method instead uses:

$$|I_{(j+1)}|^{-1} \sum_{i \in I_{(j+1)}} (a_{i,j+1}/a_{ij}) = \sum_{k=0}^{j+1} \rho_k / \sum_{k=0}^{j} \rho_k, \qquad (7.1.3.2.1)$$

where $|I_{(j+1)}|$ denotes the order (i.e. the number of members) of the set $I_{(j+1)}$.

7.1.3.3   *Projection of outstanding claims*

Projection is precisely as for the inflation-adjusted chain ladder method (Section 7.1.2.3).

7.1.3.4   Comment

It is clear from Sections 7.1.3.1 to 7.1.3.3 that there is a great similarity between the inflation-adjusted chain ladder and payment ratio methods. A comparison of the respective estimation equations, (7.1.2.2.1) and (7.1.3.2.1), makes clear the exact nature of this similarity.

Note that the left side of (7.1.3.2.1) is the arithmetic average of the payment ratios $a_{i,j+1}/a_{ij}$. The left side of equation (7.1.2.2.1) can be written in the form:

$$\sum_{i \in I_{(j+1)}} a_{ij}(a_{i,j+1}/a_{ij}) \Big/ \sum_{i \in I_{(j+1)}} a_{ij},$$

which is the weighted average of the same payment ratios with weights a_{ij}.

Thus the inflation-adjusted chain ladder and payment ratio methods are the same apart from a difference in weighting in the formation of averages.

The efficiency of these different weightings was the subject of comment by Taylor and Matthews (1977, Section 6.9), who proved that:

> "*methods which take means and then ratios of these means tend to be superior to methods which take ratios and then means of these ratios.*"

In other words, the inflation adjusted chain ladder model appears preferable to the payment ratio method on the ground of statistical efficiency. As the efficiency of chain ladder methods is thought to be low (Section 7.1.1.4), this may constitute a case for abandonment of the payment ratio method.

The comment made about the chain ladder methods, that estimation could be based on ratios $c_{i,j+1}/c_{ij}$ rather than $a_{i,j+1}/a_{ij}$, holds equally for the payment ratio method. But it is more common in the case of the latter method for such a procedure to be used in practice. In fact, Sawkins (1979, pp.445,497) treats the two alternatives as virtually equal.

7.1.4 *The payments per unit of risk method —*
     NS/MAC/NN/P/T,I,E type

7.1.4.1   Model

The method is described by Cumpston (1976), though it may well have appeared elsewhere prior to that date.

The model is less general than that of the inflation-adjusted chain ladder or payment ratio method. Instead of (7.1.2.1.2), it is:

$$c_{ij} = n_i \mu \rho_j, \qquad (7.1.4.1.1)$$

where it can be seen that average claim size is assumed to be independent of period of origin (but see the remarks in Section 7.1.4.4).

The last equation can be written as:

$$c_{ij} = n_i q_j, \qquad (7.1.4.1.2)$$

where

$$q_j = \mu \rho_j$$
$$= \text{payments (inflation-adjusted) in}$$
$$\qquad \text{development period } j \text{ per claim incurred} \qquad (7.1.4.1.3)$$

The model can be made more general if (7.1.4.1.1) to (7.1.4.1.3) are replaced by:

$$c_{ij} = e_i q_j, \qquad (7.1.4.1.4)$$

where e_i is a measure of the volume of **exposure** (or the number of **units of risk**) in period of origin i, and q_j denotes payments (inflation-adjusted) in development period j per unit of risk.

7.1.4.2.   Estimation

By (7.1.4.1.4)

$$\sum_{i \in I_j} c_{ij} = q_j \sum_{i \in I_j} e_i,$$

whence

$$q_j = \sum_{i \in I_j} c_{ij} / \sum_{i \in I_j} e_i. \qquad (7.1.4.2.1)$$

7.1.4.3.   *Projection of outstanding claims*

Outstanding claims in respect of period of origin i at the end of development period j are:

$$p_{ij}^* = \sum_{k=j+1}^{\infty} c_{ik}^*$$

$$= \sum_{k=j+1}^{\infty} c_{ik}\lambda_{i+k}/\lambda_u$$

$$= e_i \sum_{k=j+1}^{\infty} q_k\lambda_{i+k}/\lambda_u. \qquad (7.1.4.3.1)$$

7.1.4.4.   *Comment*

In practice, the application of the payments per unit of risk method tends to follow much less rigid lines than are presented here.

The restriction that $\mu_i = \mu$ in (7.1.4.1.1) is recognised as a serious one, and users of the method are inclined to attempt to allow for changes in μ_i. A drift in the μ_i may well induce drifts in the values of c_{ij}/e_i (with changing i) which make up the weighted average (7.1.4.2.1). In practice, an attempt would usually be made to detect any such trends. If they are detected, allowance would usually be made for them by changing the weighting in the weighted average (7.1.4.2.1), thus:

$$q_j = \sum_{i\in I_j} w_{ij}c_{ij} / \sum_{i\in I_j} w_{ij}e_i, \qquad (7.1.4.4.1)$$

where the w_{ij} are weighting factors. For example, if claims experience is available up to and including payment period b, and it appears that a discontinuity in experience occurred between payment periods $b' - 1$ and b', then the weights might be chosen as:

$$w_{ij} = 1, \qquad b' \le i+j < b$$
$$= 0, \qquad i+j < b'.$$

Alternatively, w_{ij} might be dependent on period of origin i rather than payment period $i + j$; or the w_{ij} might be such as to the project some observed trend into the future.

It is interesting to observe that, contrary to the methods dealt with in Sections 7.1.1 to 7.1.3, there is no distinction between the versions of the payments per unit of risk method based on the c_{ij} and the a_{ij} respectively. For, by (7.1.4.1.4),

$$a_{ij} = \sum_{k=0}^{j} e_i q_k$$
$$= e_i q'_j, \qquad\qquad (7.1.4.4.2)$$

where $q'_j = \sum_{k=0}^{j} q_k$. Also

$$q'_j = \sum_{i \in I_j} a_{ij} / \sum_{i \in I_j} e_i. \qquad\qquad (7.1.4.4.3)$$

Equations (7.1.4.4.2) and (7.1.4.4.3) are of the same form as (7.1.4.1.4) and (7.1.4.2.1) respectively. They lead to identical results.

The payments per unit of risk method does not possess the self-correcting mechanism referred to in Section 7.1.2.4 and possessed by the preceding two methods.

It might be noted that the method of projection normally associated with the payments per unit of risk method is the direct future payments method (see Section 5.4). This is in contrast with the methods of Sections 7.1.1 to 7.1.3 which are normally associated with the ratio method of projection. It cannot be stressed too strongly, however, that any of the three methods of projection presented in Section 5.4 could be combined with any of the methods of analysis encountered to this point.

7.1.5.   *The separation method —*
NS/MAC/NN/P/T, I, E type

7.1.5.1   *Model*

It may be noted that the separation method has been classified as of the same type as the payments per unit of risk method of Section 7.1.4. The models for the two methods are in fact the same, viz. (7.1.4.1.4); or written in an equivalent form,

$$c_{ij}^* = e_i q_j \lambda_{i+j} / \lambda_u$$
$$= e_i (q_j / \lambda_u) \lambda_{i+j}. \qquad (7.1.5.1.1)$$

The essential difference between the two methods is that the payments per unit of risk method takes claims escalation λ to be given, whereas the separation method treats it as unknown.

As in the payments per unit of risk method, e_i may denote any measure of volume of exposure.

For reasons which will become apparent in Section 7.1.5.2, it is customary to rewrite (7.1.5.1.1) in the form

$$c_{ij}^* = e_i \rho_j \lambda_{i+j} \qquad (7.1.5.1.2)$$

where

$$\rho_j = q_j / \lambda_u, \qquad (7.1.5.1.3)$$

and the claims escalation index has its base value λ_u set so that

$$\sum_{j=0}^{\infty} \rho_j = 1 \qquad (7.1.5.1.4)$$

That is, by (7.1.5.1.3) and (7.1.5.1.4), λ_u is so chosen that

$$\lambda_u = \sum_{j=0}^{\infty} q_j$$

$=$ total payments (inflation-adjusted to values of period u) per unit of exposure (by (7.1.4.1.3))

$=$ average claim amount (inflation-adjusted to values of period u) per unit of exposure . $\qquad (7.1.5.1.5)$

Johnson (1980) has given this interpretation of λ_u. Note that, by (7.1.5.1.3) and (7.1.5.1.5),

$$\rho_j = q_j / \sum_{j=0}^{\infty} q_j, \qquad (7.1.5.1.6)$$

so that ρ_j does in fact denote the proportion of a period of origin's (inflation-adjusted) claim payments payable in development period j, consistently with earlier sections.

7.1.5.2.   *Estimation*

For estimation purposes it is convenient to rearrange (7.1.5.1.2) so that only the unknowns stand on the right-hand side:

$$b_{ij}^* = c_{ij}^*/e_i = \rho_j \lambda_{i+j}. \qquad (7.1.5.2.1)$$

The term b_{ij}^* can be interpreted as claim payments (not inflation-adjusted) in development period j of period of origin i, per unit of exposure in period of origin i.

The problem then is to obtain the parameters ρ_j and λ_{i+j} given an array of values b_{ij}^*.

At this point we impose a restriction on the "shape" of the array of values b_{ij}^*. For the moment it will be required that the array be triangular in the sense that it appears as follows:

				Development period			
		0	1	2	...	k-2	k-1	k
Period	0	b_{00}^*	b_{01}^*	b_{02}^*	...	$b_{0,k-2}^*$	$b_{0,k-1}^*$	$b_{0,k}^*$
of	1	b_{10}^*	b_{11}^*	b_{12}^*	...	$b_{1,k-2}^*$	$b_{1,k-1}^*$	
Origin	2	b_{20}^*	b_{21}^*	b_{22}^*	...	$b_{2,k-2}^*$		
	.	.	.					
	.	.	.					
	.	.	.					
	k	b_{k0}^*						

By (7.1.5.2.1), this is equivalent to:

		Development period					
		0	1	2	...	$k-2$	$k-1$	k
Period	0	$\rho_0\lambda_0$	$\rho_1\lambda_1$	$\rho_2\lambda_2$	...	$\rho_{k-2}\lambda_{k-2}$	$\rho_{k-1}\lambda_{k-1}$	$\rho_k\lambda_k$
of	1	$\rho_0\lambda_1$	$\rho_1\lambda_2$	$\rho_2\lambda_3$	...	$\rho_{k-2}\lambda_{k-1}$	$\rho_{k-1}\lambda_k$	
origin	2	$\rho_0\lambda_2$	$\rho_1\lambda_3$	$\rho_2\lambda_4$	...	$\rho_{k-2}\lambda_k$		
	.	.	.	.				
	.	.	.	.				
	.	.	.	.				
	k	$\rho_0\lambda_k$						

It is also assumed for the time being that claim payments beyond development period k are negligible,

$$i.e. \qquad b_{ij}^* = 0, \qquad j > k,$$
$$i.e. \qquad \rho_j = 0, \qquad j > k,$$

for then (7.1.5.1.4) becomes

$$\sum_{j=0}^{k} \rho_j = 1. \tag{7.1.5.2.2}$$

The solution of this type of problem was first given by Verbeek (1972). He obtained maximum likelihood estimates of the ρ_j, λ_{i+j} under the assumption that the (i,j)-cell of the array contains a Poisson variate with mean $\rho_i\lambda_{i+j}$ and all cells are mutually stochastically independent.

Taylor (1977a) showed that exactly the same method could be obtained by heuristic means and without any distributional assumptions.

The procedure makes use of the fact that each column has a common factor of ρ_j and each (north-east to south-west) diagonal a common factor of λ_{i+j}.

Let

$$v_j = \text{sum along the j-th column;}$$
$$d_h = \text{sum along h-th diagonal.}$$

Then

$$v_j = \sum_i b^*_{ij} = \rho_j \sum_{l=0}^{k-j} \lambda_{j+l}; \qquad\qquad (7.1.5.2.3)$$

$$d_h = \sum_{i+j=h} b^*_{ij} = \lambda_h \sum_{l=0}^{h} \rho_l. \qquad\qquad (7.1.5.2.4)$$

It follows that

$$\rho_j = v_j / \sum_{l=j}^{k} \lambda_l, \qquad\qquad (7.1.5.2.5)$$

$$\lambda_h = d_h / \sum_{l=0}^{h} \rho_l. \qquad\qquad (7.1.5.2.6)$$

By (7.1.5.2.5), ρ_k can be obtained if λ_k is available, ρ_{k-1} if λ_{k-1} and λ_k are available, etc. Thus if the λ_l can be obtained in the order $\lambda_k, \lambda_{k-1}, \ldots, \lambda_0$, then the ρ_j can be calculated in the order $\rho_k, \rho_{k-1}, \ldots, \rho_0$. However, by (7.1.5.2.6), calculation of λ_k requires knowledge of $\rho_0, \ldots, \rho_k$.

Here (7.1.5.2.2) is useful. It allows (7.1.5.2.6) to be written as:

$$\lambda_h = d_h / \left[1 - \sum_{l=h+1}^{k} \rho_l \right]. \qquad\qquad (7.1.5.2.7)$$

In this case, calculation of λ_h requires knowledge of $\rho_{h+1}, \ldots, \rho_k$. Thus, (7.1.5.2.5) and (7.1.2.5.7) may be used to obtain values of the parameters in the order $\lambda_k, \rho_k, \lambda_{k-1}, \rho_{k-1}, \ldots, \lambda_0, \rho_0$. The starting point in these calculations is, by (7.1.5.2.7):

$$\lambda_k = d_k. \qquad\qquad (7.1.5.2.8)$$

We now wish to relax the assumption that $\rho_j = 0$ for $j > k$. Suppose that

$$\sum_{j=k+1}^{\infty} \rho_j = \rho \tag{7.1.5.2.9}$$

Then (7.1.5.2.2) becomes:

$$\sum_{j=0}^{k} \rho_j = 1 - \rho \tag{7.1.5.2.10}$$

Note that

$$b_{ij}^* = \rho_j \lambda_{i+j} = \rho_j' \lambda_{i+j}' \tag{7.1.5.2.11}$$

Where

$$\rho_j' = \rho_j / (1 - \rho) \qquad \text{and} \qquad \lambda_{i+j}' = \lambda_{i+j}(1 - \rho) \tag{7.1.5.2.12}$$

By (7.1.5.2.10) and (7.1.5.2.12),

$$\sum_{j=0}^{k} \rho_j' = 1$$

and, by (7.1.5.2.11) the problem reduces to the same one as before but in terms of parameters ρ_j', λ_{i+j}', instead of ρ_j, λ_{i+j}. Note that, by (7.1.5.2.12),

$\rho_j' =$ payments (inflation-adjusted to values of some common period) in development period j, per unit of total claims paid up to the end of development period k;

$\lambda_{i+j}' =$ average amount paid (inflation-adjusted to values of period $i + j$) up to the end of development period k per unit of exposure.

For $\rho > 0$, development periods $k + 1$ and later would need to be dealt with on the basis of some extraneous information.

It is also possible to make some relaxation of the assumption that the array of b_{ij}^* is triangular. It has been shown by Taylor (1977b) that the same method of parameter estimation may be applied in cases where:

(i) a north-west subtriangle of the triangular array of data is missing;

(ii) the array of data forms a parallellogram (or equivalently there are missing north-west and north-east subtriangles).

These two situations are represented by the following two diagrams.

Period of origin	Development period							
	0	1	...	s	s+1	...	k-1	k
0	Missing north-west triangle				$b^*_{0,s+1}$	...	$b^*_{0,k-1}$	b^*_{0k}
1				b^*_{1s}	$b^*_{1,s+1}$	...	$b^*_{1,k-1}$	
.								
.								
s		b^*_{s1}	...					
s+1	$b^*_{s+1,0}$	$b^*_{s+1,1}$	...					
.								
.								
k-1	$b^*_{k-1,0}$	$b^*_{k-1,1}$						
k	$b^*_{k,0}$							

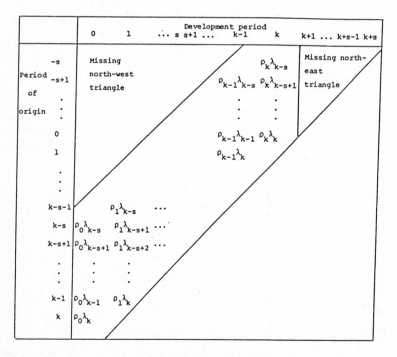

Taylor showed that in each of these two cases, the runoff array could be treated as a complete triangle but with zeros placed in the triangles of missing information. Then equations (7.1.5.2.5) and (7.1.5.2.7) still work.

The above form of representing a runoff array has become more or less traditional in the literature. However, in the last case, if the diagram is distorted somewhat, the separation method becomes quite transparent. The distortion consists of replacing the year of origin axis by a year of payment axis, thus:

	Development period				
	0	1	...	k-1	k
Period k-s	$\rho_0\lambda_{k-s}$	$\rho_1\lambda_{k-s}$	...	$\rho_{k-1}\lambda_{k-s}$	$\rho_k\lambda_{k-s}$
of k-s+1	$\rho_0\lambda_{k-s+1}$	$\rho_1\lambda_{k-s+1}$	...	$\rho_{k-1}\lambda_{k-s+1}$	$\rho_k\lambda_{k-s+1}$
origin .	.	.	.	.	.
.	.	.	.	.	.
k-1	$\rho_0\lambda_{k-1}$	$\rho_1\lambda_{k-1}$	...	$\rho_{k-1}\lambda_{k-1}$	$\rho_k\lambda_{k-1}$
k	$\rho_0\lambda_k$	$\rho_1\lambda_k$	...	$\rho_{k-1}\lambda_k$	$\rho_k\lambda_k$

For this special case, the model becomes a familiar two-factor multiplicative model in which the two factors are labelled by row and column respectively.

In the last diagram v_j is still a column sum, but d_h becomes a row sum.

By (7.1.5.2.2),

$$d_h = \lambda_h \sum_{j=0}^{k} \rho_j = \lambda_h$$

and

$$v_j = \rho_j \sum_{h=0}^{s} \lambda_{k-h}.$$

Thus

$$\lambda_h = d_h \qquad\qquad (7.1.5.2.13)$$

and

$$\rho_j = v_j / \sum_{h=0}^{s} \lambda_{k-h}$$

In words,

$$\lambda_h = \text{sum of row } h;$$

and

$$\rho_j = \frac{\text{sum of column } j}{\text{sum of all entries in array}}.$$

7.1.5.3.   *Projection*

Once values of ρ_j and λ_{i+j} have been obtained, it is a simple matter to substitute back into (7.1.5.1.2) to obtain values of c^*_{ij} for future payment years.

Outstanding claims may then be projected by any of the methods dealt with in Section 5.4.

7.1.5.4.   *Comment*

The reason for the existence of the separation method is that it seeks to estimate claims escalation rather than take it as given. This can be useful in dealing with any body of data which contains significant superimposed inflation (see Section 7.1.2.4).

One must, however, exercise caution in the interpretation, From a naive viewpoint $(\lambda_{i+j+1}/\lambda_{i+j} - 1)$ might be taken as claims escalation (subject, of course, to sampling error) between payment periods $(i + j)$ and $(i + j + 1)$. Note, however, that in the original paper Taylor (1977a), pointed out that this was not necessarily the case and that the ratio $\lambda_{i+j+1}/\lambda_{i+j}$ was a measure of all *"exogenous influences"* specific to the payment periods in question. These influences would certainly include claims escalation but might include others such as changes in speed of finalization of claims. Any *"period of origin effects"* such as changes in the mix of the portfolio would also help to confuse the situation.

Changing speed of finalization is probably the most serious of these problems. Allowance for this leads to a consideration of methods of the $\cdot/\cdot/N/\cdot/\cdot$ type which is deferred to Sections 7.3, 8.2 and 8.3.

The sampling errors in the ratios $\lambda_{i+j+1}/\lambda_{i+j}$ can be substantial in smaller portfolios. Again care is needed in interpretation.

Methods of estimation other than that presented in Section 7.1.5.2 are dealt with in the literature. In each case the model (7.1.5.1.2) is retained. Taylor and Matthews (1977) deal with a couple of minimum χ^2 versions of the separation method, in which values of ρ_j, λ_{i+j} are obtained by minimization of a certain weighted sum of squared differences between b_{ij}^* and $\rho_j \lambda_{i+j}$.

Taylor (1979) presented a **geometric separation method** in which the sums of (7.1.5.2.3) and (7.1.5.2.4) are replaced by products and the estimates of ρ_j, λ_h corresponding to (7.1.5.2.5) and (7.1.5.2.7) contain geometric means of various observations. The method of estimation presented in Section 7.1.5.2 was referred to as the **arithmetic separation method**.

In the same paper Taylor presented a **regression separation method**. The model (7.1.5.2.1) is rewritten as a **linear form**:

$$\log b_{ij}^* = \log \rho_j + \log \lambda_{i+j}.$$

The problem is then treated as a regression problem with observations b_{ij}^* and regression coefficients $\log \rho_j$, $\log \lambda_{i+j}$. Taylor showed that ordinary least squares estimation leads to the same results as the geometric separation method.

The regression separation method has been mentioned in this section because it has the same origin as the other separation methods. However, it might more properly be included under stochastic methods.

7.2   Models of the $NS/MAC/NN/I/\cdot$ type

7.2.1 *Monitoring the track record (chain ladder method) —*
      $NS/MAC/NN/I/T, Y$ *type*

7.2.1.1.   Model

As pointed out by Craighead (1980), the essence of the chain ladder
method is that it is *"one of extrapolating from known data by using ratios
drawn, as averages, from earlier cohorts"*.

Viewed in this abstract way, the method is apparently available for
application to figures other than claim payments as in Section 7.1.1. One
possibility is to apply it to "estimated amounts incurred", where the
amount incurred in respect of period of origin i, estimated as at the end
of development period j, is taken as the total of claim payments up to the
end of development period j plus the physical estimate of outstanding claims
(possibly plus an IBNR provision).

Let

$$O_{ij}^* = O_{..i.j.} = \text{ physical estimate at end of development period } j$$
$$\text{of claims outstanding in respect of period of origin}$$
$$i \text{ (possibly with an IBNR provision added).}$$

Define

$$I_{ij}^* = A_{ij}^* + O_{ij}^* = \text{ insurer's estimate, as at end of development period}$$
$$j, \text{ of claims incurred in period of origin } i.$$

Note that the use of the $*$ superscript on O indicates that physical
estimates are intended to include an allowance for future inflation. Comment
on this point is made in Section 7.2.1.4.

Truckle (1978) has suggested effectively that the chain ladder method
be applied to the i_{ij}^* instead of the a_{ij}^* as in Section 7.1.1. Actually, Truckle
worked with average claim sizes, i.e. i_{ij}^*/n_i, but this is equivalent to working
with just the i_{ij}^*. His working also involved another difference from the chain
ladder method on which we comment in Section 7.2.1.2. Truckle referred

to this method of assessing outstanding claims as "monitoring the track record".

Since it is being suggested that the chain ladder method be applied simply with a_{ij}^* replaced by i_{ij}^*, it is apparent that the model involved must have the same structure as (7.1.1.1.1), i.e.

$$i_{ij}^* - i_{i,j-1}^* = \alpha_i^* \rho_j^*, \qquad (7.2.1.1.1)$$

where the ρ_j^* will, of course, have meaning different from that ascribed in earlier sections (see e.g. Section 6.3). In fact, (7.2.1.1.1) is better written as:

$$i_{ij}^* - i_{i,j-1}^* = \alpha_i^* \xi_j^*, \qquad (7.2.1.1.2)$$

where

$\xi_j^* =$ proportion of amount incurred in a given year of origin recognised by the change of physical estimates between the ends of development periods $j-1$ and j.

Corresponding to (7.1.1.1.2) is:

$$\sum_{j=0}^{\infty} \xi_j^* = 1. \qquad (7.2.1.1.3)$$

7.2.1.2.   *Estimation*

The method of estimation is as in Section 7.1.1.2 (basic chain ladder) with a_{ij}^* replaced i_{ij}^*. Thus, corresponding to (7.1.1.2.2),

$$\sum_{i \in I_{(j+1)}} i_{i,j+1}^* / \sum_{i \in I_{(j+1)}} i_{ij}^* = \sum_{k=0}^{j+1} \xi_k^* / \sum_{k=0}^{j} \xi_k^*. \qquad (7.2.1.2.1)$$

The difference between this method of estimation and the one actually used by Truckle (1978) in his worked example is that, in (7.2.1.2.1), he recognised only the last two periods of experience. Thus, if tabulated experience is of a triangular form given in the first diagram of Section 7.1.5.2, then $I_{(j)}$ is taken as the set of accident periods

$$\{k - j - 1 \quad , \quad k - j\}.$$

7.2.1.3.   *Projection of outstanding claims*

The method of projection is as in Section 7.1.1.3 with a_{ij}^* replaced by i_{ij}^*. Thus, corresponding to (7.1.1.3.1),

$$p_{ij}^* = i_{ij}^* \prod_{k=j}^{K} \beta_k^* - a_{ij}^*, \qquad (7.2.1.3.1)$$

where for this section only, β_j^* denotes the right side of (7.2.1.2.1).

7.2.1.4.   *Comment*

The basic idea behind the track record method is that the manner in which revisions of amounts incurred have taken place in the past ought to provide some guidance as to the manner in which such estimates at a given balance date will be revised in future.

Although this idea is both simple and respectable, the method presented above suffers from several logical difficulties.

Firstly, consider the fact that no adjustment is made for claims escalation. It was shown in Section 7.1.1.1 that such a procedure in the basic chain ladder method, as applied to claim payments, was justified on the assumption of a constant rate of claims escalation from period to period.

Consider whether the same assumption justifies the absence of an inflation adjustment in the present case. Suppose that, in inflation-adjusted terms, the adjustment of physical estimates with increasing development period is consistent as between different periods of origin.

One must be careful about what is meant here by "consistent". To some extent the meaning will depend on the basis on which the physical estimates have been constructed; and in particular whether they are intended to represent outstanding claims in current or inflated values.

Suppose the former. Then the most natural interpretation of "consistent", we would suggest, is that;

$$i_{ij} - i_{i,j-1} = \alpha_i \xi_j, \qquad (7.2.1.4.1),$$

which is the inflation-adjusted version of (7.2.1.1.2).

Now, if the inflation adjustment has been to values of base period u, then

$$i_{ij} = a_{ij} + o_{ij} = \sum_{k=0}^{j} c_{ik} + o_{ij}$$

$$= \lambda_u \left[\sum_{k=0}^{j} \frac{c_{ik}^*}{\lambda_{i+k}^{(c)}} + \frac{o_{ij}^*}{\lambda_{i+j}^{(o)}} \right], \qquad (7.2.1.4.2)$$

where $\lambda^{(c)}$ is the escalation index applying to claim payments (spread over a period) and $\lambda^{(o)}$ to estimated outstandings (estimated at the end of a period).

Thus, by (7.2.1.4.2),

$$i_{ij} - i_{i,j-1} = \lambda_u \left[\frac{c_{ij}^*}{\lambda_{i+j}^{(c)}} + \frac{o_{ij}^*}{\lambda_{i+j}^{(o)}} - \frac{o_{i,j-1}^*}{\lambda_{i+j-1}^{(o)}} \right]$$

$$= \frac{\alpha_i \left[\dfrac{c_{ij}^*}{\lambda_{i+j}^{(c)}} + \dfrac{o_{ij}^*}{\lambda_{i+j}^{(o)}} - \dfrac{o_{i,j-1}^*}{\lambda_{i+j-1}^{(o)}} \right]}{\displaystyle\sum_{k=0}^{\infty} \frac{c_{ik}^*}{\lambda_{i+k}^{(c)}}}. \qquad (7.2.1.4.3)$$

In the case of a constant rate of claims escalation, this becomes:

$$i_{ij} - i_{i,j-1} = \frac{\alpha_i \left[c_{ij}^* \lambda^{\frac{1}{2}} + o_{ij}^* - o_{i,j-1}^* \lambda \right]}{\displaystyle\sum_{k=0} c_{ik}^* \lambda^{j-k+\frac{1}{2}}}$$

$$(7.2.1.4.4)$$

which, by (7.2.1.4.1), is said to be of the form $\alpha_i \xi_j$.

Now consider $i_{ij}^* - i_{i,j-1}^*$. An expression for this can be obtained by treating λ as unity in (7.2.1.4.3). Thus,

$$i_{ij}^* - i_{i,j-1}^* = \frac{\alpha_i^* \left[c_{ij}^* + o_{ij}^* - o_{i,j-1}^* \right]}{\displaystyle\sum_{k=0}^{\infty} c_{ik}^*}. \qquad (7.2.1.4.5)$$

It is certainly not obvious that $(7.2.1.4.4)$ of the form $\alpha_i \xi_j$ implies $(7.2.1.4.5)$ of the form $\alpha_i^* \xi_j^*$. In fact, the production of counterexamples is quite easy.

However, useful results can be obtained if it is required that

$$c_{ij}^* = \alpha_i \rho_j \lambda^{i+j-u}, \tag{7.2.1.4.6}$$

as in the basic chain ladder method (see $(7.1.1.1.3)$), and required separately that

$$\frac{c_{ij}^*}{o_{i,j-1}^*} = g_j^*, \qquad \text{independent of } i, \tag{7.2.1.4.7}$$

i.e. payments in development year j are always a certain proportion of the physical estimates held at the start of that year.

Then

$$o_{ij}^* = c_{i,j+1}^* g_{j+1}^{*-1} \tag{7.2.1.4.8}$$

and

$$
\begin{aligned}
o_{ij} &= o_{ij}^* \lambda^{u-(i+j+\frac{1}{2})} \\
&= c_{i,j+1}^* g_{j+1}^{*-1} \lambda^{u-(i+j+\frac{1}{2})} \\
&= c_{i,j+1} g_{j+1}^{-1}
\end{aligned} \tag{7.2.1.4.9}
$$

where

$$g_{j+1} = g_{j+1}^* \lambda^{-\frac{1}{2}} \tag{7.2.1.4.10}$$

Consequently, $(7.2.1.4.3)$ becomes:

$$
\begin{aligned}
i_{ij} - i_{i,j-1} &= \frac{\alpha_i \left[\dfrac{c_{ij}^*}{\lambda^{i+j}} + \dfrac{c_{i,j+1}^* g_{j+1}^{*-1}}{\lambda^{i+j+\frac{1}{2}}} - \dfrac{c_{ij}^* g_j^{*-1}}{\lambda^{i+j-\frac{1}{2}}} \right]}{\displaystyle\sum_{k=0}^{\infty} \frac{c_{ik}^*}{\lambda^{i+k}}} \\
&= \frac{\alpha_i \left[\rho_j + \rho_{j+1} g_{j+1}^{-1} - \rho_j g_j^{-1} \right]}{\displaystyle\sum_{k=0}^{\infty} \rho_k \lambda^{j-k}},
\end{aligned}
$$

by $(7.2.1.4.6)$ and $(7.2.1.4.10)$. Thus,

$$i_{ij} - i_{i,j-1} = \alpha_i \xi_j,$$

where

$$\xi_j = \frac{\rho_j + \rho_{j-1}g_{j+1}^{-1} - \rho_j g_j^{-1}}{\displaystyle\sum_{k=0}^{\infty} \rho_k \lambda^{j-k}} \tag{7.2.1.4.11}$$

Similarly, (7.2.1.4.5) yields:

$$i_{ij}^* - i_{i,j-1}^* = \frac{\alpha_i^* \left[\rho_j \lambda^j + \rho_{j+1}g_{j+1}^{*-1} \lambda^{j+1} - \rho_j g_j^{*-1} \lambda^j \right]}{\displaystyle\sum_{k=0}^{\infty} \rho_k \lambda^k}.$$

$$= \alpha_i^* \xi_j^*. \tag{7.2.1.4.12}$$

To sum up, if physical estimates are meant to represent outstanding claims in current values, then (7.2.1.4.1) might be a reasonable model.

If (7.2.1.4.6) and (7.2.1.4.7) are also accepted, then (7.2.1.4.12) can also be taken as the model. We return to this theme in Section 7.2.3.1.

If physical estimates are meant to represent outstanding claims in inflated values, a similar treatment to the above can be given.

Note, however, that the models (7.2.1.4.1) and (7.2.1.4.12) have been shown to hold only when the rate of inflation is constant, and (7.2.1.4.6) and (7.2.1.4.7) hold.

7.2.2. *Fitted incurred loss ratio method —*
      NS/MAC/NN/I/T,Y type

7.2.2.1   Model

Let us return to (7.2.1.1.2), the basic model equation of the track record method. It can be rewritten:

$$i_{ij}^* = \alpha_i^* \sum_{k=0}^{j} \xi_k^*.$$

If both sides of the equation are divided by premium earned in period of origin i, then the left side is transformed to a loss ratio. The result is:

$$l_{ij}^* = l_i^* \sum_{k=0}^{j} \xi_k^*, \qquad (7.2.2.1.1)$$

where l_{ij}^* denotes the loss ratio associated with period of origin i and based on (inflated) physical estimates at the end of development period j; and $l_i^* = l_{i\infty}^* =$ ultimate loss ratio experienced in period of origin i.

Now the sequence of equations (7.2.2.1.1) for $j = 0, 1, 2, \ldots$ may be regarded as points on the curve:

$$l_i^*(t) = l_i^* h^*(t), \qquad (7.2.2.1.2)$$

where the continuous-time variable t replaces the discrete-time variable j, and h is a function of t such that:

$$h^*(j+1) = \sum_{k=0}^{j} \xi_k^*.$$

It is possible to choose some parametric family of curves, say $\{h^*(t; \Omega)\}$ with set of parameters Ω, which is thought to provide a reasonable representation of the possible $h^*(\cdot)$. Then the model (7.2.2.1.2) becomes:

$$l_i^*(t) = l_i^* h^*(t; \omega), \qquad \text{some } \omega \in \Omega. \qquad (7.2.2.1.3)$$

The value of ω will be unknown.

This is the generalized statement of a method presented by Craighead (1979, pp.245-258). Details of his special case are given in Section 7.2.2.4.

7.2.2.2   *Estimation*

Estimation of the l_i^* and the parameters ω is essentially an exercise in curve fitting, and the usual methods of such fitting may be used.

7.2.2.3   *Projection of outstanding claims*

Let the parameters l_i^*, ω be estimated by $\hat{l}_i^*$, $\hat{\omega}$ respectively. Then $l_i^*(t)$ is estimated by:

$$\hat{l}_i^*(t) = \hat{l}_i^* h^*(t; \hat{\omega}).$$

Multiplication of $\hat{l}_i^*$ by premium earned in period of origin i produces an estimate $\hat{i}_i^*$ of claims incurred in period of origin i. Then outstanding claims at the end of development period j are estimated as:

$$\hat{i}_i^* - a_{ij}^*.$$

7.2.2.4   *Comment*

Craighead's parametric form was:

$$h^*(t;\omega) = 1 - \exp[-(t/B)^C],$$

where ω is the 2-vector (B, C).

The essential idea in the fitting of l_i^*, B, C appears to have been generalized least squares, where the loss function to be minimized was:

$$\sum_{i,t} t[l_i^*(t) - l_i^* h^*(t;\omega)]^2 \qquad (7.2.2.4.1)$$

where the summation goes over all pairs (i,t) for which an observation $l_i^*(t)$ is available.

In fact, Craighead appears to have experienced some difficulty through not having an algorithm which could minimize (7.2.2.4.1) with respect to l_i^*, B and C simultaneously. His final procedure was less formal than generalized least squares.

Craighead (1980) mentions that the ideas underlying this and the chain ladder (track record) methods are similar.

7.2.3 *Projected physical estimates (inflation-adjusted)*
method — NS/MAC/NN/I/T,Y,I type

7.2.3.1   *Model*

Section 7.2.1.4 has commented on the absence of an inflation adjustment from the track record method.

The obvious solution is to apply the required inflation adjustment. One would then be dealing with values of i_{ij} as in Section 7.2.1.4.

One might consider (7.2.1.4.1) as a model, i.e.

$$i_{ij} - i_{i,j-1} = \alpha_i \xi_j, \qquad (7.2.3.1.1)$$

i.e., as pointed out in Section 7.2.1.1 in connection with (7.2.1.1.2), a proportion ξ_j of the amount incurred in a period of origin is recognised in development period j.

But one may well enquire as to the reasons why this should be so. As an example, consider an extreme case of two periods of origin consisting of identical claims experiences except that, at the end of development period 2, the positions are:

period of origin 1 : zero paid, $1M physical estimates;

period of origin 2 : $1M paid, no claims outstanding (and no IBNR claims);

where all amounts are in current values. One might be inclined to ask how any further amount of claims incurred might be recognised in the future in respect of period of origin 2, barring reopened or unexpected IBNR claims.

In circumstances such as these, (7.2.3.1.1) simply does not appear a likely representation of the future of the two periods of origin.

Note that recognition in a period of any part of claims incurred in a given period of origin amounts to a revision of opinion (apart from inflation effects) as to the physical estimates held at the beginning of the period. It seems more natural that such revisions be related to the opening amount of physical estimates rather than amount incurred.

On this basis, the model of the claims incurred process is:

$$i_{ij} - i_{i,j-1} = \eta_j o_{i,j-1}. \qquad (7.2.3.1.2)$$

The meaning of η_j may be more easily understood if the last equation is written as:

$$\eta_j = (i_{ij} - i_{i,j-1})/o_{i,j-1}$$
$$= (c_{ij} + o_{ij} - o_{i,j-1})/o_{i,j-1},$$

i.e.
$$1 + \eta_j = (c_{ij} + o_{ij})/o_{i,j-1} \qquad (7.2.3.1.3)$$

$$= \frac{\text{claims paid in development period } j}{\text{opening outstandings.}} + \text{closing outstandings}$$

On the basis of this relation it is reasonable to refer to $1 + \eta_j$ as the (inflation adjusted) **development factor** of period j.

A knowledge of the sequence $\{\eta_j\}$ will not be sufficient to project future values of i_{ij} (or c_{ij} or o_{ij}). It is apparent from (7.2.3.1.2) that such a projection requires also the projection by some means of the sequence of values of o_{ij} (for the value of i in question). Clearly, the more rapidly outstanding claims run off, the less effect do the η_j have.

Thus, to enable projection, the model requires some sort of statement of the rate of runoff. We adopt (7.2.1.4.9):

$$c_{ij} = g_j o_{i,j-1}. \qquad (7.2.3.1.4)$$

The factor g_j might be referred to as the **payment-to-provision factor**.

The model consists of (7.2.3.1.2) and (7.2.3.1.4).

7.2.3.2   *Estimation*

Define

$$I_{(j-1,j)} = I_{j-1} \cap I_j.$$

By (7.2.3.1.3),

$$\sum_{i \in I_{(j-1,j)}} (c_{ij} + o_{ij}) = \frac{(1 + \eta_j)}{\sum_{i \in I_{(j-1,j)}} o_{i,j-1}}.$$

Hence,

$$1 + \eta_j = \frac{\displaystyle\sum_{i \in I_{(j-1,j)}} (c_{ij} + o_{ij})}{\sum_{i \in I_{(j-1,j)}} o_{i,j-1}}. \qquad (7.2.3.2.1)$$

Similarly,

$$g_j = \frac{\displaystyle\sum_{i \in I_{(j-1,j)}} c_{ij}}{\sum_{i \in I_{(j-1,j)}} o_{i,j-1}}. \qquad (7.2.3.2.2)$$

7.2.3.3   Projection of outstanding claims

The projection proceeds by explicit construction of the claim payments and physical estimates of future periods, (7.2.3.1.4) and (7.2.3.1.3) respectively providing the equations generating the projection, viz.

$$c_{ij} = g_j o_{i,j-1},\tag{7.2.3.3.1}$$

$$o_{ij} = (1 + \eta_j) o_{i,j-1} - c_{ij}.\tag{7.2.3.3.2}$$

Combination of these two equations yields:

$$o_{ij} = (1 + \eta_j - g_j) o_{i,j-1},$$

whence

$$o_{ik} = o_{i,j-1} \prod_{l=j}^{k} (1 + \eta_l - g_l).\tag{7.2.3.3.3}$$

Then, by (7.2.3.3.1) and (7.2.3.3.3),

$$c_{ik} = o_{i,j-1} g_k \prod_{l=j}^{k-1} (1 + \eta_l - g_l).\tag{7.2.3.3.4}$$

Then the required estimate of outstanding claims at the end of development period j is:

$$p_{ij} = \sum_{k=j+1}^{\infty} c_{ik}$$

$$= o_{ij} \sum_{k=j+1}^{\infty} g_k \prod_{l=j+1}^{k-1} (1 + n_l - g_l).\tag{7.2.3.3.5}$$

The factor following o_{ij} in this formula is of the same type as the "correction factors" mentioned by Skurnick (1973, p.23).

7.2.3.4.   Comment

It is apparent from the development of Sections 7.2.1 to 7.2.3 that the projected physical estimates method is a refinement of the track record method. To the knowledge of the author, it has not appeared previously in the literature. It has, however, been put into practice by the author for some time.

It is useful to consider the merits of $\cdot/\cdot/\cdot/I/\cdot$ type methods discussed in Section 7.2 relative to those of the $\cdot/\cdot/\cdot/P/\cdot$ type methods of Section 7.1 and several sections to come.

Note that the methods of the former group depend on physical estimates whereas the latter do not. In particular, (7.2.3.3.5) shows that outstanding claims of period of origin i are estimated by the projected physical estimates method as proportional to the physical estimates. Equation (7.2.1.3.1) shows outstanding claims estimated by the track record method as being proportional to incurred claims on the basis of the physical estimates. Thus under this method the effect of the physical estimates on the estimated outstandings will still be substantial but less than under the projected physical estimates method. Under the fitted incurred loss ratio method, because of the curve-fitting procedure, the effect of the most recent physical estimates will be less again, but still substantial.

This situation in which the statistical estimates of outstanding claims are strongly influenced by the corresponding physical estimates is to be contrasted with that surrounding the methods of $\cdot/\cdot/\cdot/P/\cdot$, type which are entirely independent of physical estimates.

Which type of method is likely to prove superior?

In my view a proper objective response to this question can be given only in the spirit of Section 1.3. That is, the superiority or otherwise of one method of analysis over another can be assessed properly only by some measurement, in terms of the fit of the model to the data, of the likely variation in projected outstanding claims. Perhaps with some qualification, one method of analysis can be regarded as superior to another if it has smaller mean square deviation (from the underlying true value) associated with its estimate of outstanding claims. We return to a formal discussion of the issue in Chapter 14.

In the meantime it is possible, on the basis of general reasoning, to make an observation on the likely comparative merits of $\cdot/\cdot/\cdot/P/\cdot$ and $\cdot/\cdot/\cdot/I/\cdot$ type models.

Consider a long-tailed class of business, and specifically outstanding claims in respect of an old period of origin, i.e. a period in respect of which only the claim payment tail remains to be paid out. Only a small number of claims will remain outstanding. It is likely that the amounts payable in respect of these claims will vary widely from one claim to another; varying perhaps from cases in which the last trivial remnants of legal fees remain outstanding in respect of claims already essentially settled, to other cases in which large actions at law have been commenced but, as yet, only small amounts paid. In some of these latter cases, if liability is disputed, there may be doubt as to whether the ultimate settlement will involve a very large or very small sum.

To summarize all this in statistical terms, any model fitted to past experience of claim payments and possible claim numbers will associate relatively large uncertainty (mean square deviation) with the parameters which describe the claim payment tail. Conversely, the corresponding uncertainties associated with the early and middle parts of payment delay distribution will usually be relatively small.

What this means is that outstanding claims estimated on the basis of such a model will be relatively uncertain as regards the more recent periods of origin, but less so as regards the less recent periods of origin.

Contrast this with the use of physical estimates. Most insurers are able to obtain reasonably accurate physical estimates in respect of the more developed periods of origin even if these may be expressed in current values and require a statistical allowance for claims escalation and investment return. Even where the physical estimates in current values require adjustment, it will usually be reasonably small and predictable by means of the projected physical estimates method.

On the other hand, the physical estimates associated with the less developed periods of origin will be less certain; the adjustments required to them larger (partly because of IBNR claims); and uncertainty associated with the projected physical estimates method correspondingly greater.

Thus, it appears that outstanding claims might be estimated most reliably by application of a $\cdot/\cdot/\cdot/P/\cdot$ type method to the most recent periods of origin and a $\cdot/\cdot/\cdot/I/\cdot$ type method to the older periods of origin. In between, some blend of the two methods is probably required.

In the light of the methodology currently at one's disposal, the choice of which method is to be applied to which period of origin has probably to be made on a largely **ad hoc** basis. In principle, however, the proper procedure would appear to be as follows:

(i) apply the $\cdot/\cdot/\cdot/I/\cdot$ method to obtain estimated outstandings in respect of each period of origin;

(ii) apply the $\cdot/\cdot/\cdot/P/\cdot$ method to obtain estimated outstandings in respect of each period of origin;

(iii) consider all possible selections of periods of origin to which the $\cdot/\cdot/\cdot/P/\cdot$ and $\cdot/\cdot/\cdot/I/\cdot$ methods are to be applied and, for each such selection, estimate the variance of total estimated outstandings;

(iv) on the basis of (iii), choose that combination of the $\cdot/\cdot/\cdot/P/\cdot$ and $\cdot/\cdot/\cdot/I/\cdot$ methods by period of origin which minimizes the variance of outstanding claims.

Clearly, though, there remains some work to be done before such an orderly approach becomes practicable.

It is sometimes asserted that the $\cdot/\cdot/\cdot/I/\cdot$ type methods have no proper place in the actuarial repertoire. One may, for example, encounter this view in dealing with an insurance company executive who is seeking "an independent actuarial" assessement of the Company's physical estimates. In such circumstances, he may put considerable emphasis on the **independence** required and maintain that the $\cdot/\cdot/\cdot/I/\cdot$ type methods, being based on physical estimates, are not in fact independent of them at all.

While there is no doubt of the dependency of the $\cdot/\cdot/\cdot/I/\cdot$ type methods on physical estimates, yet the view that such methods ought to be banished from the actuary's tool-kit seems to me unreasonable. What should be required of the actuary is an unbiased and **objective** analysis. What he should require of himself is a minimization of the statistical uncertainty associated with his final estimate. Just which items of information are used in satisfying these objectives is immaterial.

The fact is that the ensemble of past physical estimates represents information. It seems to me philosophically deficient, and in some cases professionally negligent, to adopt a blanket principle of ignoring it.

If, for example, physical estimates had developed in the past according to such a perfect pattern that there seemed every reason to regard their future development as quite predictable, then commonsense would dictate that one consider very carefully before adopting an estimate of outstanding claims significantly in conflict with this projected development.

This is, in effect, saying no more than that, if the parameters involved in a $\cdot/\cdot/\cdot/I/\cdot$ type model are estimated with very low variances, and hence outstanding claims are estimated according to that model also with very low variances, then one ought to be hesitant about rejecting that projection in favour of another with much larger associated uncertainty.

Of course, it may be argued that physical estimates of the past should not be used by the actuary because they have been recorded incorrectly or their behaviour has been erratic. But this is quite a different argument from the one that physical estimates should not be used just because they are physical estimates. Recording inaccuracy will probably, and erratic physical estimation will certainly, manifest itself in the form of variability in the raw data and therefore uncertainty in the resulting estimates of outstandings. This latter uncertainty, if sufficiently large **would** represent, in statistically quantified form, a valid reason for rejection of the model.

It should also be remembered that physical estimates will often provide the first warning of any sudden changes in experience, such as a shift in the level of court awards, the underwriting of a poor block of business by a new underwriting manager in a particular branch, etc.

Naturally, it is not suggested that, in the event of sudden change in physical estimates, the actuary must rush blindly ahead and adjust his own estimates accordingly. But such an event should provoke questions, e.g. Are company executives aware of the change? Can they explain it? Are their explanations merely vague assertions or do they point to extra data which the actuary might be able to collect and analyse? On what basis (if any) are physical estimates made? What was the basis at the last balance date? Have the estimators been issued with any instruction since the last balance date which might have affected the level of their estimates? Is the change in estimates confined to a particular branch, say, or is it more general? Has there been any substantial recent change in the staff making the estimates? and so on.

7.3   Models of the $NS/MAC/N/ · /·$ type

7.3.1 *Models of the $NS/MAC/N/I/·$ type*

To the author's knowledge there exist no models of the $NS/ · /N/I/·$ type.

7.3.2 *Payments per claim finalized (per claim handled)*
    method — $NS/MAC/N/P/E, F, I, T$ *type*

7.3.2.1   *Model*

The essentials of this method appear to have been introduced by Fisher and Lange (1973). It seems to have been rediscovered by Sawkins. A description is given by Sawkins (1979). The basic thrust is to include in the model an allowance for the effect on claim payment experience of a change in the insurer's activity in dealing with claims. Thus, if heavy payment experience is a result of an increase in the speed of finalization of claims, an attempt is made to give due recognition to the fact.

There is no doubt that in many cases a change in number of finalizations of claims will affect the volume of payments. In these cases number of finalizations needs to appear as an explanatory variable in the model. The difficulty is, of course, in the identification of the relationship.

For the moment we withhold comment on the various forms of model falling within the category now being treated. Such matters are dealt with in Section 7.3.2.4. In this section we confine our attention to presentation of those models which appear in the literature.

For the sake of definiteness, presentation will be made in terms of the payment per claims finalized method, though variants of this with identical model structure are possible as is pointed out below.

The basic assumption of the payments per claim finalized model is that, in any given development period, (inflation-adjusted) claim payments are directly proportional to the number of claims finalized; that the constant of proportionality, the payment per claim finalized, is independent of period of origin; but may (and probably will) vary with development period.

Thus the model is:

$$c_{ij} = n_{ij}\sigma_j, \tag{7.3.2.1.1}$$

or

$$s_{ij} = c_{ij}/n_{ij} = \sigma_j, \tag{7.3.2.1.2}$$

where s_{ij} denotes the **payments per claim finalized** (inflation adjusted) in development period j of period of origin i, and σ_j is the corresponding model amount, assumed to depend on development period j but not period of origin i.

It is to be noted that, while the s_{ij} are intended to represent something resembling average claim size, they do not in fact do so precisely. Whereas the denominator in (7.3.2.1.2) relates to just those claims which were finalized in the relevant period, the numerator relates to other claims as well. The numerator includes all payments made in that period, and therefore:

(i) excludes partial payments made in earlier periods in respect of the n_{ij} finalized claims;

(ii) includes partial payments made in development period j in respect of claims other than the n_{ij} finalized claims, i.e. in respect of claims to be finalized in development periods $j+1$, $j+2$,. . ..

Thus, there is a lack of correspondence between numerator and denominator of s_{ij}. Comment on the significance of this, and possible ways of avoiding it is given in Section 7.3.2.4.

Estimates of the σ_j will not be adequate for projection of outstanding claims. The σ_j describe only the amounts of claim payments expected in respective future development periods **per claim finalized** in those periods. A projection of claim payments will require an auxiliary projection of numbers of claims finalized in the respective future development periods. Whether the requirement of this additional projection has a destabilizing effect on the method as a whole is a matter of considerable significance, and this is also discussed in Section 7.3.2.4 as well as Section 8.2.4.

In any event, if a projection of numbers of finalizations is to be performed, then an auxiliary model of the finalization process is required.

The most obvious model is

$$n_{ij} = n_i \phi_j. \qquad (7.3.2.1.3)$$

We shall write

$$F_{ij} = N_{ij}/N_i,$$

and refer to the random variable F_{ij} as the **speed of finalization** of claims in development period j of period of origin i. The model (7.3.2.1.3) can be rewritten as:

$$\sum_{k=j}^{\infty} n_{ik} = n_i \sum_{k=j}^{\infty} \phi_k.$$

This and (7.3.2.1.3) yield:

$$n_{ij}/\sum_{k=j}^{\infty} n_{ik} = \phi_j/\sum_{k=j}^{\infty} \phi_k$$

$$= \psi_j, \qquad \text{say} \qquad (7.3.2.1.4)$$

As will be seen in Section 7.3.2.3, the model (7.3.2.1.3) is unsatisfactory in some respects, and (7.3.2.1.4) may be preferable.

7.3.2.2   Estimation

Summation of (7.3.2.1.1) over period of origin i gives:

$$\sigma_j = \sum_{i \in I_j} c_{ij} / \sum_{i \in I_j} n_{ij}. \tag{7.3.2.2.1}$$

The estimation of ϕ_j is made by the same method:

$$\phi_j = \sum_{i \in I_j} n_{ij} / \sum_{i \in I_j} n_i. \tag{7.3.2.2.2}$$

The alternative model (7.3.2.1.4) of claims finalization is rewritten as:

$$n_{ij} = \psi_j \sum_{k=j}^{\infty} n_{ik}$$

and estimation is then as in (7.3.2.2.1) and (7.3.2.2.2):

$$\psi_j = \sum_{i \in I_j} n_{ij} / \sum_{i \in I_j} \sum_{k=j}^{\infty} n_{ik}. \tag{7.3.2.2.3}$$

7.3.2.3   Projection of outstanding claims

Outstanding claims at the end of development period j of period of origin i are:

$$p_{ij} = \sum_{k=j+1}^{\infty} c_{ik},$$

and

$$c_{ik} = n_{ik} s_{ik}$$
$$= n_{ik} \sigma_k,$$

by (7.3.2.1.2).

The projection problem thus consists of projection of the $n_{ik}, k = j+1, j+2, \ldots$, the values of σ_j having been obtained by means of (7.3.2.2.1).

Now, according to the "obvious" model, (7.3.2.1.3), n_{ik} is given by:

$$n_{ik} = n_i \phi_k, \qquad (7.3.2.3.1)$$

where n_i is presumed known and the ϕ_k will have been found by means of (7.3.2.2.2).

However, this projection of numbers of finalizations is unsatisfactory in one respect. Note that the projected number of claims to be finalized in development periods $j + 1$ and later is:

$$\sum_{k=j+1}^{\infty} n_{ik} = n_i \sum_{k=j+1}^{\infty} \phi_k, \qquad (7.3.2.3.2)$$

and by definition, this must represent the number of claims (reported or unreported) outstanding at the end of development period j. But this number of outstanding claims is the sum of the number of outstanding reported claims, which is a factual figure, in the insurer's records, and the number of IBNR claims, which will have been calculated with greater or lesser certainty. In particular, for well-developed accident years, only a handful of IBNR claims will remain, so that the correct value of (7.3.2.3.2) will be known with near-certainty. This number may conflict with the number projected by means of (7.3.2.3.2).

An example of the kind of problem which arises is provided by the following hypothetical table.

Accident period i	Number of claims incurred n_i	Number of claims n_{ij} finalized in development period j (a)					Total number finalized in all development years
		j=0	j=1	j=2	j=3	j=4	
0	100	25	25	20	20	10	100
1	100	30	30	20	15	10	105
2	100	35	30	25	17.5	10	117.5
3	100	40	35	21.7	17.5	10	124.2
4	100	45	30	21.7	17.5	10	124.2
Values of ϕ_j		0.350	0.300	0.217	0.175	0.100	$\sum_{j=0}^{4} \phi_j = 1.042$

Note: (a) *Figures above the staircase represent recorded past experience; below the staircase, projected in accordance with (7.3.2.3.1).*

Clearly, the problem in this example arises from the persistent change which has occurred in speed of finalization. Under this condition, the averaging process used in (7.3.2.2.2) leads to the absurd conclusion that, in respect of each incomplete period of origin, the number of claims ultimately to be finalized exceeds the number incurred!

A simple **ad hoc** device for eliminating this absurdity consists merely of rescaling the projected numbers of finalizations so that they add to the correct numbers incurred. The algebraic expression of this device goes as follows.

The number of claims from period of origin i to be finalized in future development periods is projected as:

$$n_i \sum_{k=j+1}^{\infty} \phi_k, \tag{7.3.2.3.3}$$

by (7.3.2.3.2).

The actual number to be finalized is:

$$n_i - \sum_{k=0}^{j} n_{ik} = n_i \left(1 - \sum_{k=0}^{j} f_k\right). \tag{7.3.2.3.4}$$

Thus, the projected numbers $n_i \phi_k$ of finalizations need to be rescaled from (7.3.2.3.1) to:

$$n'_{ik} = n_i \phi_k \left(1 - \sum_{l=0}^{j} f_l\right) \Big/ \sum_{l=j+1}^{\infty} \phi_l. \tag{7.3.2.3.5}$$

With this correction the above table becomes the following.

Accident period i	Number of claims incurred n_i	Number of claims n_{ij} finalized in development period j (a)					Total number finalized in all development years
		$j=0$	$j=1$	$j=2$	$j=3$	$j=4$	
0	100	25	25	20	20	10	100
1	100	30	30	20	15	5	100
2	100	35	30	25	6.4	3.6	100
3	100	40	35	11.0	8.9	5.1	100
4	100	45	20.8	15.1	12.2	6.9	100
Values of ϕ_j		0.350	0.300	0.217	0.175	0.100	$\sum\limits_{j=0}^{4} \phi_j = 1.042$

Note: (a) *See preceding table.*

It is to be emphasised that the adjustment from n_{ij} to n'_{ij} in (7.3.2.3.5) is **ad hoc**. It has no basis in the models discussed in Section 7.3.2.1. It is for this reason that model (7.3.2.1.4) may be preferred to (7.3.2.1.3) as a model of numbers of claims finalizations. The former of these leads to a projection of numbers of finalizations which does not contain the anomaly treated above, as will now be shown.

By (7.3.2.1.4),

$$n_{ik} = \psi_k \sum_{l=k}^{\infty} n_{il}, \qquad k = j+1,\ j+2,\ldots \qquad (7.3.2.3.6)$$

where it is recalled that outstanding claims are being projected as at the end of development period j. Now (7.3.2.3.6) can be written more usefully in the form:

$$n_{ik} = \psi_k \left[\sum_{l=j+1}^{\infty} n_{il} - \sum_{l=j+1}^{k-1} n_{il} \right] \qquad (7.3.2.3.7)$$

Then (7.3.2.3.7) can be used to calculate n_{ik}, $k = j+1,\ j+2,\ldots$ recursively, thus:

$$n_{i,j+1} = \psi_{j+1} \sum_{l=j+1}^{\infty} n_{il},$$

$$n_{i,j+2} = \psi_{j+2} \left[\sum_{l=j+1}^{\infty} n_{il} - n_{i,j+1} \right],$$

etc.

Note that the term $\sum_{l=j+1}^{\infty} n_{il}$ represents the number of claims incurred but not finalized by the end of development period j.

We ignore the theoretically possible case of an infinite runoff of finalizations. We assume that for some value of k, say K, $\psi_k = 1$. Then, by (7.3.2.3.6),

$$n_{iK} = \sum_{l=K}^{\infty} n_{il}. \tag{7.3.2.3.8}$$

Hence, the number of claims unfinalized at the end of development period K is:

$$\sum_{l=K+1}^{\infty} n_{il} = \sum_{l=K}^{\infty} n_{il} - n_{iK}$$
$$= 0,$$

by (7.3.2.3.8).Then, by (7.3.2.3.6),

$$n_{ik} = 0, \qquad k = K+1, K+2, \ldots \tag{7.3.2.3.9}$$

Thus, (7.3.2.3.6) shows that for $k = j+1, \ldots, K-1$ (where $\psi_k < 1$), the projected number of claims finalized in a development period is less than the number unfinalized at the start of that period; then (7.3.2.3.8) shows that, in development period K, all remaining claims are projected as finalized; and (7.3.2.3.9) shows that no further finalizations are projected in subsequent development periods.

With the further use of this alternative model, the projection of future numbers of finalizations becomes the following.

Accident period i	Number of claims incurred n_i	Number of claims n_{ij} finalized in development period j (a)					Total number finalized in all development years
		j=0	j=1	j=2	j=3	j=4	
0	100	25	25	20	20	10	100
1	100	30	30	20	15	5	100
2	100	35	30	25	6.4	3.6	100
3	100	40	35	13.0	7.6	4.4	100
4	100	45	24.4	15.9	9.3	5.4	100
Values of ψ_j		0.350	0.444	0.520	0.636	1	

Note: (a) *See preceding table.*

7.3.2.4   Comment

Sections 7.3.2.1 to 7.3.2.3 have discussed **payments per claim finalized** for the sake of definiteness. But most of the general principles outlined there are of wider applicability.

For example, Sawkins (1979, pp.460-463) analyses **payments per claim handled** where the number of claims handled in a period is the number active at any time during that period. The model follows exactly the same structure as laid out in Section 7.3.2.1, i.e. equations (7.3.2.1.1) and (7.3.2.1.3) with n_{ij} appropriately redefined.

This idea is abstracted somewhat by Taylor (1980) who uses the term **claim number units** to cover either numbers finalized or numbers handled. The essential point is that, in some way or other, (7.3.2.1.1) is intended to recognise the fact that claim payments in a period are correlated with "claims activity", defined in whatever way. The variable N_{ij} is the measure of this claims activity in development period j of period of origin i, and might be number of claims finalized, number handled, or some other number.

Just which definition of claim number unit should be adopted depends on which (if any) is thought to conform with the basic model equation

(7.3.2.1.1). For example, in a class of business in which it is normal for finalization of a claim to coincide with payment of the bulk of the amount involved, it might be reasonable to adopt (7.3.2.1.1) with n_{ij} representing number of claims finalized (though this conclusion is qualified somewhat later in this section and Section 7.3.3.1).

On the other hand, in a class of business in which the normal procedure is to pay claims in the form of annuities (such as **some** Australian workers' compensation claims), it might be more reasonable to adopt (7.3.2.1.1) with n_{ij} representing number of claims handled.

Another variation of the model (7.3.2.1.1) is introduced by working with **cumulative** claim payments. In this case (7.3.2.1.1) is replaced by:

$$a_{ij} = \sum_{k=0}^{j} c_{ik} = \sigma_j \sum_{k=0}^{j} n_{ik}, \qquad (7.3.2.4.1)$$

where the meaning of σ_j is now different from the meaning ascribed to it in (7.3.2.1.1); it now denotes (inflation-adjusted) payments per claim finalized **up to the end of development year** j.

It is to be noted that this model will not normally be compatible with (7.3.2.1.1). For that model gives:

$$a_{ij} = \sum_{k=0}^{j} c_{ik} = \sum_{k=0}^{j} n_{ik}\sigma_k$$

$$= \overline{\sigma}_j \sum_{k=0}^{j} n_{ik}, \qquad (7.3.2.4.2)$$

where $\overline{\sigma}_j$ is a weighted average of the σ_k:

$$\overline{\sigma}_j = \sum_{k=0}^{j} n_{ik}\sigma_k / \sum_{k=0}^{j} n_{ik}. \qquad (7.3.2.4.3)$$

Now (7.3.2.4.2) is of the same form as (7.3.2.4.1) except that $\overline{\sigma}_j$ is dependent on the weights $n_{ik}/\sum_{k=0}^{j} n_{ik}$, i.e. on the distribution of finalizations over development years. Thus, for given constants σ_j in (7.3.2.1.1), the $\overline{\sigma}_j$ in (7.3.2.4.2) wil not necessarily be constant (for differing speeds of finalization), and so (7.3.2.4.1) will not be compatible with (7.3.2.1.1).

For this reason, the choice between models (7.3.2.1.1) and (7.3.2.4.1) is not merely one of convenience as was the choice between use of cumulative and non-cumulative claim payments in the basic chain ladder method (remarked at the end of Section 7.1.1.2). Rather it is a choice between two quite distinct models. This is a rather fundamental point not always emphasised in writings on claims analysis. For example, Sawkins (1979,pp.460-463) discusses the cumulative and non-cumulative versions of the payments per claim handled method as if they were interchangeable, no mention being made of the fact that they actually represent quite different models.

In view of this model difference, it is natural to enquire whether there is any reason to prefer either (7.3.2.1.1) or (7.3.2.4.1) in practice. The principles involved in an examination of this question are relatively complex. We return to them in Section 8.2.4. At this point, we may anticipate slightly and state that, in practice, both of the methods discussed above possess shortcomings which, on occasions, are considerable. Their use is therefore likely to be restricted to relatively unrefined analysis. Under these circumstances, the choice between them, though in principle more than just a matter of convenience, is likely to be made in this way in practice.

It was noted in Section 7.3.2.1 that *"there is a lack of correspondence between numerator and denumerator of s_{ij}"*. Partial payments were identified as the reason for this. These remarks, made in relation to the non-cumulative version of the payments per claim finalized method treated in Sections 7.3.2.1 to 7.3.2.3, apply equally to the cumulative version.

The cumulative version is now considered further. A correspondence between numerator and denumerator is achieved if cumulative payments up to a given point of development are made to exclude all partial payments in respect of claims still unfinalized at that point of development.

Thus, corresponding to a_{ij}, claim payments up to the end of development period j of period of origin i, we define:

$a^f_{ij} =$ amount (inflation-adjusted) of claim payments in respect of all claims finalized by the end of development period j of period of origin i.

It may be useful, for the purpose of comparison, to express a_{ij} and a^f_{ij} in terms of the basic notation introduced in Section 3.1. We have

$$a_{ij} = \sum_{k=0}^{j} c_{..i.k..},$$

and

$$a_{ij}^f = \sum_{k=0}^{j} c_{..i...k},$$

with the c's adjusted for inflation.

When a_{ij}^f replaces a_{ij} in (7.3.2.4.1), so that:

$$a_{ij}^f = \sigma_j^f \sum_{k=0}^{j} n_{ik}, \qquad (7.3.2.4.4)$$

then σ_j^f becomes a genuine average claim size. It is in fact that average (inflation-adjusted) size of all claims finalized up to the end of development period j of period of origin i.

It is sometimes suggested that, because of the correspondence between numerator and denumerator of σ_j^f, not possessed by σ_j, the model (7.3.2.4.4) is more "logical" than, and therefore to be preferred to, (7.3.2.1.1). A rough examination of this proposition is made below.

Regardless of the "logicality" or otherwise of any particular method of analysis, we regard one method as superior to another if it produces no larger bias and a smaller variance in its estimate of outstanding claims. Note that, just for this subsection, we are departing from our temporary practice of not recognising the stochastic nature of the claims process.

Now, the random variable statement corresponding to (7.3.2.4.1) is:

$$A_{ij} = S_{ij} \sum_{k=0}^{j} n_{ik}, \qquad (7.3.2.4.5)$$

where S_{ij} is being taken as a conditional random variable, conditional on the n_{ik}. We have

$$E[S_{ij}] = \sigma_j. \qquad (7.3.2.4.6)$$

By (7.3.2.4.5) and (7.3.2.4.6),

$$E[\sum_{i \in I_{(j)}} A_{ij}] = \sigma_j \sum_{i \in I_{(j)}} \sum_{k=0}^{j} n_{ik}$$

$$= \sigma_j \sum_{i \in I_{(j)}} m_{ij}, \qquad (7.3.2.4.7)$$

where we have written

$m_{ij} = \sum_{k=o}^{j} n_{ik}$ = number of claims finalized up to the end of development period j of origin period i.

Then an unbiased estimator of σ_j is:

$$\hat{\sigma}_j = \sum_{i \in I_{(j)}} A_{ij} / \sum_{i \in I_{(j)}} m_{ij}. \qquad (7.3.2.4.8)$$

Then

$$V[\hat{\sigma}_j] = \sum_{i \in I_{(j)}} V[A_{ij}] / [\sum_{i \in I_{(j)}} m_{ij}]^2 \qquad (7.3.2.4.9)$$

where it has been assumed that different periods of origin are stochastically independent.

If cumulative payments on finalized claims A_{ij}^f are used in place of A_{ij}, then equations (7.3.2.4.5) to (7.3.2.4.9) are replaced by:

$$A_{ij}^f = S_{ij}^f \sum_{k=0}^{j} n_{ik}, \qquad (7.3.2.4.10)$$

$$E[S_{ij}^f] = \sigma_j^f. \qquad (7.3.2.4.11)$$

$$E[\sum_{i \in I_{(j)}} A_{ij}^f] = \sigma_j^f \sum_{i \in I_{(j)}} m_{ij} \qquad (7.3.2.4.12)$$

$$\hat{\sigma}_j^f = \sum_{i \in I_{(j)}} A_{ij}^f / \sum_{i \in I_{(j)}} m_{ij}. \qquad (7.3.2.4.13)$$

$$V[\hat{\sigma}_j^f] = \sum_{i \in I_{(j)}} V[A_{ij}^f] / [\sum_{i \in I_{(j)}} m_{ij}]^2 \qquad (7.3.2.4.14)$$

Equations (7.3.2.4.9) and (7.3.2.4.14) are comparable.

Let us now consider how the variances arrived at above influence the variance of estimated outstanding claims. We consider a projection of outstanding claims by the ratio method (see Section 5.4).

When the A_{ij} (rather than the A_{ij}^f) are used, the ultimate average claim size is estimated as:

$$(\hat{\sigma}_\infty / \hat{\sigma}_j) A_{ij} / m_{ij},$$

whence outstanding claims at the end of development period j are estimated as:

$$\hat{P}_{ij} = \left(\frac{\hat{\sigma}_\infty n_i}{\hat{\sigma}_j m_{ij}} - 1 \right) A_{ij}, \qquad (7.3.2.4.15)$$

Similarly, when the A_{ij}^f are used, outstanding claims are estimated as:

$$\hat{P}_{ij}^f = \frac{\hat{\sigma}_\infty n_i}{\hat{\sigma}_j^f m_{ij}} A_{ij}^f - A_{ij}, \qquad (7.3.2.4.16)$$

where we have made use of the fact that $\hat{\sigma}_\infty^f = \hat{\sigma}_\infty$.

It is informative to rewrite $\hat{P}_{ij}$ and $\hat{P}_{ij}^f$ as:

$$\hat{P}_{ij} = (\hat{\sigma}_\infty n_i)(m_{ij}^{-1} A_{ij}/\hat{\sigma}_j) - A_{ij}; \qquad (7.3.2.4.17)$$
$$\hat{P}_{ij}^f = (\hat{\sigma}_\infty n_i)(m_{ij}^{-1} A_{ij}^f/\hat{\sigma}_j^f) - A_{ij}. \qquad (7.3.2.4.18)$$

These two equations make clear the fact that the comparison between $V[\hat{P}_{ij}]$ and $V[\hat{P}_{ij}^f]$ depends very much on a comparison between $V[m_{ij}^{-1} A_{ij}/\hat{\sigma}_j]$ and $V[m_{ij}^{-1} A_{ij}^f/\hat{\sigma}_j^f]$.

Now, since A_{ij} is included in $\hat{\sigma}_j$, these two variables will not be independent. However, provided that the order of the set $I_{(j)}$ is not too low, the dependency will not be great. For a rough analysis, we shall take $A_{ij}, \hat{\sigma}_j$ to be stochastically independent. Similarly for $A_{ij}^f, \hat{\sigma}_j^f$. Then the analysis of Appendix A can be applied. Because of (7.3.2.4.9) and (7.3.2.4.14), equations (A.7) of Appendix A hold. Then, by (A.8):

$$V[m_{ij}^{-1} A_{ij}/\hat{\sigma}_j] = Kw^2 + Kw(1+w)^2 + w, \qquad (7.3.2.4.19)$$

where

$$K = [\sum_{k \in I_{(j)}} m_{kj}]^2 / m_{ij}^2,$$

$$\mu = E[\hat{\sigma}_j]$$

$$w = V[\hat{\sigma}_j]/E^2[\hat{\sigma}_j].$$

A similar expression holds for $V[m_{ij}^{-1} A_{ij}^f/\hat{\sigma}_j^f]$.

Thus, provided μ does not vary too much according to whether the A_{ij} or A_{ij}^f are being used, i.e. provided σ_j and σ_j^f do not differ too much, the comparison between $V[m_{ij}^{-1} A_{ij}/\hat{\sigma}_j]$ and $V[m_{ij}^{-1} A_{ij}^f/\hat{\sigma}_j^f]$ depends mainly on the comparison between w and w^f, the respective coefficients of variation of $\hat{\sigma}_j$ and $\hat{\sigma}_j^f$, i.e. by (7.3.2.4.9) and (7.3.2.4.14), the coefficients of variation of A_{ij} and A_{ij}^f.

Now

$$w = \frac{M_{ij}v_j^f + (N_i - M_{ij})v_j^p}{[M_{ij}\mu_j^f + (N_i - M_{ij})\mu_j^p]^2}, \tag{7.3.2.4.20}$$

where μ_j^f, v_j^f denote the mean and variance of the amount of a claim finalized by the end of development period j; μ_j^p, v_j^p denote the mean and variance of the amount paid on a claim unfinalized at the end of development period j; and it is assumed (for convenience) that these two variables are stochastically independent.

Equation (7.3.2.4.20) can be rewritten as:

$$w = w^f \times \frac{1 + (N_i/M_{ij} - 1)(v_j^p/v_j^f)}{[1 + (N_i/M_{ij} - 1)(\mu_j^p/\mu_j^f)]^2} \tag{7.3.2.4.21}$$

It is apparent that for some values of the ratios v_j^p/v_j^f and μ_j^p/μ_j^f, the earlier development periods, when $M_{ij} << N_i$, will lead to

$$w < w^f. \tag{7.3.2.4.22}$$

When this last inequality holds, (7.3.2.4.17) to (7.3.2.4.19) are likely, as explained above, to lead to

$$V[\hat{P}_{ij}] < V[\hat{P}_{ij}^f]. \tag{7.3.2.4.23}$$

The fact that this last relation occurs under certain circumstances means that, under those circumstances, outstanding claims are more efficiently estimated by the payments per claim finalized method based on total payments than on payments only in respect of finalized claims.

It is not possible to state verbally just what are the circumstances which lead to this result, though a mathematical statement can be based on (7.3.2.4.21). In cases where the proportion of total claim payments relating to claims unfinalized at the valuation date is significant, so that μ_j^p/μ_j^f is significant, there is a distinct possibility that more efficient estimation of outstanding claims will be achieved by the use of total claim payments.

One might summarize all of this by saying that, in certain circumstances, the loss of homogeneity (and the consequent instability) of payments per claim finalized caused by inclusion of partial payments is more than offset, in terms of statistical efficiency, by the additional information provided by those partial payments.

We come now to the question, raised in Section 7.3.2.1, of whether outstanding claims projected by the payments per claim finalized method are destabilized by the requirement of that method that projected outstanding claim payments be based on an auxiliary projection of future numbers of finalizations.

Consider the following situation. For many years speed of finalization and payments per claim finalized have been stable. Suddenly, in the latest year, there has been a substantial increase in speed of finalization, affecting all years of origin.

Because of the lengthy period of averaging, this change will have little effect on the values of σ_j and ψ_j obtained from (7.3.2.2.1) and (7.3.2.2.3). However, equation (7.3.2.3.7), projecting future numbers of finalizations, will project generally earlier finalization than would have been projected had the old regime of speeds of finalization persisted (since there are now smaller numbers unfinalized than the old regime would have produced).

The result of this is that some future finalizations with which would have been associated σ_{j+1} payments per claim finalized will now have σ_j associated with them; others which would have had σ_{j+2} will now have σ_{j+1}; and so on.

But suppose that, in fact, there has been absolutely no change from one period of origin to another in the sequence of (inflation-adjusted) claim payments already made and to be made in the future, apart from changes of timing. This fact will conflict with the projected changes in payments per claim finalized discussed in the preceding paragraph. Consequently, the payments per claim finalized method will produce a biased estimate of outstanding claims.

The situation is represented diagrammatically below.

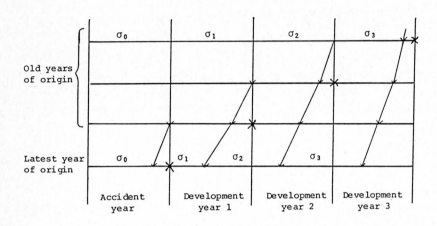

The ×'s denote the current valuation date marked on
the time-lines of the various years of origin.

Fig. 4 *Diagrammatic representation of speed of finalization*

The diagram shows the time-line of each of the last four years of origin.
It is assumed that identical sequences of claim payments are associated with
the different years of origin, but the timing of those sequences differs. Thus,
the arrows in the diagram indicate how a particular claim finalization is
shifted on the time-line as one progresses from one year of origin to the
next.

The vertical arrows show how no change in speed of finalization occurred
in years prior to the last before the valuation date (marked by ×). Then
arrows appearing in the last year and in future years (to the right of a ×)
show how the increased speed of finalization has produced a clustering of
finalizations towards the left ends of the time-lines.

Values of σ_j are marked on the most and least recent of the four years
of origin represented. Because of the meaning given to the arrows above, σ_j
denotes payments per claim finalized (we assume the non-cumulative version)

between the two arrows between which it appears.

Thus, whereas payments per claim finalized in development year 2 were σ_2 for the earliest of the four years of origin, they will be something resembling tche average of σ_2 and σ_3 in the latest of the four. A projection based on (7.3.2.2.1), (7.3.2.2.3) and (7.3.2.3.7) will effectively assume that this last value is between σ_2 and σ_3 but close to σ_2.

If σ_j increases monotonically with j, which appears to be the case in some lines of business, then the above reasoning shows that the payments per claim finalized method will lead to under-estimation of outstanding claims in the particular circumstances under consideration.

The problem emerging here is clearly that, in the circumstances set out, payments per claim finalized cannot be effectively indexed by development year. If this is so, then the whole basis of the models treated in Sections 7.3.2.1 to 7.3.2.3 (see equation (7.3.2.1.1)) is overturned. It is for this reason that an earlier passage of this subsection stated that use of the models treated in Sections 7.3.2.1 to 7.3.2.3 was *"likely to be restricted to relatively unrefined analysis"*.

7.3.3 *The Reduced Reid method — NS/MAC/N/P/E,F,I,T type*

7.3.3.1   Model

It may first be noted that this method has the same taxonomic classification as the payments per claim finalized method (Section 7.3.2). The reason for this is that the Reduced Reid method is merely the payments per claim finalized method, but with the use of development periods, as defined hitherto, replaced by the use of **operational time**.

The concept of operational time is now discussed.

A particular problem with the payments per claim number unit methods was identified at the end of Section 7.3.2.4. The problem was illustrated in **Fig. 4**. To recapitulate it briefly: When different periods of origin experience precisely the same sequences of claim payments arranged in precisely the same order, but with these sequences differently compressed or extended on the time-line, misleading results are likely to be obtained by the use of real time to index estimates of the parameters of the claims process.

The answer to this problem is fairly simple. The clue is given by the fact that the *"sequences of claim payments [are] arranged in precisely the same order"*, or so it is assumed for the moment. It will be shown in Sections 7.3.3.4 and 8.2.1 that this condition may be weakened considerably. In these circumstances it is clearly sensible to index parameters of the claims process, not by real time, but by the point to which the relevant period of origin has developed, i.e. by the proportion of incurred claims which have been finalized. This proportion is defined as the **operational time**.

The concept of operational time is not a new one. It appears to date back at least to the early days of Risk Theory (Lundberg, 1909) (its definition is a little different but the idea involved was the same). It is certainly included as standard material in modern Risk Theory (Bühlmann, 1970, pp. 49-51; Seal, 1969, pp 90-96). It was introduced to claims analysis by Reid (1978, p.221) in his method (Section 8.2), and used by Taylor (1980, p.273) in the development of Reduced Reid method .

To be precise, we define:

$t_i(j)$ = operational time, for origin period i, corresponding to real development time j, i.e. j (not necessarily integral) periods after the beginning of the period of origin

= proportion of claims incurred in period of origin i which have been finalized by real development time j

= $m_i(j)/n_i$

where

$m_i(j)$ = number of claims incurred in period of origin i which have been finalized by real time j.

Clearly for j integral,

$$m_i(j) = m_{i,j-1}$$

so that

$$t_i(j) = m_{i,j-1}/n_i.$$

Also, $t_i(j)$ is a non-decreasing function of j, and

$$0 = t_i(0) \leq t_i(j) \leq t_i(\infty) = 1$$

Note that $t_i(j)$ is defined in terms of **realizations**, $m_i(j)$ and n_i, of random variables. Although it would be possible to define operational time as a random variable, $M_i(j)/N_i$, we do not do so, as it is used in this volume only as an index of claim size dependent on the realization of the claims finalization process.

The effect of replacing real time by operational time is to remove the sort of distortion observed in **Fig.   4**, which can be redrawn in terms of operational time as below.   In **Fig.5**, as in **Fig.4**, the arrows join corresponding finalizations in consecutive years of origin. The broken lines indicate how a particular development year-end has shifted on the operational time-line as one progresses from one year of origin to the next.

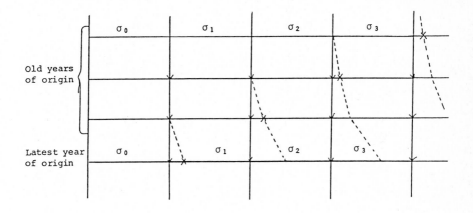

The ×'s denote the current valuation date marked on the operational time-line of the various years of origin.

Fig. 5. *Diagrammatic representation of speed of finalization (in terms of operational time)*

The significant point about the diagram is that average payment per claim finalized is σ_j within the j-th operational time-zone $(j = 0, 1, 2, \ldots)$ of **any** year of origin. This must follow, of course, from the assumption made in Section 7.3.2.4 that *"there has been absolutely no change from one period of origin to another in the sequence of claim payments already made and to be made in the future"*.

The hypothesis that this assumption holds was called by Taylor (1980) the **hypothesis of invariant order.**

If it does hold, then the objection raised against the payments per claim finalized method in **Fig.   4** can be overcome by the use of operational time. In this event the model equation (7.3.2.1.1) of the payments per claim finalized method is replaced by:

$$c_i(t_j, t_{j+1}) = n_i(t_{j+1} - t_j)\,\sigma(t_j, t_{j+1}), \qquad (7.3.3.1.2)$$

where

$[t_0, t_1, \ldots, t_r]$ is some partition of the complete operational time-interval $[0,1]$;

$(t_j, t_{j+1}]$ is the j-th operational time-zone;

$c_i(t_j, t_{j+1}) =$ (inflation-adjusted) payments in the j-th operational time-zone of period of origin i;

$\sigma(t_j, t_{j+1}) =$ (inflation-adjusted) payments per claim finalized in the j-th operational time-zone of period of origin i.

Note that, by the definition of operational time, the product $n_i(t_{j+1} - t_j)$ denotes the number of claims finalized in the j-th operational time-zone.

Apart from a couple of slightly messy details, the payments per claim finalized method (one of its versions) of Section 7.3.2 can be applied. The resulting method is known as the Reduced Reid method (Taylor, 1980).

The details requiring attention are as follows.

Firstly, whatever partition $[t_0, t_1, \ldots, t_r]$ is chosen, the required payments $c_i(t_j, t_{j+1})$ (fixed j, various i) will not normally be available directly from the data. The payments which will be available are the

$$c_{ij} = c_i(t_i(j), t_i(j+1)). \qquad (7.3.3.1.3)$$

The values of $t_i(j)$ will vary with i. In fact, the whole array of $t_i(j)$ $(i,j$ varying) might very well contain no repetitions. Thus, for fixed j, the values of $t_i(j+1)$ and $t_i(j)$ in (7.3.3.1.3) are unlikely to equal the values of $t_{i+1}(j+1)$ and $t_{i+1}(j)$ respectively. Then c_{ij} and $c_{i+1,j}$ will not relate to the same operational time-zone.

If $t_i(j-1)$ and $t_i(j)$ are sufficiently close that $c_i(x, y)$ can be assumed linear in x, y for $t_i(j-1) \le x \le y \le t_i(j)$, for each j, then an approximation to $c_i(t_j, t_{j+1})$ can be obtained by linear interpolation. If k and $l(> k)$ are such that

$$t_i(k-1) \le t_j \le t_i(k);$$
$$t_i(l-1) \le t_{j+1} \le t_i(l);$$

then

$$c_i(t_j, t_{j+1}) = \frac{t_i(k) - t_j}{t_i(k) - t_i(k-1)} c_{i,k-1} + \sum_{h=k}^{l-2} c_{ih} + \frac{t_{j+1} - t_i(l-1)}{t_i(l) - t_i(l-1)} c_{i,l-1}$$

$$(7.3.3.1.4)$$

Secondly, there will not be a "natural" partition of the operational time-interval $[0, 1]$ in the way in which there is for real time (development years, quarters, etc.). A decision will have to be made about this. Obviously, the finer the partition, the more information is gathered on the function $\sigma(\cdot, \cdot)$, provided the information is genuine. It is clear from (7.3.3.1.4) that, if the partition is so fine that there are more than $j + 1$ operational time-zones spanning the real time interval $[0, t_i(j)]$ where j is the most recent development period, then no more information about $\sigma(\cdot, \cdot)$ is obtained than would be by the use of just j operational time-zones.

Thus the partition $[t_0, \ldots, t_r]$ ought to be chosen to correspond in some rough way with the division of the real time-line into development periods.

The model (7.3.3.1.2) is completed by the addition of (7.3.2.1.3) or (7.3.2.1.4) modelling finalizations. Note, however, that the modelling of finalizations is unnecessary for the estimation of outstanding claims in current values. It is necessary, of course, if outstanding claims are to be estimated in inflated or discounted values. These facts will become more clear in Section 7.3.3.3.

Just as the above version of the Reduced Reid method has been developed in parallel with the payments per claim finalized method based on non-cumulative payments, it is possible to develop an alternative version of the Reduced Reid method based on cumulative claim payments.

In this case, the model equation (7.3.3.1.2) is replaced by:

$$c_i(0, t_j) = n_i t_j \sigma(0, t_j),$$

which may be abbreviated to:

$$c_i(t_j) = n_i t_j \sigma(t_j), \qquad (7.3.3.1.5)$$

with the notation:

$$c_i(t_j) \equiv c_i(0, t_j);$$
$$\sigma(t_j) \equiv \sigma(0, t_j).$$

As for the version of the Reduced Reid method based on non-cumulative payments, the required values of $c_i(t_j)$ are obtained by linear interpolation.

Equation (7.3.3.1.4) is used with $t_j = 0$, and becomes:

$$c_i(t_{j+1}) = \sum_{h=0}^{l-2} c_{ih} + \frac{t_{j+1} - t_i(l-1)}{t_i(l) - t_i(l-1)} c_{i,l-1} \qquad (7.3.3.1.6)$$

for $t_i(l-1) \leq t_{j+1} \leq t_i(l)$.

7.3.3.2   Estimation

As stated in Section 7.3.3.1, the Reduced Reid method is essentially the same as the payments per claim finalized method except for the change from real to operational time. Therefore, estimation of payments per claim finalized parallels (7.3.2.2.1):

$$\sigma(t_j, t_{j+1}) = \sum_{i \in I_{j,j+1}} c_i(t_j, t_{j+1}) / \sum_{i \in I_{j,j+1}} n_i(t_{j+1} - t_j), \qquad (7.3.3.2.1)$$

where

$I_{j,j+1} =$ set of periods of origin for which operational time period $(t_j, t_{j+1}]$ is tabulated.

If a projection of future numbers of finalizations is required, the relevant parameters are estimated by means of (7.3.2.2.2) or (7.3.2.2.3).

If the version of the Reduced Reid method based on cumulative claim payments is in use, (7.3.3.2.1) is replaced by:

$$\sigma(t_j) = \sum_{i \in I_{(0,j)}} c_i(t_j) / \sum_{i \in I_{(0,j)}} n_i t_j. \qquad (7.3.3.2.2)$$

If the version based on cumulative claim payments in respect of finalized claims only is in use, (7.3.3.2.1) is replaced by:

$$\sigma^f(t_j) = \sum_{i \in I_{(0,j)}} c_i^f(t_j) / \sum_{i \in I_{(0,j)}} n_i t_j, \qquad (7.3.3.2.3)$$

where $\sigma^f(t_j), c_i^f(t_j)$ denote the same as $\sigma(t_j)$, $c_i(t_j)$ except that they relate only to claims finalized by operational time t_j.

7.3.3.3.   *Projection of outstanding claims*

We begin by taking up the remark made in Section 7.3.3.1 that projection of future numbers of finalizations will not be necessary in the projection of outstanding claims in current values.

Consider, for example, the version of the method based on non-cumulative claim payments. Estimation will have been carried out by means of (7.3.3.2.1). Consider period of origin i, and suppose that the valuation date coincides with the end of development period k, i.e. operational time $t_i(k)$.

The outstanding claims are:

$$p_{i,k-1} = p_i(t_i(k)),\qquad (7.3.3.3.1)$$

where

$p_i(t) =$ outstanding claims (inflation-adjusted) at operational time t of period of origin i.

Now

$$p_i(t) = n_i(t_j - t)\sigma(t, t_j) + \sum_{l=j}^{r-1} n_i(t_{l+1} - t_l)\sigma(t_l, t_{l+1}),\qquad (7.3.3.3.2)$$

where

$$t_{j-1} \le t \le t_j.$$

Combining (7.3.3.3.1) and (7.3.3.3.2):

$$p_{i,k-1} = n_i[t_j - t_i(k)]\sigma(t_i(k), t_j) + \sum_{l=j}^{r-1} n_i(t_{l+1} - t_l)\sigma(t_l, t_{l+1}),\qquad (7.3.3.3.3)$$

where

$$t_{j-1} \le t_i(k) \le t_j.$$

Unless care has been taken to arrange it, $t_i(k)$ will not coincide with any of the extremities t_l of the operational time-zones. In this case, $\sigma(t_i(k), t_j)$ will not have been estimated by (7.3.3.2.1). However, provided that the operational time-interval $(t_{j-1}, t_j]$ is sufficiently short, the following approximation, based on linear interpolation, can be adopted:

$$\sigma(t_i(k), t_j) = \sigma(t_{j-1}, t_j) + \frac{\frac{1}{2}(t_j + t_i(k)) - \frac{1}{2}(t_{j-1} + t_j)}{\frac{1}{2}(t_j + t_{j+1}) - \frac{1}{2}(t_{j-1} + t_j)}[\sigma(t_j, t_{j+1}) - \sigma(t_{j-1}, t_j)]$$

$$= \sigma(t_{j-1}, t_j) + \frac{t_i(k) - t_{j-1}}{t_{j+1} - t_{j-1}}[\sigma(t_j, t_{j+1}) - \sigma(t_{j-1}, t_j)].\qquad (7.3.3.3.4)$$

In the first version of (7.3.3.3.4) linear interpolation has been carried out treating $\sigma(t, u)$ as a function of a single variable, average operational time, i.e. $\sigma(t, u)$ has been treated as $\sigma(\frac{1}{2}(t + u))$.

Thus, (7.3.3.3.3) gives outstanding claims in current values without any reference to a projection of future numbers of finalizations. If outstanding claims in inflated or discounted values require to be estimated, then it will be necessary to estimate not only their totality in current values, as in (7.3.3.3.3), but also their incidence over time.

Numbers of future finalizations could be projected by exactly the same methods as in Section 7.3.2.3 — see particularly (7.3.2.3.1) and (7.3.2.3.7). These represent the "standard" methods presented there. It should be borne in mind, however, that, for the reasons discussed in Section 7.3.2.4, the payments per claim finalized method provides only a rather rough analysis, in which case the "standard" methods of projecting future numbers of finalizations might be inappropriate. The Reduced Reid method, on the other hand, represents an attempt to refine the payments per claim finalized method, and in this situation a more conscientious approach to the projection of future numbers of finalizations may be required.

It may be appropriate to assume that the speed of finalization observed in the last one or two years will be maintained in the future. It may be possible to obtain information concerning the reasons for any recent changes in speed of finalization and, on the basis of this information, make a subjective forecast of future speeds of finalization. Although there is scope for error in the use of either standard methods or subjective forecasts, it should be remembered that the distribution of future numbers of finalizations over time has absolutely no effect on the estimated total outstanding claims in current values; only the difference between this and the total in inflated and discounted values is affected. The scope for error here will usually be fairly limited.

In any event, estimates of the future number of finalizations n_{ih} in development period h of period of origin i will be obtained by some means or other. It is then necessary to estimate the corresponding claim payments.

Once future numbers of finalizations have been estimated, the operational time-interval associated with n_{ih} can be calculated as $(t_i(h), t_i(h+1)]$, where

$$t_i(h) = m_{i,h-1}/n_i, \qquad t_i(h + 1) = m_{ih}/n_i.$$

Then

$$c_{ih} = n_{ih}\sigma(t_i(h), t_i(h + 1)). \tag{7.3.3.3.5}$$

The values of σ required will not usually be directly available from the estimates formed by (7.3.3.2.1). Interpolation can be used as in (7.3.3.3.3). Thus, if

$$t_u \leq t_i(h) \leq t_{u+1}, \ldots, t_{v-1} \leq t_i(h+1) \leq t_v, \qquad (7.3.3.3.6)$$

then (7.3.3.3.5) can be expanded:

$$c_{ih} = n_i \Big\{ [t_{u+1} - t_i(h)]\sigma(t_u, t_{u+1}) + \sum_{l=u+1}^{v-2} [t_{l+1} - t_l]\sigma(t_l, t_{l+1})$$
$$+ [t_i(h+1) - t_{v-1}]\sigma(t_{v-1}, t_v) \Big\}. \qquad (7.3.3.3.7)$$

Corrections can be made, if desired to the two end terms, the ones involving operational time intervals $(t_i(h), t_{u+1}]$ and $(t_{v-1}, t_i(h+1)]$, to allow for the fact that they are "off centre" in the time zones $(t_u, t_{u+1}]$ and $(t_{v-1}, t_v]$ on which the σ values are based.

In the event that $v = u + 1$, so that the set of values $\{t_{u+1}, \ldots, t_{v-1}\}$ appearing in (7.3.3.3.6) is empty, (7.3.3.3.5) becomes just:

$$c_{ih} = n_{ih}\sigma(t_u, t_{u+1}). \qquad (7.3.3.3.8)$$

Once again, a correction of the type mentioned in the preceding paragraph can be made if desired.

Precisely the same principles as above can be applied to the projection of outstanding claims when estimation has been based on cumulative claim payments (see (7.3.3.2.2) and (7.3.3.2.3)).

For example, if (7.3.3.2.2) has been used for estimation, (7.3.3.3.2) is replaced by:

$$p_i(t) = p_i(0) - c_i(t)$$
$$= n_i\sigma(\infty) - c_i(t). \qquad (7.3.3.3.9)$$

In this case, the incidence of future claim payments constituting $p_i(t)$ is again determined by means of (7.3.3.3.7), but noting that

$$\sigma(t_l, t_{l+1}) = c_i(t_l, t_{l+1})/n_i(t_{l+1} - t_l)$$
$$= [m_i(t_{l+1})\sigma(t_{l+1}) - m_i(t_l)\sigma(t_l)]/n_i(t_{l+1} - t_l)$$
$$= [t_{l+1}\sigma(t_{l+1}) - t_l\sigma(t_l)]/(t_{l+1} - t_l). \qquad (7.3.3.3.10)$$

Similarly, if (7.3.3.2.3) has been used for estimation, (7.3.3.3.2) is replaced (as in (7.3.3.3.9)) by:

$$p_i(t) = p_i(0) - c_i(t)$$
$$= n_i \sigma^f(\infty) - c_i(t). \qquad (7.3.3.3.11)$$

Note, however, that it will not be possible to determine the incidence of the claim payments contained in this $p_i(t)$ on the basis of the model underlying the Reduced Reid method based on cumulative claim payments in respect of finalized claims only.

7.3.3.4   *Comment*

There is not a great deal of comment to be made concerning the Reduced Reid method . As remarked in Section 7.3.3.1, the method is simply a variation of the payments per claim finalized method, but using operational time instead of real time as an explanatory variable in the model.

Therefore, any comment applicable to the payments per claim finalized method (unless directed to the difference referred to in the preceding paragraph), such as those made in Section 7.3.2.4, will usually have a counterpart applying to the Reduced Reid method .

A major comment to be made here is the one foreshadowed in Section 7.3.3.1. There, and in Sections 7.3.3.2 and 7.3.3.3, it was assumed, for simplicity of exposition, that "different periods of origin experience precisely the same sequences of claim payments arranged in precisely the same order". It was stated that this condition may be weakened considerably.

A much weaker condition is given by Taylor (1983). Consider a distribution function $G(x : t)$ of size x of a single claim finalized at operational time t (t being regarded as a parameter of the d.f. rather than a random variable).

The expected payment per claim finalized in the operational time interval $(t_1, t_2]$ is:

$$\sigma(t_1, t_2) = (t_2 - t_1)^{-1} \int_{t_1}^{t_2} dt \int_{-\infty}^{\infty} x d_x G(x : t)$$
$$= \text{function of just } t_1, t_2, \qquad (7.3.3.4.1)$$

which is essentially the assumption on which the Reduced Reid method of Section 7.3.3.1 is based.

This is a version of the argument given by Taylor (1981b).

Thus the hypothesis of invariant order, used to justify the Reduced Reid method , has been weakened to a stochastic condition which requires that the joint d.f. of claim size and delay in payment of an individual claim does not vary from one period of origin to another.

We conclude this section by pointing to a major shortcoming of both the payments per claim finalized and Reduced Reid methods. Both methods assume that payments per claim finalized (adjusted for inflation) for a given development period , defined in either real or operational time, are independent of speed of finalization (e.g. (7.3.2.1.1) and (7.3.3.1.2)). What is the justification of such an assumption?

This question is examined by Taylor (1981b). He shows that, for small η:

$$\sigma(t_1 - \eta, t_2 + \eta) = \sigma(t_1, t_2) + [\eta/(t_2 - t_1)] \times [\overline{x}(t_2) + \overline{x}(t_1) - 2\sigma(t_1, t_2)],$$
$$(7.3.3.4.2)$$

where

$$\overline{x}(t) = \int_{-\infty}^{\infty} x d_x G(x, t).$$

Now the operational time intervals $(t_1, t_2]$ and $(t_1 - \eta, t_2 + \eta]$ appearing in (7.3.3.4.2) may be viewed as representing the same development period with slightly different speeds of finalization. Note that these two operational time intervals have the same average values of operational time.

Thus, (7.3.3.4.2) shows that, as speed of finalization changes but average operational time of the development period under consideration is held constant, payments per claim finalized do not remain constant. Rather, they are changed by a term which is directly dependent on η, the parameter defining the change in speed of finalization.

In fact, it is shown by Taylor (1981b) that

$$\sigma(t_1 - \eta, t_2 + \eta) \gtreqless \sigma(t_1, t_2) \qquad (7.3.3.4.3)$$

according as

$$\overline{x}(t) \text{ is } \begin{cases} \text{convex to the } t\text{-axis without being linear on } [t_1, t_2] \\ \text{linear in } t \text{ on } [t_1, t_2] \\ \text{concave to the } t\text{-axis without being linear on } [t_1, t_2] \end{cases}$$

It follows that the Reduced Reid method cannot be expected to provide a realistic representation of the claims process except in the fortuitous circumstance that $\bar{x}(t)$, the instantaneous payment per claim finalized at operational time t, is a linear function of t.

How this shortcoming of the model ought to be dealt with is taken up in Section 8.2.

8.   STOCHASTIC MACRO-MODELS

8.1   Stochastic payments per unit of risk method —
$S/MIC/NN/P/T, I, E, D$ type

8.1.1 *Model*

Pollard (1983) has produced a stochastic version of the payments per unit of risk method dealt with in Section 7.1.4. Although that author does not so characterize the method, it should be apparent from the following that it is in fact as described above.

Sections 8.1.1 to 8.1.4 use the notation introduced in Section 3 except that all claim amounts are assumed to have been adjusted for claims escalation. In this notation, the model is:

$$c_{z.i.j..} = q_j + \epsilon_{zij}, \tag{8.1.1.1}$$

where we recall that z indexes individual claims and where ϵ_{zij} is a stochastic error term with zero mean.

If expected values are taken through (8.1.1.1) and the result summed over all values of z relating to period of origin i, one obtains:

$$E[c_{..i.j..}] = n_i q_j. \tag{8.1.1.2}$$

Comparison of (8.1.1.2) with (7.1.4.1.2) reveals that the model (8.1.1.1) is just a stochastic version of the payments per unit of risk model.

There is one more ingredient in the model. It concerns the form of the stochastic error terms. The form of the ϵ_{zij} in (8.1.1.1) is not specified. However, the central limit theorem is invoked to establish approximately that (8.1.1.2) can be written as:

$$c_{..i.j..} = n_i q_j + \epsilon_{ij}, \tag{8.1.1.3}$$

where ϵ_{ij} is now a normal random variable with zero mean and covariance matrix $n_i V$, say. That is, the matrix V contains as its (j,k)-element the covariance between ϵ_{ij} and ϵ_{ik} (i.e. between the payments in respect of a single claim in development periods j and k respectively), which is assumed independent of period of origin i. In taking the matrix $n_i V$, Pollard assumes payments in respect of distinct individual claims to be stochastically independent.

Thus Pollard's model consists of (8.1.1.3) and:

$$\mathrm{Var}[\epsilon_i] = n_i V, \tag{8.1.1.4}$$

where ϵ_i here denotes the column vector whose j-th component is ϵ_{ij}.

One might question the use of the central limit theorem on a sum of random variables (the payments in respect of individual claims) rather than their mean. However, we do not pause here but return to the question of normality more generally in Section 8.1.4.

8.1.2 *Estimation*

The model expressed in (8.1.1.3) and (8.1.1.4) contains as parameters just the vector of values q_j and the covariance matrix V. These are the parameters which need to be estimated. In principle, the dimension of $q = (q_1, q_2, \ldots)$, and hence of V, is unlimited. In practice, of course, it is limited to some convenient finite integer. Then estimation of claims in respect of higher development periods than this becomes a subsidiary problem falling outside the scope of the formal method discussed here.

In Pollard's paper the parameters q and V are estimated from data in respect of individual claims. We comment in Section 8.1.4.

The suggested estimators are the sample mean and sample (biased) covariance matrix based on these data. That is, q_j is estimated by the mean of all the observations $c_{z.i.j..}$ for fixed j. Similarly, the (j,k)-element of V is estimated by the empirical covariance of all the pairs of observations $(c_{z.i.j..}, c_{z.i.k..})$ for fixed j, k.

Symbolically, q_j is estimated by:

$$\hat{q}_j = \sum_{\substack{z, \\ i \in I_j}} c_{z.i.j..} / \sum_{i \in I_j} n_i. \tag{8.1.2.1}$$

If the sum over z indicated in (8.1.2.1) is taken, it becomes:

$$\hat{q}_j = \sum_{i \in I_j} c_{..i.j..} / \sum_{i \in I_j} n_i. \tag{8.1.2.2}$$

Equation (8.1.2.2) can be seen to have a form identical with (7.1.4.2.1), the equation displaying the estimator used by the (non-stochastic) payments per unit of risk method. Thus, as far as the non-stochastic component (8.1.1.3) of Pollard's method are concerned, both model and estimation are as for the payments per unit of risk method.

8.1.3 *Projection of outstanding claims*

It was pointed out in Section 8.1.1 that, apart from the addition of a stochastic structure, the model set up there was precisely the payments per unit of risk model of Section 7.1.4. It was further pointed out in Section 8.1.2 that, once again apart from the stochastic structure, estimation was as for that earlier model.

It is interesting, therefore, to note that the method of projection suggested by Pollard is quite diferent from that described in Section 7.1.4.3 in connection with the payments per unit of risk method. The addition of a stochastic structure increases the range of options available in the choice of projection formula.

Effectively, this is achieved by making use of the estimated covariances forming the matrix V. To explain the process verbally, if a positive (say) covariance has been observed in the past between claim payments (of individual claims) in development periods j and $k(> j)$, and if in the period of origin now in question claim payments (for all claims) show a historically high value in the past development period j, then it is assumed that the payments in the future development period k are likely to emerge historically high also.

The precise details of this procedure are as follows, Consider a period of origin which has developed to the end of development period k. The inverse matrix V^{-1} is partitioned:

$$V^{-1} = \begin{bmatrix} V_{11}^I & V_{12}^I \\ V_{21}^I & V_{22}^I \end{bmatrix},$$

where the partitioning is determined by the submatrix V_{11}^I, which is the $(k + 1) \times (k + 1)$ covariance matrix in respect of development periods $0, 1, \ldots, k$.

The vector q is similarly partitioned:

$$q = \begin{bmatrix} q_{(1)} \\ q_{(2)} \end{bmatrix},$$

i.e. the partitioning separates the first $k + 1$ components of q from the remainder.

Let c denote the $(k + 1)$-dimensional vector consisting of the $c_{..i.j..}$, $j = 0, 1,\ldots, k$.

Then Pollard uses a standard statistical result for a multivariate normal model described by (8.1.1.3) and (8.1.1.4). The result is that the vector of outstanding claims, consisting of the $c_{..i.j..}$, $j = k + 1, k + 2,\ldots$, has expectation conditional on c equal to:

$$nq_{(2)} - \left(V_{22}^I\right)^{-1} V_{21}^I (c - nq_{(1)}), \tag{8.1.3.1}$$

where, for consistency with the rest of the notation in this formula, the subscript on the symbol n has been suppressed.

Pollard also notes that the associated covariance matrix is:

$$n \left(V_{22}^I\right)^{-1}. \tag{8.1.3.2}$$

Thus, the vector of outstanding claims of the period of origin in question is estimated by (8.1.3.1) with $q_{(2)}$ and V_{21}^I, V_{22}^I replaced by their estimates obtained in Section 8.1.2.

As Pollard notes, the first member of (8.1.3.1) (after replacement by its estimator) is the estimate of the outstanding claims vector in the absence of any information about the effect of past experience of period of origin i on future experience of that same period of origin .

As this line of reasoning suggests, and as (8.1.2.2) confirms, the first member of (8.1.3.1) is precisely the payments per unit of risk estimate of outstanding claims. The second member represents a corrective term which takes into account the stochastic structure added in Section 8.1.1. to the earlier model of Section 7.1.4.

8.1.4 *Comment*

Pollard covers a number of related topics in his paper.

He provides a χ^2 test for consistency between individual periods of origin in respect of the hypothesised parameters q_j. In the notation used in Section 8.1.3, the relevant test statistic is:

$$\chi^2 = (c - nq_{(1)})^T V_{11}^{-1} (c - nq_{(1)})/n, \tag{8.1.4.1}$$

where the T denotes matrix transposition, and V_{11} is the pricipal $(k + 1) \times (k + 1)$ submatrix of V.

On the normality assumptions made in Section 8.1.1., and on the hypothesis that all periods of origin conform with the model (8.1.1.3) and (8.1.1.4), the test statistic (8.1.4.1) is distributed as a χ^2-square with $k + 1$ degrees of freedom. Large values of this statistic are indicative of violation of the model assumptions.

The question of how one should proceed when such violation is indicated is discussed. The suggestion is made that changes in speed of finalization might account for inconsistent payment patterns as between different periods of origin. There is some discussion of simple methods of correction for this distortion.

The methods considered have in common that the correction must be based on some simple formula describing the changes in speed of finalization. For example, Pollard's major example is based upon the assumption

" *that there has been an acceleration in claim payments such that a payment, which, in the past, would have been made at time τ, is now made at time $\tau/(1 + \alpha)$.* "

In the author's experience, it is unusual to find changes in speed of finalization conforming to such neat and convenient rules. Changes tend to occur in a discrete fashion.

The numerical example presented in Pollard's paper might appear to contradict this. In that example the very simple formula described above for an acceleration of finalizations works perfectly in removing a gross inconsistency between the run-off patterns of different periods of origin. However, as I understand from private communication with Professor Pollard, they are manufactured. One presumes that they were so manufactured that the simple formula mentioned above would indeed work.

While Pollard mentions that the formula changing speed of finalization can be complexified if necessary, there are nevertheless two fundamental drawbacks involved in the concepts on which the method is based.

Firstly, the method does not seem to include a facility for exploratory data analysis with the objective of estimating the real effects of changing speed of finalization, which might not be mathematically expressible in an elegant form. Thus, quite apart from the difficulties of mathematical expression, no procedure is laid down according to which the user of the method is able to arive at a description of the effects of speed of finalization. This is a theme to which we shall return in Section 8.2, particularly 8.2.4.

Secondly, Pollard states that

> " *More complicated structural changes in the run-off pattern require more complicated models, and possibly more parameters ... The temptation to overparameterise must be resisted.*"

This situation, in which the model appears to represent the data in an unsatisfactory way if regard is not had to speed of finalization yet the model can be modified to include this variable properly only at the expense of considerable expansion of the parameter set, suggests that a fundamental overhaul of the model structure may be in order.

The question of how speed of finalization might be incorporated in the model with economy of parameters is considered in Section 8.2. It will be seen there that this variable may, under certain circumstances, be incorporated with a **decrease** in the number of parameters (as compared with some of the "standard" models).

Of course, the stochastic structure of the model, and particularly the expression (8.1.3.2) which is taken as the covariance matrix of the projected vector of outstanding claims in respect of period of origin i, admit the possibility of estimating the second moments associated with the first moment estimates.

While it is not seen as the function of this survey to go into great detail concerning estimation of second moments, there are a couple of matters arising from the treatment of second moments in Pollard's paper.

As has been pointed out by Bartholomew (1975), there are three distinct types of error which can arise in estimation exercises of the sort attempted here:

(i) estimation error,

(ii) statistical error,

(iii) specification error.

Error (iii) is considered first. It refers to the fact that if the real (unknown) model structure differs from that assumed in a modelling exercise, the difference will manifest itself in larger deviations of observations from the fitted model than from the true underlying parametric structure. The result will be overestimation of the stochastic variation inherent in the modelled process. Thus, the estimates of second moments associated with the first moment estimates are likely to be overstated.

One can summarise this point in the slogan

> " *Good models produce estimates with small confidence intervals. Bad models produce estimates with large confidence intervals.* "

The relevance of this to the model of Section 8.1.1 is clear when one considers its simplicity and the fact (Taylor, 1982a) that in specific cases it has proven demonstrably and comprehensively lacking in explanatory power. It seems that, as far as specification error is concerned, expression (8.1.3.2) will often overestimate the covariances involved.

Of course, accusations of this type of error can be brought against virtually all models since it is highly unlikely that any model always captures all the features of the modelled process. However, the payments per unit of risk method is generally accepted as a crude method, and therefore particularly renegade in failing to model the claims process realistically.

It may be noted that a fundamental assumption built into the model is that the covariance matrix does not change with period of origin. This appears, in turn, to involve the implicit assumption that whatever inflation correction has been made to the claim payments is accurate. For any errors in these corrections will induce covariances between calendar (or experience) periods and, since these are not taken into account in the estimation of V, they will manifest themselvres as variations in V from one period of origin to another. Moreover, if V actually reflects calendar period covariances, it is highly unlikely that those observed in the past will provide much of a guide to the future as is assumed in the basic projection formulas (8.1.3.1) and (8.1.3.2).

Errors of types (i) and (ii) above are discussed in the claims reserving context by Taylor and Ashe (1983). They refer to the distinction between:

(i) "**estimation error**" arising from the fact that their estimates of outstanding claims are functions of estimated parameter values which, because of the stochastic nature of the claims process, are random variables,

(ii) "**statistical error**" arising from the fact that, even if one were able to obtain estimates of the parameter values which were correct with certainty, random error would still enter into the realization of the outstanding claims since these themselves are regarded as random variables.

It appears that the covariance estimate (8.1.3.2) includes allowance for statistical but not estimation error. Estimates of outstanding claims are obtained by means of (8.1.3.1). This includes, most importantly, the terms $q_{(1)}$ and $q_{(2)}$ which, according to the method, are estimated by means of (8.1.2.1). This process of estimation will induce estimation error in $q_{(1)}$ and $q_{(2)}$, and hence in (8.1.3.1).

In the one model with which the author has experience of estimation and statistical error (Taylor and Ashe, 1983), both made significant contributions to the total variance of the estimated outstandings. It is difficult to extrapolate from this to other models, but it appears that omission of either type of error might render estimated second moments seriously deficient.

In summary, then, it appears that second moments estimated by means of (8.1.3.2) are probably:

 (i) overstated due to specification error,

(ii) understated due to the omission of estimation error.

It was mentioned in Section 8.1.1 that the model regards (inflation-adjusted) claim payments in respect of period of origin i and development period j as approximately normally distributed. Pollard expresses caution about this assumption, referring to the fact that in the higher development periods of some classes of business payments in respect of individual claims *"will tend to have distributions which are markedly skew, and there may be some concern that the number of claims is not large enough to ensure the multi-variate normality"*.

The caution is, of course, well warranted. The skewness which does exist in some of these distributions is exemplified by the data given by Buchanan and Lester (1982). However, the problem may be less than it appears.

It seems that whether or not non-normality presents problems depends to some extent on just what is being estimated. For example, if one were particularly concerned with estimating future payments in development year 6 of year of origin 1980 in a medium-sized Australian Liability portfolio, then problems would almost certainly arise from non-normality considerations. On the other hand, if one were concerned only with the total amount of outstanding claims in respect of the same portfolio, problems of this type migh be much less serious. This total amount consists of the sum of all the individual amounts relating to particular combinations of period of origin and development period. Probably, in some of these combinations the application of the central limit theorem will be appropriate, in others not. However, the applicability of the theorem to the total outstandings will be greater than to any of the individual cells. Quite possibly, then, there is no objection to the use of the central limit theorem in this case.

Section 8.1.1 made a further reservation about the use of the central limit theorem in the context described there. Doubt was expressed about its application to a sum of random variables rather than a mean. The greater part of this doubt can be cleared up if the whole of the model, estimation and projection (Sections 8.1.1, 8.1.2 and 8.1.3) are re-expressed to deal with **average amount outstanding per claim incurred** in the relevant period of origin rather than total amount outstanding. This would overcome the above objection.

Of course, at the very end of this procedure it would be necessary to rescale all estimates in order that the final results relate to total outstanding claims. At this point the central limit theorem might cease to be applicable. One would then be left with estimates of outstanding claims and the associated second moments, but **without** any indication of the distributional properties of the estimates. Nevertheless, this approach has the advantage of rigorous reasoning.

Finally, we consider one or two points arising out of the estimation procedures used in Section 8.1.2. It was noted in that section that the estimation of parameters q and V required individual claim histories. Naturally, these will not always be readily available. If available, they will certainly need to be processed by computer, yet they might not be in a form readily assimilated by the system of the person carrying out the estimation.

On the other hand, an advantage of gathering raw data is that the opportunity for its corruption by its owner will usually be less than is the case for summary data.

8.2   The see-saw method —
$S/MAC/N/P/E, F, I, T, S, Y$ type

8.2.1 *Model*

This method can be viewed as a refinement of the Reduced Reid method dealt with in Section 7.3.3. The refinement relates not only to the stochastic nature of the see-saw model, but the model of expected claim payments EC_{ij} has also been refined.

Relation (7.3.3.4.3) shows that a change in speed of finalization will induce a change in expected payments per claim finalized which will be positive, zero or negative according to the convexity properties of the instantaneous payments per claim finalized.

Taylor (1982a) alluded to the empirical finding that a rise in speed of finalization appeared usually to be accompanied by a fall in payments per claim finalized. This led him to refer to a method which recognised the dependence of expected payments per claim finalized on speed of finalization in the (i, j)-cell.

The formal introduction of this dependency requires the concept of instantaneous speed of finalization which is now defined.

Let
$$f_i(j) = \partial t_i(j)/\partial j = [\partial m_i(j)/\partial j]/n_i$$

= **instantaneous speed of finalization at real development time** j, in the sense that:

$f_i(j)dj$ = proportion of claims incurred in period of origin i which were finalized in the infinitesimal real time interval $(j, j + dj)$.

We note here that, at the observational (as opposed to expectational) level, there are conceptual difficulties associated with the differentiation of operational time since (at the observational level) this is a step function. For the moment we brush these difficulties aside by imagining that we are dealing with infinitely large numbers n_i of claims incurred. In Section 8.2.4 we return to a more honest recognition of this difficulty.

Even given that payments per claim finalized are a function of just two variables, operational time and speed of finalization, there is, of course, no obvious indication of the functional form involved.

A simple recourse is to assume that the function is sufficiently smooth to be modelled by a piecewise linear function. This was done in the original see-saw model (Taylor 1982a) where it was assumed that $\dot{\sigma}_{ij}$ was linear in $\bar{t}_{ij}$ and f_{ij} for j within certain limits, and where

$$\bar{t}_{ij} = \tfrac{1}{2}[t(j) + t(j+1)]$$

= average operational time passed through during development period j.

To be more precise, let the operational time-interval $[0, 1]$ be given the partition $\{u_0, \ldots, u_r\}$. We assume σ_{ij} to be linear in $\bar{t}_{ij}$, f_{ij} for $\bar{t}_{ij} \in (u_k, u_{k+1}]$. In order to obtain continuity in $\bar{t}_{ij}$ as this variable passes from one interval $(u_k, u_{k+1}]$ to the next, one may define **confined operational time**:

$$\bar{t}_{ij}^{(k)} = \bar{t}_{ij} \wedge u_k$$
$$= \min(\bar{t}_{ij}, u_k). \qquad (8.2.1.1)$$

One may then write:

$$S_{ij} = \alpha + \sum_{k \in S} \beta_k \bar{t}_{ij}^{(k)} + \sum_{k \in \mathcal{T}} \gamma_k f_{ij}^{(k)} + e_{ij}, \qquad (8.2.1.2)$$

where $S, \mathcal{T} \subset \{1, \ldots, r\}$, α and the β_k, γ_k are constants, and $f_{ij}^{(k)}$ is defined as:

$$f_{ij}^{(k)} = \begin{cases} f_{ij}, & \text{if } \bar{t}_{ij} \in (u_{k-1}, u_k] \\ 0, & \text{otherwise.} \end{cases} \qquad (8.2.1.3)$$

The term e_{ij} represents a stochastic error term whose characteristics are partly described in (8.2.1.22) below.

The definition (8.2.1.3) is chosen so as to allow $\partial \sigma_{ij}/\partial f_{ij}$ to vary as operational time $t_i(j)$ varies. Note, however, that $f_{ij}^{(k)}$ is a discontinous function of f_{ij}, whence (8.2.1.2) will **not** ensure continuity of σ_{ij} as a function of f_{ij}.

The approximation of σ_{ij} by a continuous piecewise linear function of two variables in a form amenable to estimation of its parameters is not a simple problem. But, in any case, it is not pursued here because the need to do so is removed by the invariant version of the see-saw method expounded below.

It may be noted at this point that the procedure actually followed by Taylor (1981a) was slightly different from the above. Confined operational time was taken not as (8.2.1.1) but as:

$$\bar{t}_{ij}^{(k)} = \begin{cases} u_{k-1} & \text{if } u_{k-1} > t_{ij}; \\ \bar{t}_{ij} & \text{if } u_{k-1} \leq t_{ij} \leq u_k; \\ u_k & \text{if } t_{ij} > u_k. \end{cases} \qquad (8.2.1.4)$$

Definitions (8.2.1.1) and (8.2.1.4) lead to identical results when $S = \{1,\ldots,r\}$. But when l, say, $\notin S$,(8.2.1.4) generates a constant contribution of operational time to σ_{ij} in the operational time interval $[u_{l-1}, u_l]$. Thus, (8.2.1.4) forces:

$$\partial \sigma_{ij}/\partial \bar{t}_{ij} = 0 \qquad for \quad \bar{t}_{ij} \in (u_{k-1}, u_k).$$

The alternative definition of confined operational time, (8.2.1.1) does not force this result and is therefore to be preferred.

The preamble to the above development of the see-saw method contained a statement that we have no obvious indication of the functional dependence of σ_{ij} on f_{ij}. For this reason, the rough expedient of taking σ_{ij} piecewise linearly dependent on f_{ij} was adopted.

It is possible, however, to proceed rather more rigorously than the above phenomenological procedure. This leads to a different see-saw model, called the **invariant see-saw model** (Taylor,1983).

The assumption on which this see-saw model is based is that foreshadowed towards the end of Section 7.3.3.4. For convenience, it is restated below. In assumptions 1a, 1b, 1c, 2 and 3 below, all claim payments discussed are taken to be in constant money values, i.e. the effects of claims escalation have been removed.

Assumption 1a. For each value of operational time $t \in [0, 1]$, there exists a d.f. $G(x : t)$ of size x of an individual claim finalized at that operational time.

In fact, this assumption is a little too restrictive. It includes no assumption about partial payments. The following assumption is a weakened version of Assumption 1a which rectifies this shortcoming. Slightly more technical language is required to introduce the concepts associated with partial payments.

Assumption 1b (weakened version of Assumption 1a). For each value of operational time $t \in [0, 1]$, there exists a d.f. $G(x : t)$ of the amount x of claim payments between consecutive finalizations (counting in these claim payments the amount paid in finalization of the first but not the second of the finalizations) within an infinitesimal operational time-interval containing t (where, in order to achieve consecutive finalizations within an infinitesimal operational time-interval, we are effectively assuming an infinitely large number of claims incurred).

Although the infinitely large number of claims incurred mentioned here will never be realised in practice, there is of course nothing objectionable in simply describing the model as if such an infinite sample were observable.

Occasionally it will be possible to weaken Assumption 1b even further. This is done as follows.

Assumption 1c (weakened version of Assumption 1b). For each value of operational time $t \in [0, 1]$, there exists a d.f. $G(x : t)$, and for each period of origin i there exists a constant K_i, such that $G(K_i x : t)$ or $G(x + K_i : t)$ is the d.f. of the amount x of claim payments between consecutive finalizations (counting in these claim payments the amount paid in finalization of the first but not the second of the finalizations) within an infinitesimal operational time-interval containing t (where, in order to achieve consecutive finalizations within an infinitesimal operational time-interval, we are effectively assuming an infinitely large number of claims incurred).

Remark. The d.f.'s $G(x : t)$ required in each of Assumptions 1a to 1c would be implied in each case by a postulate of a joint d.f. $G(x, t)$ of claim size x (or its extended meaning as given in Assumptions 1b and 1c) and operational time t. Then the required $G(x : t)$ would be the marginal d.f. of $G(x, t)$. Assumptions 1a to 1c as stated are weaker than the corresponding requirement of a joint d.f. The three possible types of assumption which have been considered as justification of the Reduced Reid and see-saw models are, in order of strength:

hypothesis of invariant order

↓

existence of joint d.f. $G(x, t)$

↓

existence of conditional d.f. $G(x : t)$.

Assumption 1c is the same as Assumption 1b except for the effect of the constants K_i. These allow for rescaling or translation of the claim size random variables from one period of origin to another. As long as only a single period of origin is considered, Assumptions 1b and 1c are identical.

It is not difficult to conjure up circumstances in which all of Assumptions 1a, 1b and 1c will be violated. Comment on this aspect of the matter is given in Section 8.2.4. Nonetheless, a selection of one from these three assumptions represents a reasonably realistic point of departure for an investigation, albeit perhaps necessary ultimately to abandon it in the face of evidence tending to contradict it.

Note that, for a given period of origin and a given development epoch, Assumptions 1b and 1c both imply that expected payments per claim finalized (during an infinitesimal operational time-interval) depend on only the value of operational time corresponding to that epoch. In the earlier notation,

$$\lim_{\delta \to 0} \sigma(t, t + \delta) \quad \text{depends only on } t. \qquad (8.2.1.5)$$

This carries one rather significant implication for the amount of outstanding claims at a particular date. Consider a given period of origin i at a valuation date corresponding to (real) development time b. Because of (8.2.1.5), the amount of claims outstanding (in current values) at time b is:

$$\int_b^\infty n_i f_i(j) E_i(t_i(j)) dj, \qquad (8.2.1.6)$$

where $E(t)$ has been temporarily written for expression (8.2.1.5) (and of course the period of origin subscript added).

If the variable of integration in (8.2.1.6) is changed from real time j to operational time $t(j)$, the amount of claims outstanding becomes:

$$\int_{t(b)}^\infty n_i E_i(t) dt \qquad (8.2.1.7)$$

It is now necessary to return to the real world by departing from models involving infinitesimal time-intervals. Consequently, it will not be possible to use parameters such as $E_i(t(j))$ corresponding to the instant j of (real) development time. Instead it will be necessary to use a function like E_i, but dependent on the development period $(j, j + 1]$.

The new function is now dependent on the whole set of parameters:

$$E_i(t_i(k)), \qquad k \in (j, j + 1] \qquad (8.2.1.8)$$

For example, it will be necessary to consider:

$$\sigma_{ij} = \int_j^{j+1} n_i f_i(k) E_i(t_i(k)) dk \Big/ \int_j^{j+1} n_i f_i(k) dk. \qquad (8.2.1.9)$$

The set (8.2.1.8) depends in turn on the speed of finalization experienced in development period j. A greater (lesser) speed of finalization will increase (decrease) the set of functions $E(\cdot)$ involved.

For practical purposes it is necessary to consider what concise **approximate** representations of the set (8.2.1.8) are available. They will need to be approximate as long as one wishes to consider only a finite set in place of (8.2.1.8), a restriction dictated by practice.

Now, as has already been pointed out at the end of Section 7.3.3.4, when one works with **finite development periods**, expected payments per claim finalized become dependent on not only operational time but also speed of finalization. In the reference cited there (Taylor, 1981b) it is shown that:

$$\sigma_i(t - \eta, t + d + \eta) = \sigma_i(t, t + d) + \frac{\eta}{d} \left[I(t + d) + I(t) - 2\sigma_i(t, t + d) \right],$$

where $I(\cdot)$ is a particular function defined there and η is small. This is just a restatement of the result already cited in (7.3.3.4.2).

As noted in that paper, the dependence on η reflects the dependence of σ_{ij} on speed of finalization in development period j.

If the separation of $t_i(j)$ and $t_i(j+1)$ is sufficiently small, then (8.2.1.9) indicates that the last relation can be replaced approximately by:

$$\sigma_i(t - \eta, t + d + \eta) = E_i(t + d/2) + 2(\eta/d) \left[I(t + d/2) - E_i(t + d/2) \right].$$
$$(8.2.1.10)$$

Now $t + d/2$ is the average operational time in the interval $(t - \eta, t + d + \eta)$ under consideration.

Thus, setting $t - \eta$, $t + d + \eta$ equal to $t_i(j)$, $t_i(j + 1)$ in (8.2.1.10) shows that σ_{ij} is approximately a function of $[t_i(j) + t_i(j + 1)]/2$ and f_{ij}.

This leads to the following.

Assumption 2 (approximation to Assumption 1b).

The expected payments per claim finalized in a given development period of a given period of origin (adjusted for inflation) are a function of just the two variables:

(i) average operational time traversed in that development period ,

(ii) speed of finalization experienced in that development period .

Strictly, it should be noted from the above discussion that this approximation will not necessarily be a good one if:

> either (i) the interval of operational time covered by the development period in question is not sufficiently short,

> or (ii) variations in speed of finalization, as between different periods of origin, are not sufficiently small.

Another key to the reasoning below is the following.

Assumption 3 (actually a deduction from Assumption 1c).

For any given point of development time of any given period of origin , the expected amount of outstanding claims , deflated to current values, is invariant under all variations of future speed of finalization.

This "assumption" is in fact no more than a verbal statement of (8.2.1.7) which expreses the amount of outstanding claims in a form which is manifestly independent of speed of finalization.

Assumptions 2 and 3 provide the basis for an investigation of the form of models, involving payments per claim finalized , which might reasonably be adopted. The question to be considered is:

Which functions σ_{ij} of just the two variables, $[t_i(j) + t_i(j + 1)]/2$ and f_{ij}, are such as to ensure the invariance of:

$$\sum_{j=b}^{\infty} n_i f_{ij} \sigma_{ij},\qquad (8.2.1.11)$$

under all the admissible changes of the f_{ij}, $j = b$, $b + 1$, etc.

Since the total number of claims still to be finalized is presumed known, these admissible changes must satisfy:

$$\sum_{j=b}^{\infty} n_i f_{ij} = \text{const.,} \qquad (8.2.1.12)$$

where the constant on the right side is in fact equal to the number of claims remaining to be finalized.

It will be found simpler to work with continuous functions rather than the discrete ones appearing in (8.2.1.11) and (8.2.1.12). For this reason $E_i(t)$ in the earlier expressions will be replaced by $E_i(t, f_i(t))$. Thus the expected claim size paid at operational time t is treated as a function of not only t but also the (instantaneous) speed of finalizations prevailing at t.

Of course, as follows from any of the Assumption 1b or 1c, E_i is not, in fact, dependent on this speed. However, it does no harm, despite the null-dependence, to enter $f_i(t)$ as an argument. The use of the continuous function $E_i(.,.)$, treated as depending on two variables, will serve as an approximation to the corresponding discrete-time function involved in (8.2.1.11), this latter being truly a function of two variables.

Using this rather back-handed approach, we rewrite the problem expressed in (8.2.1.11) and (8.2.1.12) in the following form:

Which functions $E(f, t)$ of just the two variables, t = operational time and f = instantaneous speed of finalization, are such as to ensure the invariance of:

$$\int_b^{\infty} n_i f_i(j) E(t_i(j), f_i(j)) dj, \qquad (8.2.1.13)$$

under all the admissible changes of the $f_i(j)$, $j > b$, i.e. under all changes of the $f_i(j)$, $j > b$ which satisfy:

$$\int_b^{\infty} n_i f_i(j) dj = \text{const.,} \qquad (8.2.1.14)$$

with the constant on the right side equal to the number of claims remaining to be finalized.

Expression (8.2.1.13) and equation (8.2.1.14) are the continuous-time analogues of the discrete-time (8.2.1.11) and (8.2.1.12). Expression (8.2.1.13) is merely a restatement of (8.2.1.6), the amount of claims outstanding (in current values), at time b, with E_i, a function of just operational time in (8.2.1.6), taken as a function of the two variables, operational time and speed of finalization.

Taylor (1983) used a standard variational calculus argument (see e.g. Gelfand and Fomin, 1963) to deduce that the admissible forms of dependency of σ_{ij} on f_{ij} make up a very restricted set indeed. In fact, it is shown that:

$$E_i(t_i(j), f_i(j)) = \beta(t_i(j)) + \gamma/f_i(j), \qquad (8.2.1.15)$$

for some function $\beta(\cdot)$ and constant γ.

Equation (8.2.1.15) gives an expression for the instantaneous payments per claim finalized. An alternative expression, in terms of a whole period's payments can be derived from (8.2.1.15):

$$EQ_{ij} = \int_j^{j+1} f_i(k) E_i(t_i(k), f_i(k)) dk$$

(similar to (8.2.1.9))

$$= \int_j^{j+1} f_i(k) \beta(t_i(k)) dk + \gamma \quad \text{[by (8.2.1.15)]}$$

e. expect payments per claim

      incurred in (i, j)-cell $=$ component identical with Reduced Reid method (i.e. a payments per claim finalized method)

            $+$ component identical with the payments per claim incurred method, but restricted so that payment per claim incurred does not vary with development period .

It is possible to develop an approximation to (8.2.1.15) corresponding to (8.2.1.2) in which piecewise linear functions are used. Using the same notation as in (8.2.1.2), one can write:

$$S_{ij} = \alpha + \sum_{k \in S} \beta_k \bar{t}_{ij}^{(k)} + \gamma/f_{ij} + e_{ij}. \qquad (8.2.1.17)$$

The similarity between models (8.2.1.2) and (8.2.1.17) is to be noted. The only difference between the two lies in the manner in which speed of finalization features in payments per claim finalized . The appearance in (8.2.1.17) is in a much simpler form than in (8.2.1.2).

Note that, despite this simplification, the variation of σ_{ij} with f_{ij}, the main purpose of the elaborateness of the earlier formula, is still admitted by (8.2.1.17). In fact,

$$\partial \sigma_{ij}/\partial f_{ij} = -\gamma/f_{ij}^2, \qquad \text{in (8.2.1.17)}, \tag{8.2.1.18}$$

compared with

$$\partial \sigma_{ij}/\partial f_{ij} = \gamma_k, \quad \text{for } \bar{t}_{ij} \in (u_{k-1}, u_k] \text{ in (8.2.1.2).} \tag{8.2.1.19}$$

Because (8.2.1.17) represents the see-saw model of (8.2.1.2) restricted by the invariance principle embodied in Assumption 3, it is called the **invariant see-saw** model (though see Section 8.2.4 for the full generality of this model).

It remains to say something of the error term e_{ij} appearing in (8.2.1.2) and (8.2.1.17). This is of course the same term in each formula, since each formula represents S_{ij}. We prefer not to be too prescriptive about the precise characteristics, as one of the features of the see-saw models which we wish to emphasise in Section 8.2.4 is their flexibility.

However, for illustrative purposes we recount the properties of e_{ij} assumed in an actual application of the invariant see-saw method (Taylor, 1983). Now C_{ij} is the sum of n_{ij} amounts paid in finalization plus a number of partial payments. This latter number is unknown but, by the statement of Assumption 1b or 1c above, its expected value will be proportional to n_{ij}. Thus, it is reasonable to write:

$$V[C_{ij}] = n_{ij} \times \text{factor independent of the } n_{ij}, \tag{8.2.1.20}$$

whence

$$V[S_{ij}] = n_{ij}^{-1} \times \text{factor independent of the } n_{ij}, \tag{8.2.1.21}$$

The second factor on the right might be thought to depend on $\bar{t}_{ij}$ and f_{ij} as does $E[S_{ij}]$:

$$V[S_{ij}] = n_{ij}^{-1} \varsigma(\bar{t}_{ij}, f_{ij}). \tag{8.2.1.22}$$

Of course, the ς functions are at a level where accurate estimation is virtually impossible. The practical expedient adopted by Taylor (1983) is to simplify (8.2.1.22) to:

$$V[S_{ij}] = n_{ij}^{-1} \varsigma_j \tag{8.2.1.23}$$

The reader is referred to Taylor (1983) for details of the estimation of the ς_j.

To summarise then, we have either the original see-saw model (8.2.1.2) or the invariant see-saw model (8.2.1.17) in each of which cases e_{ij} is an error term with zero mean and variance given by (8.2.1.23).

The only remaining topic for discussion is the shape of the distribution of e_{ij}. An opinion of this could be formed by reference to the individual claim amounts which make up S_{ij}. It is doubtful whether any respectable conclusion can be reached without individual claim data.

The use of bulk data, such as the c_{ij}, n_{ij}, etc., rather than individual claim data, raises some questions which are discussed in Taylor (1979). The difficulty is as follows. For the most interesting classes of business, e.g. liability, individual claim sizes are likely to be drawn from a long-tailed distribution. Therefore, for small experiences, the e_{ij} will be highly skewed (see e.g. Buchanan and Lester, 1982, Appendix A1). For very large experiences, the central limit theorem ensures normality of the e_{ij}. Practical cases may well fall in a difficult area in which the e_{ij} are close to normal in some (i,j)-cells, but distinctly nonnormal in others, especially for large j where n_{ij} will tend to be small. As will appear, in Section 8.2.2, applications of the models have been carried out using a statistical package in which various options as to the distribution of e_{ij} are available.

It is assumed that the e_{ij} form a stochastically independent set.

8.2.2 *Estimation*

Both of the models, (8.2.1.2) and (8.2.1.17) are straightforward linear models with heteroscedasticity described by (8.2.1.23).

If it be sufficiently accurate to assume each e_{ij} normally distributed, the maximum likelihood estimation or best linear unbiased estimation leads to regression estimates of the unknown parameters.

Because of the heteroscedasticity, the regression is of the generalized least squares type. The risk function is:

$$\sum_{i,j} n_{ij} \varsigma_j^{-1} (s_{ij} - \hat{s}_{ij})^2, \tag{8.2.2.1}$$

where the summation runs over all available (i,j)-cells, and $\hat{s}_{ij}$ is the regression estimate of σ_{ij} according to whichever of the models, (8.2.1.2) or (8.2.1.17), is in use.

In the case of the invariant see-saw model, (8.2.1.17), the risk function (8.2.2.1) is to be interpreted as regression of the s_{ij} on the $\bar{t}_{ij}^{(k)}$, f_{ij}^{-1}, with the (i, j)-cell receiving weight $n_{ij}\varsigma_j^{-1}$.

To estimate the parameters in (8.2.1.17), we write the risk function in matrix form. The values of s_{ij} for all available i, j are written as a vector $\underline{s}$ with the i, j ordered in whatever way is convenient. The $\hat{s}_{ij}$, e_{ij} are written as vectors $\underline{\hat{s}}$, $\underline{e}$ with the same ordering. The parameters α, γ and the β_k are also written in a convenient order as a vector $\underline{\omega}$. Then (8.2.1.17) can be put in the form:

$$\underline{\hat{s}} = X\underline{\omega}, \tag{8.2.2.2}$$

where the matrix X consists of 1's and values of $\bar{t}_{ij}^{(k)}$, f_{ij}^{-1} written out in the appropriate order.

The risk function (8.2.2.1) is then

$$(\underline{s} - X\underline{\omega})^T W(\underline{s} - X\underline{\omega}), \tag{8.2.2.3}$$

where W is a diagonal matrix with the weights n_{ij}/ς_j written in an order conforming with the order of the s_{ij} in $\underline{s}$.

The solution of the regression problem consisting of minimization of (8.2.2.3) is well-known (see e.g. Bibby and Toutenburg, 1977). It gives an estimate $\hat{\underline{\omega}}$ of $\underline{\omega}$ of the form:

$$\hat{\underline{\omega}} = (X^T W X)^{-1} X^T W \underline{s}. \tag{8.2.2.4}$$

Then fitted values of the s_{ij} are:

$$\underline{\hat{s}} = X\hat{\underline{\omega}} = X(X^T W X)^{-1} X^T W \underline{s}. \tag{8.2.2.5}$$

In practice, the dimensions of the matrices involved here virtually demand that the solution be obtained by means of computer. This opens the way to use of regression and other statistical packages. These may enable relaxation of the normality assumptions. For example, the numerical work presented by Taylor (1983) and Taylor and Ashe (1983) was carried out by means of the GLIM package (Baker and Nelder, 1978).

This linear modelling package carries out estimation by maximum likelihood. For normal error term $\underline{e}$, this leads to regression estimation as in (8.2.2.3) to (8.2.2.5). However, a wide range of alternative distributional assumptions is available. In numerical work some experimentation with such assumptions may repay the effort involved.

8.2.3 *Projection of outstanding claims*

If Y is another matrix like X, but such that $Y\underline{\omega}$ is the vector of values of σ_{ij} for (i,j)-cells belonging to the **future** (i.e. Y contains **future** values of $\bar{t}_{ij}^{(k)}$, f_{ij}^{-1}), then the vector of future values of σ_{ij} is estimated by:

$$\hat{\underline{s}}^{fut} = Y\hat{\underline{\omega}} = Y(X^T W X)^{-1} X^T W \underline{s}. \qquad (8.2.3.1)$$

Outstanding claims (in current values) in respect of period of origin i are estimated as:

$$\hat{\pi}_{ij} = \sum_j \hat{s}_{ij}^{fut}, \qquad (8.2.3.2)$$

which is a linear transformation of (8.2.3.1).

Similarly outstanding claims, inflated or inflated and discounted, are estimated as different linear transformations of (8.2.3.1).

Since the matrix Y relates to the future, questions arise as to the values of f_{ij}^{-1} (the $\bar{t}_{ij}^{(k)}$ follow from these) which should be entered in it. This is in fact a non-problem. The invariance principle on which the invariant see-saw method is based (see Section 8.2.1) ensures that, whatever assumptions are made about future values of f_{ij}, the same projected outstanding claims (in current values) in respect of period of origin i will result. In practice, the approximation involved in deriving (8.2.1.17) from (8.2.1.15) will destroy the invariance of these projected outstanding claims. The variation introduced by this approximation will usually not be significant, however (for an example, see Taylor, 1983).

8.2.4 *Comment*

The derivation of the invariant see-saw model settles, under the hypotheses leading to that model (see Section 8.2.1), the question of whether payments per claim finalized for individual development periods are preferable to cumulative payments per claim finalized up to the end of development periods. This question is raised in Section 7.3.2.4, and the invariant see-saw model provides an answer in favour of the former (**under the hypotheses of that model**).

At this point we may return to the issue raised in Sections 7.3.2.1 and 7.3.2.4 concerning whether or not the payment per claim finalized method was likely to be destabilized by the required auxiliary projection of numbers of claims finalized. It is seen that the invariant see-saw method, by its very design, is immune to such destabilization.

Section 8.2.1 displayed the original and invariant see-saw models as (8.2.1.2) and (8.2.1.17) respectively. The equations do not represent the end of the story, but rather the kernel of considerably more general models.

To be more specific, note that the invariance principle applies separately to separate periods of origin (see (8.2.1.13) and the constraint (8.2.1.14)), and so (8.2.1.15) applies separatley to separate periods of origin. Thus, strictly, the conclusion which should have been drawn as (8.2.1.15) is:

$$\sigma_i(t_i(j), t_i(j) + 0) = \beta_i(t_i(j)) + \gamma_i/f_i(j). \tag{8.2.4.1}$$

Such generality is rather too wide to be useful in practice since it involves too great a number of parameters relative to the number of observations. However, it does permit the modelling of special features of the experience such as superimposed inflation. For example, a form of superimposed inflation related to period of origin is included in the following modification of (8.2.1.10):

$$S_{ij} = \alpha_i + \sum_{k \in S} \beta_k \bar{t}_{ij}^{(k)} + \gamma/f_{ij} + e_{ij}, \tag{8.2.4.2}$$

in which positive superimposed inflation is indicated by α_i increasing with i.

Equation (8.2.4.2) can be derived from the use of the d.f.'s $G(x + K_i : t)$ with K_i set equal to α_i (see Assumption 1c of Section 8.2.1).

Although it is quite feasible to fit a model of form (8.2.4.2) to the data, the additional parameters, one more for each period of origin would normally be too many to be justified. A more reasonable approach will sometimes be to assume the α_i's to be approximated by a piecewise linear function. Thus, let $w_1, \ldots, w_q$ be the set of points at which this function changes slope (w_q denotes the latest observed period of origin).

Define

$$f_0(i) = 1;$$
$$f_l(i) = i \wedge w_l.$$

Then replace α_i in (8.2.4.2) as follows:

$$S_{ij} = \sum_{l=0}^{q} \alpha_l f_l(i) + \sum_{k \in S} \beta_k \bar{t}_{ij}^{(k)} + \gamma/f_{ij} + e_{ij}. \tag{8.2.4.3}$$

Alternatively, superimposed inflation related to period of experience may be modelled in a similar way:

$$S_{ij} = \sum_{l=0}^{q} \alpha_l f_l(i+j) + \sum_{k \in S} \beta_k \bar{t}_{ij}^{(k)} + \gamma/f_{ij} + e_{ij}. \qquad (8.2.4.4)$$

Equations (8.2.4.3) and (8.2.4.4) give two examples of the way in which the basic model (8.2.1.17) may be elaborated. Clearly, there are many other variations of the model which could be dealt with. Provided that the terms added to (8.2.1.17) are linear in the additional parameters which they introduce, it will be possible to continue use of the regression methods outlined in Sections 8.2.2 and 8.2.3 and of the computer packages which perform those methods.

It is hoped that the preceding few paragraphs illustrate that there is no such entity as the *"invariant see-saw method"*, described by a rigid model and set of procedures for fitting the model. Rather, the invariant see-saw should be thought of as comprising a large range of possible models of which (8.2.1.17) represents a skeletal form. The author would prefer to see a choice of model made only after extensive experimentation with alternatives.

A couple of examples of different models fitted to the same data are given by Taylor and Ashe (1983).

The above loose type of definition of model, together with the use of computer packages in estimation, permit a considerable break with the prior philosophy of claims analysis. Within the new philosophy, each exercise in claims analysis commences with a thorough exploration of the data by means of models such as (8.2.1.17) and variations of them such as (8.2.4.3) and (8.2.4.4). The aim of this exploration is not to obtain immediate results in the form of projected outstanding claims, but merely to inform oneself as far as possible about the subtleties of the data.

The substance of the change in philosophy is that the approach described in this section permits a worthwhile attempt at unravelling and comprehending the various interrelationships between factors which might wreak material consequences on the data. This is rather in contrast with the use of methods from the earlier sections. There, different models incorporated different explanatory variables, while none of those models had a real potential for incorporating all relevant variables simultaneously. As a consequence, they are likely to produce deficient insights into the processes underlying a given data set. Too often, in practice, the final choice of estimate of outstanding claims consists of peering with uncomprehending eyes at a range of results obtained from a variety of methods and lighting upon some sort of compromise figure not too close to the extremities of the range. While the use of a variety of methods is agreed by the author to be useful in the amplification of the various features to which those methods are sensitive, it is nonetheless suggested that, at some stage of the analysis, an understanding of the underlying processes is highly desirable. Compromise answers within a large range of results are not always reliable, and are always unsatisfying.

Section 8.2.1 referred to the possibility of violation of the assumptions on which the invariant see-saw method rests.

Assumptions 1a, 1b and 1c of Section 8.2.1 have the informal interpretation that, for a given development period, different periods of origin generate identical distributions of (inflation-adjusted) claim sizes if payment delays are distributed, "in expectation", identically.

An example of circumstances leading to violation of this assumption is cited by Taylor (1980, p.268) who refers to "an attack on the backlog of cases due to go to court". Such a phenomenon might have the effect of causing a surge in the settlement of large (common law) claims. The more recent periods of origin will then have a greater proportion of large claims settled in early development periods than will the older periods of origin. This amounts to violation of Assumptions 1a, 1b and 1c.

Although Assumption 3 of Section 8.2.1 is, as stated there, only a deduction from Assumption 1c, it is useful to consider its validity separately. This assumption appears likely to be valid as long as one contemplates a claim as being fixed in amount (apart from inflationary effects) as soon as the event generating it occurs; and the insurer as, rather passively, paying that amount.

In fact, the insurer will usually be an active strategist and bargainer. A change in speed of finalization may be a consequence of a change in direction of management accompanied by various other consequences. For example, the change might be due to the advent of a new claims manager who negotiates claims more aggressively. The result of this will probably be a change in the amounts of the various claims, and violation of Assumption 3.

Violation of the assumptions on which any model rests naturally implies a diminution in reliability of that model. It is useful therefore to be able to detect such a feature. Such may be revealed by a comparison of the data with the corresponding values fitted by the model. An example is given by Taylor (1983).

Section 8.2.1 mentioned the dubious treatment of number of claims incurred n_i as nonstochastic within the see-saw models. For theoretical completeness of the model, what is required is a proper stochastic treatment of n_i, conditional on the number of claims reported to date.

We mention this for completeness but record that hitherto no such project has been carried out in the literature. The reasons for this appear to be twofold (they apply to portfolios of direct insurance but with less force, or perhaps not at all, to reinsurance portfolios).

Firstly, in Australia, in some forms of long-tail business, e.g. Employers Liability, the possible variation of n_i given only n_{i0} is quite small — in fact, virtually negligible. In other classes, e.g. Compulsory Third Party, this is not the case, but n_i given $n_{i0} + n_{i1}$ is virtually nonstochastic. This means that, conditional on information usually available, n_i is close to nonstochastic except perhaps in respect of the most recent period of origin. Excess-of-loss reinsurance treaties in respect of long-tailed classes provide a striking exception.

Secondly, it appears that in practice there may be considerable secular influences on n_i whose nature is not understood and which are therefore difficult to model reliably. For example, in one Australian Compulsory Third Party experience, the ratio n_{i1}/n_{i0} has tended to exhibit fairly steady drifts over lengthy periods interspersed with isolated dramatic shifts.

This is not intended to argue that the stochastic nature of the numbers of claims incurred should not be incorporated in the see-saw model. It is intended, however, to convey the facts that:

(i) to a large extent the problem is not of financial materiality,

(ii) where it is material, the solution of the problem is unlikely to be straightforward.

Indeed, in relation to the Australian Compulsory Third Party portfolio mentioned above, it has been found that, for the most recent period of origin, n_{i0} (the only claim number information available) may not be the conditioning data leading to the best estimate of n_i. It appears that the claim frequency in the Motor Vehicle (accidental damage) class or number of rainy days in the year (which influences claim frequency in both classes) may lead to better estimates.

It was hinted in Section 8.2.1 that some difficulties may arise from the treatment of speed of finalization as a differentiable function of time, since this implicitly regards the number of claims incurred as infinite. This problem has been considered in the literature by Ashe (1982). He sets up a model parallel to the one considered as the invariant see-saw model here, but with the finite number of claims incurred recognised explicitly. He finds that the required invariance property can be obtained non-trivially only if one specifies the epoch of finalization of the last claim in each period of origin. Otherwise, his results are very similar to those given above for the invariant see-saw model. In particular, he obtains a discretized version of the basic model equation (8.2.1.15).

A couple of final points concerning the see-saw methods. An objection sometimes raised is that the method, involving regression modelling as it does, is over-refined.

It is true that the model is based on a rather more theoretical foundation than most others. However, viewed purely as a parametric representation of the data, the method in fact gives quite rough representations. For example, Taylor and Ashe (1983) quote an example in which 55 cells of data are modelled by 6 parameters. They point out that a 3-parameter model appears almost as effecient. Since the 55 cells constitute a 10×10 triangle of claims data, even the crude Payments per Unit of Risk method (Section 7.1.4) would involve the estimation of 10 parameters. Although the see-saw models involve a significantly smaller number of parameters, they nonetheless include effects due to

(i) speed of finalization,

(ii) superimposed inflation.

These are not incorporated in the Payments per Unit of Risk model. Thus, it appears that the see-saw models not only model the data more closely than the other method, but do so using a rougher model in the sense of cutting down the number of parameters. It is a well-known fact (see e.g. Seber, 1977, p.364-366) that, other things equal, the variability of an estimate from a model increases with the number of parameters used in fitting that model. Therefore, the see-saw models ought to produce estimates which have smaller confidence intervals associated with them than do many of their rivals, such as the Payments per Unit of Risk method mentioned above. This is the opposite of the conclusion implied by the above criticism that the see-saw models are over-refined.

8.3   Reid's method — $S/MAC/N/P/E, F, I, T, Y, D, P$ type

8.3.1 *Model*

The method, in its original version, is described by Reid (1978). Subsequently, he has made some modification to the original procedure (Reid,1981). We shall have occasion to refer to this below.

Reid was preoccupied with three main matters in devising his method:

(i) the effect of speed of finalization on the claim payment experience being subjected to analysis,

(ii) the fact that claims escalation may not affect all claims equally in a given period of experience, but that the escalation (within a given period) might be dependent on the extent to which the claims in question have developed (development period or operational time),

(iii) the calculation of second and perhaps higher moments of outstanding claims.

It may not seem surprising that Reid was concerned with (i) in view of the amount which has been said on this topic earlier in this volume (see Section 7.3) and in other papers (e.g. Taylor, 1980, 1981a, b, 1982a, 1983) on the significance of speed of finalization. However, it must be remembered that Reid's paper was published in 1978 and therefore pre-dates all other references to speed of finalization given here. Moreover, as will appear below, Reid's treatment of speed of finalization is rather more extensive than that of the various other methods which take it into account.

Point (ii) is novel, and does not appear to have received treatment in any other models. All models dealt with in preceding sections of this volume either ignore claims escalation or assume that it affects all claim payments equally in a given period of experience.

Underlying Reid's alternative assumption is a concern that, within a particular period of experience, it may well happern for example that large claims with a common law component (which tend to be settled at rather high operational times) are subject to claims escalation differing from that affecting "medical only" claims involving only relatively trivial medical expenses and usually settled within a few months or less of their dates of origin.

One factor which is largely responsible for the lack of recognition of this aspect of claims escalation in other models is lack of data. Consider, for example, the typical situation in which claims data are available in a form resembling that required by statute. The data are then likely to take the "shape" displayed in the first table of Section 7.1.5.2. The essential feature of this form of data is that, as far as claim payments are concerned, there is only one item of information for each separate combination of period of origin and development period. Clearly, in these circumstances there is no possibility of estimating a separate escalation effect for each such combination in addition to the other parameters needed to describe the claim payment process.

It follows, then, that Reid's method will require more data than are available in the situation described above. In fact, the method obtains more data by working with claim payments of each combination of period of origin and development period subdivided according to the sizes of the claims to which they relate. This idea, of modelling claim payments as a function of both payment delay (development time) and claim size, is one which was introduced, albeit in a simple form, by Beard (1974) some years earlier.

Point (iii) above is dealt with by the construction of a genuinely stochastic model of the claims process. This is a point which applies to all stochastic $(S/\cdot/\cdot/\cdot/\cdot$ type) models. We return to it in Section 8.3.4. It may, however, be noted that, for a given claim which has occurred (though perhaps not yet reported), the contribution of that claim to the uncertainty associated with total outstanding claims arises from the stochastic nature of the claim size. It follows, therefore, that the inclusion of claim size as an explanatory variable in the model provides the data required for an assessment of the stochastic variation inherent in the "best estimate" of outstanding claims.

Thus, Reid's model can be viewed as modelling claim payments in terms of two explanatory variables:

(i) delay from date of origin of claim to date of its payment, i.e. operational time, in much the same way as this was used as an explanatory variable in the models of Sections 7.3.3 and 8.2,

(ii) claim size as a variable which allows the generation of second (and perhaps higher) moments of outstanding claims.

In general terms Reid's method involves an assumption that all periods of origin generate identical claims experiences apart from distortions superimposed by inflationary effects and changes in speed of finalization.

In accordance with the above discussion of inflationary effects, the equation describing inflation adjustments becomes not (7.1.2.1.1) as up to this point but

$$E_i(t) = E_0(t)\lambda_i(t)/\lambda_0(t), \tag{8.3.1.1}$$

where $E_i(t)$ has the same meaning as in Section 8.2.1, and $\lambda_i(t)$ is the value of the claims escalation index appropriate to the combination of period of origin i and operational time t. Note that the claims escalation effect is expressed here in terms of some chosen base period of origin labelled 0. Further mention of this base period is made below.

Reid's model then consists of a joint d.f. $G(x, t)$ of x, the claim size (unadjusted for claims escalation), and t, the operational time at finalization of that claim. Note that this is similar to the d.f. postulated at the start of Section 7.3.3.4. There is, however, a major difference. Whereas in the earlier section $G(., .)$ represented the d.f. of claim size **with** adjustment for claims escalation, in the present section **no such adjustment is made**. For this reason, the present $G(., .)$ will apply to only one period of origin, whereas in Section 7.3.3.4 it was assumed to apply to all periods of origin. However, Section 8.3.2 will indicate the manner in which $G(., .)$ needs to be modified in order to pass from one period of origin to another.

For operational purposes Reid distinguishes one particular period of origin (usually it would be the most recent period of origin which has run off sufficiently to be regarded as essentially complete) designated the "base period" (actually "base year" in Reid's usage). In his own words, *"it is assumed that later event year's claims [i.e. claims of later years of origin] are settled in the same sequence as they would have been had they been drawn at random from the base year's distribution"*.

It is interesting that the assumption of the existence of a basic d.f. $G(., .)$ serves as justification of the Reduced Reid method (see Section 7.3.3.4), the see-saw methods (see Section 8.2) and Reid's method.

Reid appears to cloud the issue a little in his paper. After describing the operation $G(., .)$ as quoted above, he goes on to state on the same page (p.221) that *"settlements for the later event year take place in a settlement time which is an appropriately stretched or contracted version of the base year's settlement time"*. On the same page there is mention of *"the assumed identity of sequence of settling claims in all years"*. Again he states (p.233) that *"the argument hinges upon the asumption that very approximately claims are settled in a notional sequence which is not disturbed by changes in cost levels or settlement rate ..."*.

The last two quotations, though not specifically precise, indicate an assumption resembling or identical to the hypothesis of invariant order discussed in Section 7.3.3.1. The first quotation, referring to the joint d.f.

$G(.,.)$, is weaker and is sufficient to justify Reid's method. On these grounds it seems preferable.

Indeed, in much the same way as was discussed at some length in Section 8.2.1 in connection with the see-saw methods, it is possible to develop Reid's method on the basis of the weaker assumption of just a conditional d.f. $G(x:t)$.

Among actuaries Reid's method is widely regarded as complex. It is true, as will be seen in Section 8.3.2, that the method does require quite careful manipulation of the data. However, as is apparent from the above commentary, the model on which the method rests is very compactly stated indeed. It consists of:

 (i) equation (8.3.1.1) stating the mode of operation of claims escalation;

(ii) postulation of the existence of the joint d.f. $G(.,.)$ describing the manner in which claim sizes vary (in distribution) with increasing operational time.

8.3.2 *Estimation*

Since the only components of Reid's model are the d.f. $G(.,.)$ and the various claims escalation factors discussed in Section 8.3.1, it follows that the estimation problem consists just of estimating these.

There are, however, several points, not affecting any of the principles involved, which should be noted as of practical importance.

Firstly, Reid distinguishes explicitly between zero and non-zero claims. He sets up a separate d.f. for each, thus:

$$G(x,t) = pG_z(t) + (1-p)G_{nz}(x,t), \qquad (8.3.2.1)$$

where p denotes the proportion of claims which result in zero claim payments; $G_z(.)$ is the d.f. of payment delays in respect of zero claims, and $G_{nz}(.,.)$ is the joint d.f. of operational time and claim sizes in respect of non-zero claims. Clearly, the writing of $G(.,.)$ in the form (8.3.2.1) does not provide any greater generality than a general $G(.,.)$. Of course, the recognition of the two components may make for greater efficiency in the estimation of $G(.,.)$.

In the following treatment, the discussion will be simplified by the estimation of just $G(.,.)$ rather than p, $G_z(.)$ and $G_{nz}(.,.)$ separately. It should be emphasised that this simplification has been made purely for expository purposes. A practical usage of the method should have due regard to the individual components of $G(.,.)$ named above.

Secondly, there may be some difficulty with claims which suffer a long delay to finalization. For some classes of business it may well be the case that any period of origin sufficiently recent to be relevant to a projection of the future provides an incomplete base period in the sense that, as at the date of valuation, there are still claims remaining to be finalized, possibly still to be reported. Such claims form Reid's "end group".

This means, of course, that, even for the base period, the empirical version of the d.f. $G(x,t)$ is unknown at sufficiently high values of t. Essentially, Reid's suggestion is to select values of $G(x,t)$ in this region by extrapolation from the values for smaller t. Physical estimates of the claims in the "end group" might play some part in the extrapolation.

Thirdly, data on the very largest claims will necessarily be limited. They will probably be insufficient for the reliable construction of a mathematical model. Moreover, the empirical distribution will be rather "lumpy". Reid suggests truncating the empirical distribution at some relatively large value of x, say x_M. The observed claims at larger values of x form what he refers to as the "excess group". He suggests using one of the following devices:

(i) increasing the amount of available data by aggregating the data from the class of business in question with those from other classes thought to have similar characteristics,

(ii) using published material (probably industry-wide, or more or less so) on claim sizes,

(iii) grafting on to the data at the smaller values of x a "tail" selected from some particular family of statistical distributions known to have suitable properties for the representation of the tail of a claim size distribution (Reid gives special prominence to the Pareto distribution in this connection).

The "excess group" might be dealt with by some combination of these alternatives.

If alternative (ii) or (iii), or some combination thereof, is chosen as a means of arriving at a hypothetical claim size tail, difficulties will probably arise in the decision as to the distribution of these large claims with respect to t. Presumably, this decision is likely to be made largely on the basis of extrapolation from the recorded data, supplemented by guesswork.

In accordance with the above discussion, then , the estimation phase of

Reid's method will take the form of:

(i) estimation of the d.f. $G(x, t)$ directly from the data in the region $x < x_M$ and $t < t_M$, say,

(ii) extension of this truncated d.f. into the regions covered by the "excess group" $(x > x_M)$ and the "end group" $(t > t_M)$.

We now come to stage (i) of this procedure.

This will involve estimation of $G(.,.)$ by reference to **base period data only**.

Reid's original paper devoted considerable effort to the mathematical modelling of the d.f. $G(x, t)$. Motivated to some extent by the family of gamma distributions, he modelled $\log\{1 - G(x, t)\}$ by functions consisting of terms of the form:

$$x^m t^n \exp(-px - qt).$$

While it is by no means intended to condemn this approach, it seems to me to have had the unfortunate effect of diverting almost the entire discussion of Reid's method away from its essential features. After all, the essential characteristics of the method are embodied in the model described in Section 8.3.1. The question of how to fit that model to the data is an entirely different issue from the establishment of the model itself. It is perfectly acceptable in logic to adopt the model but reject estimation in the manner described above.

Yet discussion of Reid's method has tended to be concentrated on the fitting technique. One gets the distinct impression that, in many minds, the whole method either stands or falls according to one's taste for Reid's surface(distribution)-fitting technique. In my own opinion, this is not only an illogical and unfair assessment of the method but also an unfortunate impediment to sensible debate of its merits.

Reid appears to recognise the communications difficulty arising from his initial attempts at surface-fitting. More recently, he has stated (1981,p.278):

> " *Although in previous papers I have suggested the fitting of mathematical forms to this distribution [i.e. the one described by $G(.,.)$] it has been found that in many applications it suffices to use the empirical distribution ... without further graduation other than is achieved by interpolation between data values* ".

To sumarise, then, there are two available approaches to the estimation of $G(.,.)$:

(i) the fitting of a member of some mathematical family to the data,

(ii) the use of the empirical distribution of claims with repect to claim size and operational time at finalization as the true underlying distribution $G(.,.)$.

Alternative (ii) oversimplifies the problem somewhat. In Reid's papers separate estimation of the parameter p and the d.f.'s $G_z(.)$ and $G_{nz}(.,.)$ is dealt with. The interaction between p and the d.f.'s renders straightforward estimation by reference to the empirical distribution(s) impossible. Reid carries out the simultaneous estimation of p, $G_z(.)$ and $G_{nz}(.,.)$ by means of maximum likelihood. The interested reader is referred to the original writings (Reid, 1978, 1981) for details.

In this survey only alternative (ii) is considered in detail, There are two reasons for this. Firstly, and perhaps more importantly, the fitting of bivariate d.f.'s such as $G(.,.)$ to data represents quite a weighty subject in its own right. It would distort the desired emphasis of this volume to attempt a survey of this subject also. Secondly, it is not clear that Reid himself, probably the only worker with any substantial practical experience with the method, still feels any commitment to the efficacy of alternative (i).

Let us introduce some precision into our discussion of the d.f. $G(x, t)$. More commonly Reid discuuses the decumulative d.f. $H(x, t)$ representing the probability that a random claim from the relevant period of origin is finalized later then operational time t and for an amount $> x$. It is easily shown that:

$$H(x, t) = 1 - G(x, \infty) - G(\infty, t) + G(x, t), \qquad (8.3.2.2)$$

and the dual relation

$$G(x, t) = 1 - H(x, 0) - H(0, t) + H(x, t). \qquad (8.3.2.3)$$

Thus it is easy to transform from $G(.,.)$ to $H(.,.)$ and back again as the occasion demands.

Let the empirical version of the decunulative d.f. $H(.,.)$ be denoted by $\hat{H}(.,.)$. That is, $\hat{H}(x, t)$ denotes the observed proportion of claims from the base period which were finalized later than operational time t for (inflation-unadjusted) amounts $> x$.

It is possible to express $\hat{H}(.,.)$ in terms of the notation introduced in Section 3.1. Effectively, this was done in Section 3.2. Reference to that section discloses that:

$$\hat{H}(v_e, t) = \sum_{t(g) > t} n^e_{..i...g}/n_{..i....}, \qquad (8.3.2.4)$$

where i designates the base period; $n_{..i....}$ has the same meaning as $n^+_{..i....}$ in Section 3.2 but without the restriction to strictly positive claims; and, in conformity with foregoing sections, $t(g)$ denotes operational time corresponding to real time g.

As pointed out earlier in this section, the existence of the "end group" and "excess group" will complicate (8.3.2.4) somewhat in practice.

The "excess group" will require only a redefinition of n^e. As suggested above, n^e needs to be replaced by:

$$n^e_{..i...g} - n^M_{..i...g}, \qquad (8.3.2.5)$$

where (v_M, ∞) is the range of claim sizes included in the "excess group". The claim size tail is then grafted on by one of the procedures suggested earlier in this section.

Now consider the "end group" with $t > t_M$. The d.f. $\hat{H}(x, t)$ is still defined as in (8.3.2.4) but only for $t < t_M$. Thus $\hat{H}(x, t_M)$ represents the "end group". Values of $\hat{H}(x, t)$, $t > t_M$ are discarded and $H(x, t)$, $t > t_M$ estimated by one of the alternative means described above.

We consider now the question of estimation of claims escalation. This is carried out by reference to the data. No appeal is made to external information.

The effect of claims escalation is quite simply stated in (8.3.1.1). However, its estimation is rather more difficult. It is fundamental to the considerations involved that claims escalation is expressed in terms of operational time and not real time. This gives effect to the idea, expressed in Section 8.3.1, that the claims escalation affecting a claim is a function of the extent of development of the period of origin to which that claim belongs (as well, of course, as being a function of the epoch of real time at which the claim is paid).

Recall that, given two periods of origin, a given development period will not, in general, correspond to the same operational times in both. Hence, the respective experiences of the two periods of origin in the development period concerned will not be directly comparable in terms of (8.3.1.1). Correspondingly, if sets of claims of the two periods of origin are found which are comparable in the sense that they relate to the same operational time interval, (8.3.1.1) becomes applicable, but there is no simple relation between these intervals in real time and the interpretation of the claims escalation between them is not straightforward.

As in Section 8.2.1, it is necessary to work with the claims experiences of finite time intervals rather than infinitesimal intervals. Consequently, (8.3.1.1) is adapted to finite intervals:

$$\sigma_i(t_1, t_2) = \sigma_0(t_1, t_2)\lambda_i(t_1, t_2)/\lambda_0(t_1, t_2). \qquad (8.3.2.6)$$

The factor $\lambda_i(t_1, t_2)$ is in some sense the average of the values of $\lambda_i(t)$ for t between t_1 and t_2.

Now data will normally have been collected in respect of periods of origin and development periods all of equal length. That is, for each period of origin i, data will be available in respect of development periods $(j, j + 1]$ in real time. These development periods are in turn $(t_i(j), t_i(j + 1)]$ in operational time.

One may therefore consider claims escalation between operational time interval $(t_0(j), t_0(j+1)]$ of period of origin 0 and time interval $(t_i(j), t_i(j+1)]$ of period of origin i. Analogously with (8.3.1.1), let this escalation be denoted by $\lambda_{ij}/\lambda_{oj}$. It will be convenient to write $\lambda_{io:j}$ for this ratio.

Now the distribution of claim sizes and delays to finalization, in the absence of any claims escalation after the base period, has been estimated earlier by the function $\hat{G}(x, t)$. In particular the estimated proportion of the claims incurred in period of origin i which have size $> x$ and delay to finalization in the interval $(t_i(j), t_i(j + 1)]$ (development time) is:

$$\hat{H}(x, t_i(j)) - \hat{H}(x, t_i(j + 1)), \qquad (8.3.2.7)$$

still under the no-escalation assumption. When allowance is made for an escalation factor of $\lambda_{io:j}$, (8.3.2.7) becomes:

$$\hat{H}(x/\lambda_{io:j}, t_i(j)) - \hat{H}(x/\lambda_{io:j}, t_i(j + 1)), \qquad (8.3.2.8)$$

Strictly, values of $\hat{H}(., t)$ will have been observed only for $t = t_0(0), t_0(1)$, etc. As suggested above, values of this function for intermediate values of t can be obtained by linear interpolation.

Now, provided that development period j (real time) has passed, observations on the proportion displayed in (8.3.2.8) are available. There are, in fact, a number of such observations, one for each value of $x = v_e$, where the bands of claim size considered in the base period are $(v_e, v_{e+1}]$. These various observations need to be combined to provide an estimate of the single unknown in (8.3.2.8), $\lambda_{i0:j}$. Once again, Reid obtains this estimate by means of the maximum likelihood method. The likelihood function is given, up to the unknown parameter $\lambda_{i0:j}$, by (8.3.2.8).

It should be pointed out that the estimates $\hat{\lambda}_{i0:j}$ of the $\lambda_{i0:j}$ are not, in a direct sense, meaningful indicators of claims escalation. This is because any given one of these estimates relates operational time intervals of periods of origin 0 and i which are not equal. This will lead to the factor's containing a mixture of the effect of claims escalation and also the effect (in terms of change in claim size) of a shift in operational time.

Nonetheless, the factors have validity as mere abstract parameters defining the model of the claims process in periods of origins subsequent to the base period.

Further work is required to obtain estimators of claims escalation. As is implied by the last paragraph but one, it is necessary to consider identical operational time intervals in respect of periods of origin 0 and i. It is natural to adopt as those operational time intervals the ones which coincide with (real time) development periods in the base period.

Thus, one considers the real development time intervals:

$$(t_i^{-1}(t_0(j)), t_i^{-1}(t_0(j+1)))].\tag{8.3.2.9}$$

The interval displayed as (8.3.2.9) is the interval of real development time in respect of period of origin i which contains the same operational times as development period j in respect of period of origin 0 (the base period).

Apart from the effect of claims escalation, the claims of these two respective intervals of development time are, according to Assumption 1b of Section 8.2.1, equal in expected size. Therefore, a comparison of the average sizes experienced in the two intervals provides an estimate of the claims escalation which occurred between them.

Thus we define:

$$\Lambda_{ij} = \frac{\int_0^{x_M} x.d_x\left[\hat{H}_i(x, t_i^{-1}(t_0(j))) - \hat{H}_i(x, t_i^{-1}(t_0(j+1)))\right]}{\int_0^{x_M} x.d_x\left[\hat{H}_0(x, j) - \hat{H}_0(x, j+1)\right]},\tag{8.3.2.10}$$

where $\hat{H}_i(x, t)$ denotes the modelled d.f. for period of origin i. This d.f. will appear as $\hat{H}(x/\lambda_{i0:j}, t_i(j)))$ for $t = t_i(j)$, j integral, and is evaluated at intermediate points of t by interpolation. Of course, $\hat{H}_0(x, t) = \hat{H}(x, t)$.

From the argument preceding (8.3.2.10), Λ_{ij} is an estimator of the escalation of claims paid in the operational time interval $(t_0(j), t_0(j + 1)]$ between the calendar intervals:

$$(j, j + 1] \tag{8.3.2.11}$$

and

$$(i + t_i^{-1}(t_0(j)), i + t_i^{-1}(t_0(j + 1))]. \tag{8.3.2.12}$$

At this point we recall the end of Section 8.3.1. Reid's model was summed up there as consisting of just two parts, the joint d.f. $G(.,.)$ and the mode of operation of claims escalation. An estimate of the former has been found in the application of (8.3.2.3) to $\hat{H}(.,.)$. The latter has been estimated in the form of the Λ_{ij}.

The estimation of the model parameters is thus complete.

8.3.3 *Projection of outstanding claims*

As with the projection of outstanding claims by almost any method, projection on the basis of this method requires:

(i) estimation of the amounts of future claim payments in particular development periods, and expressed according to some particular convention as regards currency values (e.g. in values current at the date of evaluation),

(ii) estimation of the future effects of claims escalation,

(iii) calculation of the influence of (ii) on (i).

Item (i) is given by the function $\hat{H}(.,.)$. For example, in the notation of Section 8.3.2, the amount of outstanding claims in respect of period of origin i is estimated as:

$$n_i \int_{t(b)}^{\infty} \int_{0+}^{\infty} x.\hat{g}(x, t) \, dx \, dt, \tag{8.3.3.1}$$

where $\hat{g}(.,.)$ is the p.d.f. associated with the d.f. $\hat{G}(.,.)$ (or, equivalently, with the decumulative d.f. $\hat{H}(.,.)$).

However, the form in which this function gives the amount of outstanding claims is rather different from the form used by most earlier models in this survey. All previous models which have made explicit correction for claims escalation have done so by adjusting all claim payments to constant money values. The money values chosen might have been those current at the date of evaluation, or in some other base period. The material fact is that all payments were brought to the **same** values.

Reid's method is to be contrasted with this practice. The basic estimated d.f. $\hat{G}(.,.)$ expresses claim payments of period of origin i in the monay values of development period j of the base period of origin provided that the payments in question fell in the operational time interval $(t_i(j), t_i(j+1)]$.

Thus, although (8.3.3.1) gives outstanding claims according to a *"particular convention as regards currency values"*, as required above, the convention adopted is not such as to render (8.3.3.1) directly useful. The amount of outstanding claims given by that formula is not in current values, nor inflated values, but in a mixture of values.

In order to convert it to inflated values (or, indeed, just about any other practically meaningful values), two items are necessary:

(i) a projection of future speeds of finalization,

(ii) a projection of future claims escalation.

Item (i) will be required to assign future operatiuonal times, on which claim payments depend through $\hat{G}(.,.)$, to real time intervals. Item (ii) will obviously be required if future claims escalation is to be incorporated in the estimates of outstanding claims (clearly, (ii) will not be required just for the estimation of outstandings in current values).

Strictly, the projection of outstanding claims should follow these steps:

(i) projection of future speeds of finalization F_{ij}, thus determining the values of $t_i(j)$ for future j,

(ii) hence, calculation of the real development times $t_i^{-1}(t_0(j))$ corresponding, in operational time, to integral development periods of the base period,

(iii) choice of values of Λ_{ij} for future j, describing claims escalation between development period j of the base period of origin and the corresponding development time interval, calculated in (ii), of period of origin i,

(iv) calculation of claim payments in the development time interval (8.3.2.9) by the formula:

$$n_i \int_{t_1}^{t_2} \int_{0+}^{\infty} \Lambda_{ij}.x.\hat{g}(x,t)dx\ dt, \qquad (8.3.3.2)$$

where $(t_1, t_2]$ is based here to denote interval $(t_0(j), t_0(j+1)]$.

The results of (iv) then provide the required estimates of outstanding claims.

Steps (i) to (iv) above are conceptually straightforward. However, there may be some practical difficulties with (i) and (iii).

As regards (i), if speeds of finalization have undergone substantial change in the past, there may be little guidance as to their likely future values.

As regards (iii), the usual difficulties which exist in any forecast of inflation exist here too. The additional difficulties related to this particular method are not great. However, some care is needed since the (real) development time intervals referred to in (ii) are not integral. Thus, the factors Λ_{ij} are required to project claims escalation over non-integral periods of real time.

As mentioned by Reid (1978, p.241), in cases where past speeds of finalization have been reasonably stable, the real development time intervals (8.3.2.9) will be close to integral, and the difficulties discussed above will be minimized. Indeed, as Reid points out, the evaluation of the intervals (8.3.2.9) is necessary only in order that the forecast Λ_{ij} be associated with the correct real time intervals. In the case where stability of past experience renders it obvious that the intervals (8.3.2.9) are close to integral it may be possible to proceed directly to the forecast of the Λ_{ij} without calculation of the (8.3.2.9).

8.3.4 *Comment*

It is perhaps appropriate to comment first on the inclusion of this method as of the $S/\cdot/\cdot/\cdot/\cdot$ type. The material fact, as with all methods in this case, is that Reid's model contains an explicit stochastic structure. This is visible in the appearance in the model of an explicit distribution function $G(.,.)$ (see Section 8.3.1).

Reid himself, in commenting on the method, draws attention to the question of partial payments. He points out that the method

This simplification has one very significant consequence to which reference is made by Reid (p.241):

" *assumed ... that each claim gives rise to just one payment which defines the date of settlement of the claim. This is a simplification of the actual situation, where a claim can give rise to a number of payments culminating in a final payment*".

" *Because the approach ... aggregates these 'payments on account' into the final payment and notionally attributes these to the settlement date, any reserves constructed as forecasts of the total cost of claims to be settled beyond the accounting date must be adjusted by subtraction of whatever payments on account may have been made up to that date*".

In addition to this extremely practical matter, one needs to consider to what extent the realism and applicability of the model are affected by the existence of partial payments. It may be recalled that the partial payments were introduced in Assumption 1b of Section 8.2.1. It was pointed out there that that assumption is in fact a weaker one than that of the existence of a joint d.f. $G(.,.)$ assumed by Reid's model (see Section 8.3.1). Apparently, then, there is no particular difficulty in incorporating the basic concept of partial payments in the mechanisms underlying the Reid model.

The area in which problems do arise is that involving the estimation of claims escalation factors Λ_{ij}. The procedure described above for dealing with partial payments involves the artificial relocation of such payments in respect of a given claim at the date of settlement of that claim, however that date is determined. This, of course, must result in some distortion of the estimates of claims escalation which are based on the claims data (see Section 8.3.2).

As Reid himself remarks, "*it might be possible at the expense of considerable further elaboration to construct a model which would deal with each such payment individually*". Any attempt at a generalization of this type would of necessity involve a radical revision of the basic model. It would no longer be possible to associate a single epoch of settlement with each claim. Presumably, therfore, it would be necessary to think in terms of a distribution over development time (real or operational) of the payments making up the total cost of a claim. Thus, the d.f. $G(x, t)$ of Sections 8.3.1 to 8.3.3 would need to be replaced by a different d.f. $G(x, T(.))$, where $T(.)$ is the d.f. over time of the total claim cost x.

The remark is often made that the procedures used in the estimation of the parameters of the Reid model involve some degree of overfitting.

There may have been some validity in this criticism in its original form. An example of this can be found in the contribution of G.B. Hey (p.301) to the discussion of Reid's paper. It was suggested there that Reid's original surface-fitting procedures, involving quite extensive linear combinations of gamma-like terms, resulted in overfitting and perhaps unstable estimates of $G(.,.)$.

However, as remarked in Section 8.3.2, Reid has since forsaken this procedure for the much simpler one of using the empirical d.f. The question of overfitting needs to be considered in the light of this.

Naturally, whether or not the number of parameters to be fitted for a model is excessive must be judged in relation to the volume of data with which the fitting is to be performed. Suppose r denotes the number of cost-bands used by the Reid model. Suppose s denotes the number of development periods which must elapse before the "end group" is reached. Then there will be rs observations on the base period of origin . Similarly, there will be $r(s-1)$, $r(s-2)$, ..., r observations on subsequent periods of origin. Thus, there are $rs(s+1)/2$ observations in all.

One may observe immediately that this is many more observations than are usually available in connection with the methods discussed in earlier sections. For example, if $r = s = 8$, then there are 288 obsevations. This is to be compared with 36 observations when the chain ladder method is applied to the case $s = 8$. It is difficult not to question whether those who allege overfitting in Reid's method are failing to allow properly for the much greater volume of data used by that method.

The number of parameters involved in the general case is:

rs to describe the empirical d.f. $\hat{G}(.,.)$;

$s(s-1)/2$ to describe past claims escalation (these are the Λ_{ij}).

The above numbers of observations and parameters do not allow for zero and non-zero claims to be recognised separately in $G(.,.)$. They would be altered if such allowance were made.

Thus, the Reid method uses $rs(s+1)/2$ observations to estimate $s(2r+s-1)/2$ parameters. The payments per unit of risk method (one of the most parsimonious in parameters) discussed in Section 7.1.4 uses $s(s+1)/2$ observations to estimate s parameters.

Again considering the case $r = s = 8$, one may note that the

Reid method would use 288 observations to estimate 92 parameters. The payments per unit of risk method would use 36 observations to estimate 8 parameters. On the basis of these figures, the argument that the Reid method involves overfitting appears far from open-and-shut.

It is remarked in passing that the stochastic nature of the method permits the estimation of higher moments of the amount of outstanding claims than just the first. This matter is dealt with in Reid's paper. It involves no particular difficulties, and we do not go into detail here. It may be noted, however, that Reid does not consider **estimation error** in the sense described in Chapter 13 below. That is to say, his estimates of second moments are made as if $\hat{G}(.,.)$ were known to be a perfect description of $G(.,.)$. See, for example, Appendix 5 to Reid's paper. This will result in an understatement of variance.

9.   STOCHASTIC MICRO-MODELS

9.1   Stochastic chain ladder method —
$S/MIC/\cdot/P$ or $I/T,Y$ type

9.1.1 *Model*

We note, as was noted in Section 5.2.2, that the third level of model taxonomy (N or NN) is not meaningful in the context of micro-models. It has therefore been left unspecified in the above categorization of this method.

The stochastic version of the chain ladder method is due to Bühlmann, Schnieper and Straub (1980).

Define

$^k X_{ij}^{(m)^*} = $ **individual claim amount** in respect of claim number m as at the end of j-th development period, periods of origin and notification being i and k respectively (unadjusted for claims escalation, as the $*$ indicates).

The precise meaning of "individual claim amount" is left vague. This is deliberate, as it is desired to maintain generality of application of the method. The main requirement of $^k X_{ij}^{(m)^*}$ is:

$$\lim_{j \to \infty} {}^k X_{ij}^{(m)^*} \quad \text{exists (denote by } {}^k X_i^{(m)^*}). \tag{9.1.1.1}$$

and is equal to the final total amount paid in respect of claim number m.

The reason for the vagueness in definition of $^k X_{ij}^{(m)^*}$ can now be seen. There is more than one definition of $^k X_{ij}^{(m)^*}$ satisfying (9.1.1.1). For example, we might define:

$^k X_{ij}^{(m)^*} = $ total claim payments in respect of claim number m up to the end of development period j, OR

$^k X_{ij}^{(m)^*}$ = estimated total cost (past claim payments plus estimated outstandings) of claim number m at the end of development period j.

With this explanation of the flexibility in definition of $^k X_{ij}^{(m)^*}$, the reason for the appearance of" P or I" in the classification of the method at the start of this section becomes clear. Indeed, of the two definitions suggested above, the first falls in the P classification while the second falls in the I classification.

The individual claim amount is presented here as unadjusted for claims escalation. A completely parallel theory can be developed for $^k X_{ij}^{(m)}$, the corresponding adjusted amount.

In the development of this section, $^k X_{ij}^{(m)^*}$ is viewed as a stochastic variable. The model described below consists of placing sufficient probabilistic structure on it to enable estimation of parameters. That structure is as follows.

Distribution of number of claims

The N_i are stochastically independent and

$$N_i = \text{Poiss}(E_i \nu), \qquad (9.1.1.2)$$

where ν is a scalar parameter. Thus EN_i is proportional to exposure (or volume) E_i.

Independence of claim frequency and delay in notification

Let

$K_i^{(m)}$ = year of notification of claim number m (a random variable).

It is assumed that the sets $\{N_i\}$, $\{K_i^{(m)}\}$ are stochastically independent classes of variables in the sense that any member of the first class and any member of the second are stochastically independent.

Independence of claim frequency and claim size

It is assumed that $\{N_i\}$, $\{^k X_{ij}^{(m)^*}\}$ are stochastically independent classes of variables.

Independence between periods of origin

It is assumed that, for $i_1 \neq i_2$,

$$\{N_{i_1}, K_{i_1}^{(m)}, {}^k X_{i_1 j}^{(m)^*}\}$$

and

$$\{N_{i_2}, K_{i_2}^{(m)}, {}^k X_{i_2 j}^{(m)^*}\}$$

are stochastically independent classes of variables.

<u>Claims within a period of origin</u> The claim payments in respect of distinct claims are stochastically independent. More precisely, the classes $\{{}^k X_{ij}^{(m)^*}\}$ for various values of m are stochastically independent classes. Moreover the ${}^k X_{ij}^{(m)^*}$, with i, j, k constant and m varying, are identically distributed.

The $K_i^{(m)}$ are all i.i.d.

<u>Development of individual claim amounts over time</u>

Individual claim amounts develop from one development year to the next in accordance with

$$E[{}^k X_{i,j+1}^{(m)^*}/{}^k X_{ij}^{(m)^*} = x] = {}^k \beta_j^* x. \tag{9.1.1.3}$$

Also,

$$V[{}^k X_{i,j+1}^{(m)^*}/{}^k X_{ij}^{(m)^*} = x] = {}^k \sigma_j^2 v(x), \tag{9.1.1.4}$$

where $v(.)$ is a strictly positive function.

The meaning of (9.1.1.3) can best be discerned by comparing that equation with the definition of ${}^k \beta_j^*$ given in Section 7.1.1.2 involving equation (7.1.1.2.2).

It can be seen that there is a correspondence between that earlier section and this one:

$$a_{ij}^* \longleftrightarrow X_{ij}^*, \tag{9.1.1.5}$$

where the omission of superscripts k and m from the right side indicates summation over those indexes. As a consequence of that correspondence, β here can be placed in correspondence with the β of Section 7.1.1.2 (except that in this section different values of β are assumed applicable to different delays k in notification). If ${}^k X_{ij}^{(m)^*}$ denotes total claim payments made in respect of claim number m up to the end of development period j, which is shown above to be the one of its possible definitions, the β defined in (9.1.1.3) will have the same meaning as β defined in Section 7.1.1.2 except that here, in the stochastic framework, it is an expected value whereas in Section 7.1.1.2 it was taken as deterministic. That is, ${}^k \beta_j^*$ denotes the expected ratio of claim payments up to the end of development period $j + 1$ to those up to the end of period j, without adjustment for claims escalation.

One can establish a similar correspondence between the β of this section and that of Section 7.2.1 on the method of monitoring the track record (see particularly equation (7.2.1.2.1)). In this case ${}^kX_{ij}^{(m)^{*}}$ denotes total claim cost as estimated at the end of development period j, and ${}^k\beta_j^*$ denotes the expected value of the ratio of this statistic at the end of development period $j+1$ to the corresponding one for development period j.

The correspondence established above between the method of this section and the chain ladder method of Section 7.1.1 justifies its classification as a type of chain ladder method.

Recall also that the method of monitoring the track record is only a version of the chain ladder method. Therefore, the correspondence established between this section and Section 7.2.1 reinforces the choice of name for the method of this section.

9.1.2 *Estimation*

Bühlmann, Schnieper and Straub give several approaches to the estimation of the β values. The simplest and most direct turns on the observation that

$$ {}^kX_{ij}^{(m)^{*}} / {}^kX_{i,j-1}^{(m)^{*}} \tag{9.1.2.1} $$

is an unbiased estimator of ${}^k\beta_{j-1}^*$. Such a statement is just a formalization of the intuitive idea on which simple methods like the chain ladder method are based (see e.g. (7.1.1.2.1)).

The authors give a rough argument indicating that the variance of

$$ {}^kX_{ij}^* / {}^kX_{i,j-1}^* $$

is proportional to

$$ {}^k\sigma_{j-1}^{*2} U_{ik} / ({}^kX_{i,j-1})^2, $$

where U_{ik} is the number of claims incurred in period of origin i and notified in period k, and

$$ {}^kX_{ij}^* = \sum_m {}^kX_{ij}^{(m)^{*}}, $$

the summation extending over all claim numbers m with the relevant values of i, j and k. Then standard arguments may be used to combine the above unbiased estimators of ${}^k\beta_{j-1}^*$. The estimator of ${}^k\beta_{j-1}^*$ adopted is the weighted average of the unbiased estimators displayed above, where the weights are the reciprocals of the associated variances. That is, $^k\beta_{j-1}^*$ is estimated by:

$$\frac{\displaystyle\sum_{\substack{i \in I_j, \\ I_{j-1}}} \frac{^kX_{ij}^* \quad ^kX_{i,j-1}^*}{U_{ik}}}{\displaystyle\sum_{\substack{i \in I_j, \\ I_{j-1}}} \frac{(^kX_{i,j-1}^*)^2}{U_{ik}}}. \qquad (9.1.2.2)$$

We refer once again to the chain ladder method. It is noted that (9.1.2.2) is just a weighted average of the ratios (9.1.2.1), as in (7.1.1.2.2) of the chain ladder method. The only difference between the two formulas lies in the system of weights chosen.

The estimation proposed by Bühlmann, Schnieper and Straub is in fact slightly more complex than (9.1.2.2). However, the extra complexity arises outside the mainstream of logic heading to that formula. It is discussed briefly in Section 9.1.4.

9.1.3 *Projection of outstanding claims*

The projection formula is just a slight elaboration of that used in conjunction with the chain ladder method (see (7.1.1.3.1)). The only difference is that the method presently under consideration includes, within each period of origin, separate treatment of each notification period whereas the chain ladder does not (at least, not as presented in Section 7.1.1).

Thus, outstanding claims at the end of development period j in respect of period of origin i and notification period k are estimated as:

$$^kp_{ij}^* = {^kX_{ij}^*}(\prod_{h=j} {^k\beta_h^*} - 1), \qquad (9.1.3.1)$$

in the case where $^kX_{ij}^*$ denotes claim payments.

In the case where $^k\beta_j^*$ is independent of k, (9.1.3.1) reduces to the same form as (7.1.1.3.1). This simplified case is in fact dealt with by Bühlmann, Schnieper and Straub on p.34 of their paper.

9.1.4 *Comment*

The similarities of the method presently under consideration and the chain ladder method of Section 7.1.1 have been mentioned in Sections 9.1.1 to 9.1.3. However, it is perhaps worth stressing them in this section.

If one reviews the 6 headings in Section 9.1.1 under which the stochastic chain ladder method is set out, one finds that the first 5 of them build a stochastic structure onto the central assumption (9.1.1.3). The remaining part of the sixth heading, (9.1.1.4), also adds to the stochastic structure. As has been pointed out in the foregoing subsections, the central assumption (9.1.1.3) is in strict correspondence with the assumption (7.1.1.1.1) of the chain ladder method. Thus the model described in Section 9.1.1 can properly be viewed as identical with the chain ladder model of Section 7.1.1 (though elaborated to include dependency on notification period) with a stochastic structure added.

It is to be noted that this stochastic structure, as far as it is described in Section 9.1.1, includes no distributional specification in respect of $^k X_{ij}^{(m)^*}$. Only the form of (conditional) variance is specified (see(9.1.1.4)). The complete argument leading to estimator (9.1.2.1) was not given. However, if given in full detail (see Bühlmann, Schnieper and Straub, 1980, p.37), it is seen to require no distributional assumptions. This appears to have been recognised also by Van Eeghen (1981) who describes the stochastic chain ladder method without any reference to the distribution of $^k X_{ij}^{(m)^*}$.

The authors do, nevertheless, make the assumption (p.27) that the conditional distribution of $^k X_{ij}^{(m)^*}$ given $X_{i,j-1}^{(m)^*}$ is log-normal. One should be clear of course on where the assumptions made are required in the logic. The authors appear to have used this particular assumption only for the purpose of simulating the samples of claims data on which their numerical work is based and not in the development of the methodology.

It should be said however that, with a basic model structure of the multiplicative sort set out in (9.1.1.3), the log-normal assumption is a very natural one.

The inclusion of the stochastic chain ladder method in the class of micro-models might be queried. The following arguments might be advanced against such inclusion:

(i) the model required for the development of the method of estimation and projection does not need detailed distributional assumptions,

(ii) the principal estimator of the method (i.e. (9.1.2.2)) is only a slight variation of its counterpart in the (non-stochastic) chain ladder method.

Such argument are specious for:

(i) despite the absence of detailed distributional assumptions the model is set up in terms of individual claims,

(ii) the fact that the method produces an estimator very similar to that used by the chain ladder method is not necessarily a demerit.

Recall that the system of classification established in Section 5.2 required that micro-models "work at the individual claim level". This is true of the stochastic chain ladder method in the sense that the model itself works at the individual claim level. It has been noted above, however, that this model leads (at least in the case dealt with in Sections 9.1.2 and 9.1.3) to formulas which do not use individual claim information but information from the mass of claims in virtually the same way as do the methods based on macro-models.

Taxonomy not being the major preoccupation of this volume, we have not sought to establish a completely rigorous and unequivocal system of classification. Consequently, there is some scope for debate on just where in the hierarchy some particular model fits. However, it must be remembered that what are being classified are the **models** (which appear in subsection 1 of each method) rather than the **methods**, i.e. the methods of estimation and projection (which appear in subsections 2 and 3 of each method). On this basis, it would appear that the stochastic chain ladder is correctly classified as a micro-model.

The great similarity between the model of this section and the non-stochastic chain ladder model carries some implications of a general kind for the former. In particular, many of the criticisms which can be made of the chain ladder model of Section 7.1.1 can equally be made of the stochastic chain ladder model. Most significantly, neither model includes allowance for changes in the rate of claims escalation or speed of finalization. The first of these deficiencies can be rectified of course by introducing a stochastic inflation-adjusted chain ladder model. This would correspond to the model of Section 7.1.2. That is, the model would be exactly as in this section except that the amounts of claim payments ${}^{k}X_{ij}^{(m)*}$ would be replaced by ${}^{k}X_{ij}^{(m)}$, the inflation-adjusted versions of those payments.

The paper by Bühlmann, Schnieper and Straub estimates outstanding claims in two separate components:

(i) in respect of claims already notified (called by them "IBNER claims").

(ii) in respect of IBNR claims.

This practice has not been followed in this volume. The reason is quite simple. While the method used by the authors for projecting IBNR claims is quite straightforward, the whole area of IBNR claims estimation is a subject in its own right. A good deal could be said on it. The present survey would be materially expanded if this were attempted. Instead, only brief comment is given in Chapter 16.

There is one very significant difference between the versions of the chain ladder method currently under consideration. It concerns the linking of different periods of origin in the model.

It is apparent from an examination of the earlier sections that, in terms of the average sizes of claims incurred, different periods of origin are quite independent. This appears, for example, in (7.1.1.1.1), where average claim sizes are proportional to the parameter α_i^* dependent on period of origin i. The functional dependence of α_i^* is not restricted in any way by the model.

A different approach has been followed by Bühlmann, Schnieper and Straub, who build into their model an assumption that expected claim amounts increase exponentially from one period of origin to the next. More precisely, it is assumed that

$$E[^k X_{i,k-i}^{(m)^*}] = c_k(1 + \delta)^i, \qquad (9.1.4.1)$$

where the c_k are constants, and δ is the (constant) rate of claims escalation during a period of origin.

The c_k and δ are parameters of the model free to be estimated from the data. Methods of estimation are dealt with by the authors on pp.38-41. Three approaches are covered.

Firstly, δ and c_k are treated as unrelated parameters and estimated by a least squares procedure details of which can be found in the original paper.

Secondly, it is noted, by fixing i in (9.1.4.1), that c_k is related to an index of expected claim size according to period of notification. The authors then argue that the c_k are not in fact unrelated but should increase with increasing k. A least squares procedure is then used once again in the estimation of δ and the c_k, but this time subject to the side-condition that the c_k should be monotonically nondecreasing with k.

Thirdly, it is noted that $E[^k X_i^{(m)^*}]$, defined by (9.1.1.1), is the true index of expected claim size as a function of period of notification k. A least squares procedure is therefore used to estimate the parameters δ and the c_k, this time subject to the side-condition that, for each i, the above expectations form a sequence which is nondecreasing with k.

It should be noted that these refinements do not overcome some of the basic crudities of the method already observed. For example, the absence from the model of any allowance for changing claims escalation or speed of finalization, particularly as regards the latter factor, would be likely to wreak a fundamental change on the model, as is apparent from the detailed consideration in Chapter 8 of the appropriate manner in which speed of finalization might be introduced into a model.

9.2   Stochastic separation method —
$S/MIC/ \cdot /P/T, I, E, N, Z$ type

9.2.1 *Model*

The model is presented by Linnemann (1980, 1982). He uses a claims database, and the model is based on information which is more detailed than used by most methods covered in this review.

In the notation of Section 3.1, the data required by Linnemann comprise the following in respect of each claim:

$$i_z = \text{period of origin,}$$

$$k_z - i_z = \text{delay in notification,}$$

$$\max\{m : c_{zm} \neq 0\} = \text{number of claim payments on the claim,}$$

$j_{zm}, m = 1, 2, \text{etc} = $ numbers of complete periods from (exact) **date** of origin (not period of origin) to the dates of these payments,

$c_{zm}, m = 1, 2, \text{etc} = $ amounts of these payments.

This information can be condensed as follows:

$c_{ij}^{(z)^*} = $ total claim payments with $j_{zm} = j$ in respect of claim numbered z which was incurred in period i

$= \sum c_{zm}$, where the summation runs over values of m such that $j_{zm} = j$,

$h_{ij}^{(z)} =$ the number of payments included in this summation.

The recorded delay in notification does not appear to be used by Linnemann despite its introduction.

Linnemann's model can now be stated as:

$$E[C_{zm} : i_z = i, j_{zm} = j] = e_i \rho_j \lambda_{i+j}, \qquad (9.2.1.1)$$

where the e_i, ρ_j and λ_{i+j} are parameters to be estimated, and

$$E[H_{ij}^{(z)}] = \Pi_{ij}, \qquad (9.2.1.2)$$

a function which is periodic in i. The periodicity is intended to represent a seasonality effect. Therefore, the period is chosen as the number of periods of origin in a year. Linnemann uses quarterly periods of origin, and so sets the period of Π to 4.

It is assumed that, for each z, the C_{zm} are stochastically independent of $H_{ij}^{(z)}$.

In fact, (9.2.1.2) is simplified by the omission of the seasonal effect more than a year after the date of occurrence of the claim. Thus, (9.2.1.2) is assumed to hold for all periods j relating to the year following the date of occurrence, but for subsequent periods (9.2.1.2) simplifies to:

$$E[H_{ij}^{(z)}] = \Pi_j, \qquad (9.2.1.3)$$

independent of i.

Comparison of (9.2.1.1) with (7.1.5.1.2) reveals that Linnemann's model can be identified as similar to the separation model of Section 7.1.5.

The former does differ from the latter in one significant respect. The model of Section 7.1.5 adopts the structure of the right side of (9.2.1.1) as a representation of the **total claim payments** in the (i, j)-cell of the run-off array. Linnemann's model adopts it as the expectation of the size of a **single claim payment** in respect of an individual claim within that cell. The model of the present section is also subject to the addition of a stochastic error term to $C_{ij}^{(z)*}$ and the imposition of a seasonal influence on the claims experience of the year of origin.

9.2.2 *Estimation*

As is evident from (9.2.1.1) to (9.2.1.3), there are 4 categories of parameter to be estimated. They are the e_i, ρ_j, λ_k and Π_{ij}.

Linnemann obtains estimates by least squares procedures. He defines two quadratic loss functions as follows:

$$Q_1 = \sum_i \sum_j w_{ij}^{(C)} [c_{ij}^*/h_{ij} - e_i \rho_j \lambda_{i+j}]^2, \qquad (9.2.2.1)$$

and

$$Q_2 = \sum_i \sum_j w_{ij}^{(H)} [h_{ij}/n_i - \Pi_{ij}]^2, \qquad (9.2.2.2)$$

where the summations run over all pairs (i, j) for which the requisite data c_{ij}^* and h_{ij} are available; the $w_{ij}^{(C)}$ and $w_{ij}^{(H)}$ are suitable weights; and as usual

$$c_{ij}^* = \sum_z c_{ij}^{(z)*}, \qquad (9.2.2.3)$$

and similarly for h_{ij}, i.e. c_{ij} and h_{ij} denote the total amount of claims and the total number of claim payments respectively in the (i, j)-cell of data.

In the use of these loss functions it must be remembered that, although Π_{ij} appears in (9.2.2.2) in this generality, it is in fact constrained by (9.2.1.3).

Linnemann suggests (Section 3.3):

$$w_{ij}^{(C)} = h_{ij} \qquad (9.2.2.4)$$

and

$$w_{ij}^{(H)} = 1 \qquad (9.2.2.5)$$

as the choice of weights in (9.2.2.1) and (9.2.2.2). We comment on this choice in Section 9.2.4.

Once the loss functions Q_1 and Q_2 have been decided, it is routine, in principle, to minimize them in order to produce estimates of the parameters involved. One forms the normal equations by differentiating the loss functions by the various parameters in turn and setting the results equal to zero.

In practice, this procedure is not altogether straightforward. It is quite apparent that the normal equations derived from (9.2.2.1) will not yield estimates of the e_i, ρ_j and λ_k which are expressible in closed form in terms of the data. An iterative approach to the solution of these equations is required.

Linnemann displays the iteration formulas arising from this particular set of normal equations (see his (3.1.3) to (3.1.5)). He states that the iterative procedure leads to rapid convergence.

He also points out that the parameters of any model are not unique in that (9.2.1.1) is left unaffected if the vectors of e_i, ρ_j and λ_k are each subjected to constant multipliers whose product is unity.

The estimation of the Π are simpler, the normal equations derived from (9.2.2.2) yielding closed form estimates. It is simple to check that the estimator for Π_{ij} is the weighted average of terms h_{ij}/n_i with weights $w_{ij}^{(H)}$. Details are given by Linnemann's (3.1.7) to (3.1.9).

9.2.3 *Projection of outstanding claims*

For the most part, the projection of future claim payments is no more than the piecing together of the estimates of the e_i, ρ_j, λ_k and Π_{ij} with the structural equations (9.2.1.1) to (9.2.1.3). Then (9.2.1.2) yields:

$$E[H_{ij}] = \sum_z E[H_{ij}^{(z)}]$$

$$= n_i \Pi_{ij}. \qquad (9.2.3.1)$$

Then

$$E[C_{ij}^*] = n_i E[C_{ij}^{(z)*}]$$

$$[\text{by} (9.2.2.3)]$$

$$= n_i E[H_{ij}^{(z)}] E[C_{zm} : i_z = i, j_{zm} = j]$$

(using the independence of C_{zm} and $H_{ij}^{(z)}$)

$$= n_i \Pi_{ij} e_i \rho_j \lambda_{i+j}, \qquad (9.2.3.2)$$

by (9.2.1.1) and (9.2.1.2).

Let the parameters listed in the preceding paragraph be estimated by $\hat{e}$, $\hat{\rho}_j$, $\hat{\lambda}_k$ and $\hat{\Pi}_{ij}$.

Thus C_{ij}^* is estimated for future periods as:

$$n_i \hat{\Pi}_{ij} \hat{e}_i \hat{\rho}_j \hat{\lambda}_{i+j}. \qquad (9.2.3.3)$$

It follows that any future cash flow, e.g. outstanding claims in respect of a particular year of origin, is estimated as a sum of terms of the form (9.2.3.3).

There is really only one complication to this procedure. It relates to the fact that some of the (i,j)-cells of data will be incomplete at the date of valuation. This arises essentially from the somewhat unusual definition of j.

Recall from Section 9.2.1 that the (i,j) data cell, i.e. that containing $c_{ij}^{(z)*}$, deals with claim payments made during the $(j+1)$-th period measured from the **date** of origin. Now dates of origin are of course distributed over periods of origin.

Consider claims such that the j-th period ($j = 1,2$,etc.) measured from the date of origin contains the valuation date. Let the valuation date lie at the end of the b-th calendar period (we emphasise that in the present context all "periods" are of equal length). Then the period of origin must be the $(b-j+1)$-th calendar period. A claim which occurred at the beginning of this period will, by the valuation date, have completed j periods measured from the date of origin. A claim which occurred in the middle of the $(b-j+1)$-th calendar period, on the other hand, will, by the valuation date, have completed only $(j - \frac{1}{2})$ periods measured from the date of origin.

Thus, in projecting (9.2.3.3) in respect of calendar periods which lie in the future at the valuation date, one must take due allowance for the fact that the (i,j)-cells containing the valuation date will lie partly in the past, partly in the future. The simple consequence of this is that, in the projection expression (9.2.3.3), $\hat{\Pi}_{ij}$ needs to be replaced by $\hat{\Pi}_{ij}^{(fut)}$, the estimated number of payments per incurred claim to be made in the future, wherever the (i,j)-cell contains the valuation date.

Linnemann does not state how $\hat{\Pi}_{ij}^{(fut)}$ should be estimated from $\hat{\Pi}_{ij}$. It seems implied, however, by his equation (3.1.9) that the former might be taken as just half of the latter. This is justified by arguments of the type given above. Thus, if b and j have the meanings ascribed above, then on the average the number of periods elapsed between date of origin and the valuation date will be $(j - \frac{1}{2})$ on the assumption that dates of origin are uniformly distributed over periods.

9.2.4 *Comment*

Section 9.2.1 has referred to the similarity between the model presently under discussion and that of the separation method of Section 7.1.5. Indeed the algebraic structures of the right-hand sides of the respective model equations (9.2.1.1) and (7.1.5.1.2) are identical. Hence the reference to the present method as the **stochastic separation method**.

The model of (7.1.5.1.2) does not contain an explicit stochastic component. However, in the least squares regression version of the method of Section 7.1.5 (see Section 7.1.5.4) one may think of a normal stochastic component as implied. Then that method might also be considered as a stochastic separation method.

There is however one substantial difference between the two models (quite apart from the fact that one recognises stochasticity explicitly whereas the other does not). This difference appears on the left-hand side of the model equations. Whereas the nonstochastic separation method models **total claim payments** in development period j of period of origin i, the stochastic separation method models the **average amount per claim payment made**.

Thus, despite their algebraic similarity, the two models are quite different. Most particularly, the criticism of the nonstochastic version that it includes no allowance for changes in speed of finalization (Section 7.1.5.4) is not applicable to the stochastic version. Linnemann's intention is (see his Section 2.2) that speed of finalization for a particular period of origin and development period be reflected in the number of claim payments made in the period (e.g. see (9.2.1.2) and (9.2.3.2)). A greater speed of finalization is reflected by a greater number of claim payments.

It is of interest, of course, to consider the effectiveness of such a representation of speed of finalization. It has not been used in other methods in the literature mainly because numbers of claim payments, subdivided by period of origin and development period are not usually available. However, if available, they do have some intuitive appeal as a measure of the genuine activity in settlement of claims. Nonetheless, their appropriateness to this purpose will not always be as obvious as their superficial appeal may suggest. A brief word of caution is therefore necessary.

Consider a portfolio in which it is typical for many payments to be made in respect of an individual claim. A portfolio which paid weekly compensation to claimants (e.g. Australian workers compensation) would fit this category. Now suppose the claims settlement activity remains unchanged for many years up to and including year $j - 2$. In year $j - 1$ claims administration difficulties cause a reduction in settlement activity. This situation persists into the early part of the year j, but is then reversed during the remainder of that year. By the end of year j the claims handling situation has returned to normal.

If this situation is to be reflected properly by Linnemann's model, then the average number of claim payments should be:

(i) lower than "normal" (i.e. than in prior years) than year $j - 1$;

(ii) higher than "normal" in year j.

However, if the payment of weekly claims is say 3 weeks in arrear at the beginning of year j, the acceleration during that year might result, in some cases, in benefits in respect of three weeks being paid in a single payments instead of in three separate payments. This then would be an influence tending to lower the average number of payments per claim during year j, the year of high settlement activity.

Thus, average number of payments per claim may not always provide a completely satisfactory indicator of claims activity. Nonetheless, it is probably a reasonable such indicator in the absence of extreme shifts in the speed with which claims are being processed.

Estimation in Section 9.2.2 is carried out in terms of the quadratic loss functions Q_1 and Q_2 which involve weights $w_{ij}^{(C)}$ and $w_{ij}^{(H)}$. Naturally, some question arises as to the form which these weights should take. Linnemann's (1982) suggestions are noted in (9.2.2.4) and (9.2.2.5).

In a separate section, Linnemann gives a brief consideration of the theory according to which the weights should be selected. Considering $w_{ij}^{(C)}$, for example, he states that one should choose:

$$w_{ij}^{(C)} = n_i / V[C_{ij}^*], \qquad (9.2.4.1)$$

where $V[.]$ here denotes the variance of the argument. Some general and approximate arguments then lead from this formula to (9.2.2.4).

There are, however, some doubts in this author's mind as to the validity of (9.2.4.1). On the basis that the weight to be associated with any given cell of data should be the reciprocal of the variance of that item, which is the (fairly standard) reasoning used by Linnemann, it does not seem obvious that (9.2.4.1) follows.

The relevant data item with which the weight $w_{ij}^{(C)}$ is associated in (9.2.2.1) is c_{ij}^*/h_{ij}. This is the average size of individual payments associated with the (i, j)-cell. It can be interpreted as a weighted average of the sizes of the individual payments, where the weights themselves are random variables (depending on the numbers of payments associated with the individual claims). Thus, it would appear that $w_{ij}^{(C)}$ ought to involve the variance of individual payment sizes rather than of total payments in the cell. Of course, individual payment sizes and total payments are intimately related, and so it will be possible to express the suggested form of $w_{ij}^{(C)}$, involving the variance of individual payment size in terms of $V[C_{ij}^*]$. But it is by no means obvious that the result will be Linnemann's weight (9.2.4.1).

Further, consider the hypothetical case in which the number of payments made in respect of any given claim in the (i,j)-cell is non-random. In terms of the weighted average mentioned in the preceding paragraph, this is the case of non-random weights. A trivial calculation shows that, for this case, $w_{ij}^{(C)}$ is not given by (9.2.4.1). Now the hypothesis on which this calculation is based is of course quite unrealistic. The adoption of more realistic assumptions would change the calculated value of $w_{ij}^{(C)}$ substantially; in fact, reduce it in recognition of the additional stochastic variation of the weights in the weighted average. The change might be towards Linneman's formula (9.2.4.1). For the purpose of this volume it suffices to point out that the form (9.2.4.1) for $w_{ij}^{(C)}$ has not been established by Linnemann, is not correct in some specific cases, and in this author's opinion, is subject to considerable doubt in general.

9.3   Claim status Markov chain method —

$S/MIC/\cdot/I/I, T, Y, D, P$ **type**

9.3.1 *Model*

The method discussed in this section derives from a series of papers by Hachemeister (1976, 1978, 1980). The main ideas presented are summarized in the last of that series.

Hachemeister's main concern lay in the fact that the majority of claims reserving techniques pivoted on runoff arrays of the sort displayed in Section 7.1.5.2. Such arrays most commonly presented details of past claim payments, though they might have been supplemented by additional information (possibly also in the form of runoff arrays) in respect of numbers of claims reported, physical estimates of outstandings, etc. Hachemeister, on the other hand , emphasises the fact that each claim outstanding at a given epoch is likely to have associated with it a considerable amount of information other than its bare financial history.

This information may not be of a type which is easily quantifiable numerically. Hachemeister (1980) gives an example:

> " *The claim department Vice President decides that he will double the number of claims people who settle small claims by telephone. By not breaking down claims into telephone handled and other claims, projections of future settlements will be off.* "

The point being made here is that claims reserving is an exercise in estimation of certain parameters conditional on the accumulated information about the claims concerned, and that runoff arrays may not always constitute the most efficient conditioning information. This is particularly likely to be the case for a reinsurer. Delays in reporting of claims are lengthy. So are delays in claim payments, at least those affecting reinsurance liability. The result is that several years after the commencement of a year of origin very little claim payment experience might have accumulated. It might be the case that the claim files, often quite extensive, contain other information, possibly qualitative, which will provide a better indicator of ultimate total claim cost than the limited information accumulated in respect of recent years of origin.

Hachemeister's method of analysis provides an approach capable of taking such information into account. Of couse, the information need not **necessarily** be nonquantitative. Indeed, much of Hachemeister's discussion concerns the use of the history of physical estimates for claims reserving purposes.

The general idea of the method may be described as follows. A particular set of **claim statuses** is chosen such that, at any given moment, a given claim must have one of those statuses.

Next it is assumed that there exists a probability of transition from any particular status to any other particular status, and that such probabilities can be estimated from recorded data.

Finally it is assumed that an expected claim size can be associated with each status.

Then, given the status of any particular claim at a balance date, one may use the transition probabilities to derive probabilities of future trajectories through the statuses, and so arrive at an estimate of the ultimate expected claim size.

Let the (finite) set of claim statuses be $\mathcal{U}$.

Let $r_{st}(j, k : i)$ denote the probability that a claim from period of origin i with status s at development epoch j will have status t at development epoch $k(> j)$.

In most applications it would be assumed that transition probabilities were independent of period of origin:

$$r_{st}(j, k : i) = r_{st}(j, k), \qquad (9.3.1.1)$$

independent of i.

An alternative meaning of $r_{st}(j, k : i)$ and $r_{st}(j, k)$ but one just as useful or even more so, is obtained by letting j, k denote operational times.

Now let $G_{st}(x : j, k : i)$ denote the d.f. of claim size in respect of a claim from period of origin i which has status t at development epoch k, having had status s at epoch j.

In many applications it would be assumed that this d.f. is independent of period of origin:

$$G_{st}(x : j, k : i) = G_{st}(x : j, k), \qquad (9.3.1.2)$$

or even independent of the claim status from which transition has been made:

$$G_{st}(x : j, k : i) = G_t(x : k). \qquad (9.3.1.3)$$

Thus, in (9.3.1.3) the d.f of claim size at a given epoch is dependent on only the claim status occupied then.

Hachemeister's own approach in fact contains a further dimension of generality. In his paper both r and G are made dependent on a further parameter, the "exposure group". An "exposure group" is simply a subset of the portfolio consisting of risks which are homogeneous with respect to r and G. The motivation for these groups is apparent in Hachemeister's example, quoted above, dealing with the settling of small claims by telephone. For most purposes distinct exposure groups can be regarded as stochastically independent. It is then possible for all theory developed below ignoring the groups to be regarded as applying to just one exposure group and the results of all such groups finally combined.

On the understanding, then, that the following development will ignore exposure groups, Hachemeister's model consists of just the postulation of existence of the transition probabilities $r_{st}(j, k : i)$ and the claim size d.f.'s $G_{st}(x : j, k : i)$.

An application of the method mentioned by Hachemeister as being of particular interest is that in which claim status is defined by the physical estimate of total cost of the claim in question.

The idea behind such a procedure is much as expressed in Section 7.2.3.4. The physical estimation of the cost of a claim tends to be a difficult and unreliable business during the early life of the claim. Hard facts material to the assessment of the claim may not be to hand at this stage. In this period, the medical condition of an injured party may not have stabilized. The likelihood of legal action being brought for recovery of damages by an injured party may not be clear.

As a consequence of all these shortcomings in the available information, there may be very few claims in respect of which there is any strong reason for estimating large claim sizes early in their lifetimes;and this despite the knowledge that a significant proportion is likely ultimately to produce large settlements.

Thus, claims which have low physical estimates at say development year 2 are seen as having a certain probability of attaining large estimates by year 3.The Markov chain method provides a means of formalizing this idea. The concept involved is that of a **transition probability**, in the standard terminology of Markov chains (see e.g. Kemeny and Snell, 1960). This probability relates to the transition from a small estimated claim size at development year 2 to a large size (whatever is meant by "small" and "large") at year 3. It is represented in the above notation as $r_{SL}(2,3:i)$ where S and L denote "small" and "large" respectively.

9.3.2 *Estimation*

Section 9.3.1 makes clear that the model consists of just transition probabilities and certain d.f.'s. These are very simple concepts, and their estimation will usually be correspondingly simple (in concept).

Consider the estimation of $r_{st}(j,k)$. This is a probability of transition from status s to status t. That is, it is the conditional probability that a claim will move to status t at time k given that it occupied status s at time j.

Suppose that the restriction (9.3.1.1) is in use. If the total number of claims ever observed in status s at development epoch j (N say) is given, then the number of these observed in status t at epoch k will be a binomial variate with parameters N and $r_{st}(j,k)$ (on the assumption that all of the N have been tracked through their entire subsequent development).

Then $r_{st}(j, k)$ can be estimated in the customary way, i.e. dividing the above count with respect to status t by N, the corresponding count in status s.

Similarly, the relevant d.f. can be estimated from its associated empirical d.f. For example, suppose that the d.f. described by (9.3.1.3) is to be estimated. Suppose further that claim sizes have been adjusted for inflation, and consequently there is thought to be no reason for the d.f. to depend on either period of origin or development epoch k:

$$G_t(x : k) = G_t(x) \qquad (9.3.2.1)$$

independent of k. Then all that is necessary to estimate the right side of (9.3.2.1) is to collate all available observations on claim size in status t, and arrange them as a distribution. This will be the empirical distribution corresponding to $G_t(x)$.

In practice, it will often be desirable to carry out some smoothing of the estimates of both $r_{st}(j, k)$ and $G_t(x)$. For $G_t(x)$ would normally be expected to display reasonable continuity with respect to x, and possibly also t if this assumes numerical values. Similarly, $r_{st}(j, k)$ would normally be expected to be continuous in j and k, and possibly s and t. The smoothing may be carried out on the $r_{st}(j, j + 1)$, which then serve as the basis for further work. Some further comment on this appears in Section 9.3.3, particularly in relation to (9.3.3.1).

In practical terms, smoothing over several dimensions simultaneously like this may not be an easy task.

9.3.3 *Projection of outstanding claims*

As foreshadowed in Section 9.3.1, the projection of outstanding claims consists of two distinct stages. For each of the outstanding claims with which we are concerned, there must be:

(i) a projection of the probability that the claim ultimately occupies status m (i.e. the probability it remains in status m after some sufficiently large epoch),

(ii) for each of the probabilities found in (i) for the various values of m, the associated expected claim size must be obtained.

The required estimate of the expected value of outstanding claims is then calculated as the probability-weighted average of the average claim sizes obtained in (ii) using the probabilities found in (i).

In the following, the details of these two stages are considered.

Consider first the projection of claim status probabilities. As pointed out in Section 9.3.1, the concepts involved in the transitions between claim statuses are the familiar ones of Markov chains. In Markov chain terminology, the transition probabilities such as $r_{st}(j, j+1)$ are **single-step** transition probabilities. It will usually be these which are most conveniently estimated from the data.

The calculation of **multi-step** transition probabilities can be carried out by the usual means, the Chapman-Kolmogorov equation (Feller, 1950):

$$r_{st}(j, k) = \sum_{u \in U} r_{su}(j, j+1) r_{ut}(j+1, k). \qquad (9.3.3.1)$$

Recursive use of this equation permits the building up of multi-step from single-step probabilities. According to (i) at the start of this subsection, the required probabilities are the $r_{si}(j, K)$, where K is the epoch beyond which it it assumed that no further transitions between claim statuses occur. Naturally, in practice the probabilities r in (9.3.3.1) are replaced by their estimates.

We now deal with claim sizes on the supposition that restriction (9.3.2.1) is in operation, in particular that claim sizes are adjusted for inflation. Suppose the development epoch of evaluation of the outstanding claims with which we are concerned is b. Consider claims from period of origin i with status s at that epoch.

Suppose there are N_{is} of them. The probability that such a claim will utlimately occupy status t and will generate a claim size no greater than x is

$$r_{st}(b, K) G_t(x). \qquad (9.3.3.2)$$

The probability that a claim from period of origin i with status s at the date of evaluation will generate a claim size no greater than x is

$$\sum_t r_{st}(b, K) G_t(x). \qquad (9.3.3.3)$$

The expected number of claims from period of origin i, outstanding at epoch b, ultimately with claim sizes no greater than x is:

$$\sum_s N_{is} \sum_t r_{st}(b, K) G_t(x). \qquad (9.3.3.4)$$

It follows that the estimated outstandings in respect of period of origin i at epoch b are:

$$\sum_s N_{is} \sum_t r_{st}(b, K) \int_0^\infty x dG_t(x), \qquad (9.3.3.5)$$

or equivalently:

$$\sum_s N_{is} \sum_t r_{st}(b, K) \int_0^\infty [1 - G_t(x)]dx, \qquad (9.3.3.6)$$

The development from (9.3.3.1) to (9.3.3.5) is not completely general. However, it can serve as an archetype of the calculations required in the estimation of outstanding claims. In cases involving more generally defined r and G, the calculations will still need to follow more or less the form of (9.3.3.1) to (9.3.3.5).

9.3.4 *Comment*

There is perhaps no harm in repeating that the development presented in Sections 9.3.1 to 9.3.3 disregards Hachemeister's "exposure groups". However, as pointed out in Section 9.3.1, there is absolutely no difficulty in expanding the above theory to accommodate them.

One point which should be noted is that, since the Markov chain method essentially forecasts the trajectories of individual claims from their (known) current statuses, it is necessarily applied to only reported claims when the definition of status involves some specific information about the claim (such as estimated size). No information on unreported claims will be at hand. It will therefore be impossible to assign statuses to them when status is defined as above.

Of course, it is possible to envisage a Markov chain in which there are only two statuses, "reported" and "unreported". Unreported claims could then feature in the model. This set of statuses represents, however, only a very weak classification.

In practice, as in the specific models dealt with below, it will be necessary to deal separately with IBNR claims. This is a matter which is taken up in Chapter 16.

It was mentioned at the end of Section 8.3.4 that stochastic models, by their very nature, permit the computation of second moments of estimated outstanding claims. Naturally, this applies to the Markov chain method as much as to any other stochastic method.

We do not go into detail since it is not the function of this volume to treat second moments. However, a couple of general matters can be touched upon.

Firstly, the theory required to develop expressions for second moments, **given the parameters of the model**, contains no difficulties. Basic expressions like (9.3.3.6) just involve compounding the binomial variates $N_i r$ with the general claim size d.f. G. This can be dealt with by standard techniques. The reader is referred to Hachemeister (1980, 189-191).

Secondly, however, there are sampling-theoretic problems arising from the fact that the parameters of the model are not known in practice but must be estimated. The concatenation of probabilities r as in (9.3.3.1), each r accompanied by a standard error, renders the computation of second moments of projected future numbers of claims in the various statuses extremely difficult.

A couple of examples of sets of claim statuses are now considered briefly.

Firstly, a very simple example. Suppose the set $\mathcal{U}$ of claim statuses consists of only 3 members:

(i) open claims assessed as "small",

(ii) open claims assessed as "large",

(iii) closed claims.

The definition of "small" and "large" might or might not be precise. Exactly what is the definition is not **particularly** important for the purpose of the present discussion.

Suppose that "small" claims, however defined, are dealt with by telephone, while "large" claims are not. This classification, together with the Markov chain method of analysis and projection, will provide an appropriate response to the situation described in Section 9.3.1 concerning telephone handled claims.

If the 3 statuses are represented by S (small), L (large) and C (closed), then one of the matrices of transition probabilities $r_{st}(j, k)$ will have the following form:

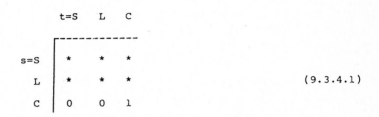

unless it is necessary to consider the possibility of reopened claims.

If such matrices were constructed for various j and $k = j + 1$, the decision of the claim department Vice President described in Section 9.3.1 as to the handling of claims by telephone would be reflected for the particular j concerned by a sudden increase in the observed values of $r_{SC}(j, j + 1)$.

Such examples as the above are too simple for most practical purposes. They might, however, serve a purpose in the case of a very small portfolio of outstanding claims. Here, the data might be so scant that refinement of the above model might not be possible.

A more comprehensive model for practical purposes is described by Hachemeister (1976). The set $\mathcal{U}$ of statuses consists of:

(i) 16 different size-ranges for open claims,

(ii) the same 16 size-ranges for closed claims,

(iii) a further status for claims closed at zero cost.

In this case, if O and C denote the sets of statuses (size ranges) for open and closed claims respectively, and Z denotes the status of having been closed at zero cost, then the transition matrix $r_{..}(j,k)$ will have the following submatrix form:

$$(9.3.4.2)$$

again provided one does not need to consider the possibility of reopened claims.

It is seen that the transition matrix contains many null entries.

One practical difficulty possessed by the Markov chain method is that, for its proper application to examples such as the above involving estimated total claim size, past claim payments should be adjusted for claims escalation in their contribution to total size. Usually, the information readily available from an insurer would consist of total claims paid to date, unadjusted for escalation. Too often, therefore, the available options involve the use of unadjusted data, which is rather unsatisfactory, or collection of data in the form of entire histories of individual claims, which is inconvenient.

In closing, we mention one specific area in which the Markov chain method, with statuses based on estimated claim sizes, is of especial use. This is the case where outstanding claims are subject to large excess of loss reinsurance recoveries. By the very nature of excess of loss reinsurance, a proper allowance for its effect on estimated outstanding claims requires in principle that the individual claims composing the total outstandings be examined with respect to their sizes, that the subset exceeding the reinsurance retention be determined, and the retention be applied to just these to determine the amount of recoveries.

Most of the methods of projection of outstanding claims discussed above contain no explicit consideration of individual claim size. In this event it is necessary to resort to indirect and approximate methods (e.g. Taylor, 1982b). The Markov chain method, on the other hand, explicitly projects expected numbers of claims in the size ranges within which they are ultimately to be settled. Thus, the projected total claim cost in each such range is easily converted into the corresponding cost net of reinsurance.

10.   DYNAMIC MODELS

10.1   General

The structure according to which the claims process was to be modelled was set out in a very general way in (4.2.5). Put into words, that formula expresses any given item of claims data as some function of a set of **parameters** (to be estimated from the data) plus random noise.

It should be noted that these parameters are of fixed value. That is, it is assumed that they do not alter their values with the passage of time. In this sense, all of the models dealt up with up to this point can be described as **static**.

It may be argued quite realistically that the parameters describing the claims process may be expected to undergo some form of drift over time with perhaps superposed shocks from time to time. Naturally, as additional data accumulate, all of the models developed in the foregoing sections will tend, to a greater or lesser extent, to track the shifts in model parameters. They will, however, do so rather more slowly than is desirable by virtue of their inherent property of assigning to data items weights which do not depend on the antiquity of the data concerned.

This type of problem is far from novel. It is the typical problem encountered in time series forecasting (see e.g. Brown, 1962). It may be noted that, in the analysis of claims data, what is being dealt with is in fact a time series, although one in which the item of data associated with any given epoch is a whole collection of information (claim payments made in the period just completed, subdivided by period of origin; numbers of claims finalized in the same period, similarly subdidvided, etc.) rather than a single scalar. Time series techniques are therefore likely to be relevant to the problem of analysis of past claims data and forecast of future experience.

Various techniques are available for the treatment of time series. This survey is not an appropriate place to review them. The interested reader may consult one of the standard texts on the subject such as that referred to above. The intention here is merely to present those techniques which have found their way into the literature concerned with claims analysis, and particularly estimation of outstanding claims.

Just as the static claims models were circumscribed by a very general statement in (4.2.5), it is useful to set out the corresponding statement in connection with those models based on a time series approach. We do this by spelling out the required modification of (4.2.5). Such models will be called **dynamic**.

Recall from the preceding discussion that the motivation for the dynamic models is the possibility of instability of the claims process parameters over time. Whereas the relevant set of parameters was denoted in (4.2.5) by Ω, we now use Ω_k to denote the set of values of these parameters during experience period k. Similarly, we use $I_{red:k}$ in place of the left side of (4.2.5). The (4.2.5) is simply reduced by:

$$I_{red:k} = E(\Omega_k) + u. \qquad (10.1.1)$$

Note however, that (10.1.1), though analogous to (4.2.5), will usually be inadequate as a dynamic model specification. This is because if (10.1.1) were not supplemented in some way the various experience periods k would **decouple** and the parameter set Ω_k for a particular k would be estimated solely from $I_{red:k}$, the data relating to that k.

Thus the time series approach will normally be useful only if some model "linkage" between the Ω_k for the various k is established. This would normally take the form:

$$\Omega_{k+1} = W(\Omega_k, \Omega_{k-1}, \ldots) + v, \qquad (10.1.2)$$

where $W(., ., \ldots)$ is some function and v is a random variable.

In the applications considered below, the function $W(., ., \ldots)$ is always linear. An attempt to consider nonlinearity would introduce substantial difficulty.

One feature of the dynamic models described by (10.1.1) and (10.1.2) is that any static model (4.2.5) can be easily converted into the corresponding dynamic model (10.1.1) and the necessary parameter linkage (10.1.2) added. This means that in the following discussion of particular dynamic "models" there is no necessity for precise formulation of that part of the model described by (10.1.1). Indeed, these dynamic "models" are not models in the same sense as those formulated in the foregoing sections. Rather they represent **procedures**, applicable to virtually any of those earlier models (by conversion of (4.2.5) into form (10.1.1)), which revise the estimators involved in those earlier models in such a way as to recognise the linkage (10.1.2) and increase the weight given to more recent data.

10.2   Autoregressive models

10.2.1 *Model*

As foreshadowed in Section 10.1, it will be necessary to formulate the model to be treated here in only the vaguest manner. The formulation takes the form of two restrictions on (10.1.1) and (10.1.2).

Firstly, (10.1.2) is specialised to:

$$I_{red:k} = \Omega_k + u, \tag{10.2.1.1}$$

where $I_{red:k}$ and Ω_k are now vectors of data and parameters respectively. That is, there is assumed a direct correspondence between the items of data available and the parameters requiring estimation.

Secondly, the function $W(.,.,\ldots)$ is assumed linear.

Substitution of (10.1.2) in (10.2.1.1) yields:

$$I_{red:k+1} = W(\Omega_k, \Omega_{k-1}, \ldots) + u + v. \tag{10.2.1.2}$$

Then application of (10.1.2) to the right side of (10.2.1.2) gives:

$$I_{red:k+1} = W(I_{red:k}, I_{red:k-1}, \ldots) + w, \tag{10.2.1.3}$$

where w is a new random variable.

Expression of the model in the form (10.2.1.3) gives, apart from the stochastic component, data from experience period $k+1$ as a linear function of data from periods k and earlier. The problem of estimating $W(.,.,\ldots)$ can then be interpreted as a problem of autoregression of the sequence $I_{red:k}$.

This approach has been followed by Lemaire (1982). As has already been mentioned above, there is no need in principle for us to go into detail as to the particular model (10.2.1.3) used. However, as a matter of interest we mention that Lemaire's specific model was:

$$C_{ij} = aC_{i-1,j} + bC_{i,j-1} + c + w_{ij}, \qquad (10.2.1.4)$$

where a, b and c are unknown parameters and w_{ij} has the same meaning as above except that it is specific to period of origin i and development period j.

It is apparent that claim payments from the (i,j)-cell are modelled in terms of the experience of the preceding period (i.e. experience period) at the same and preceding development period. Thus, it is tacitly assumed that:

(i) claim payments made in development period j are likely to undergo shifts from one period of experience to another;

(ii) the magnitude of such shifts is likely to be influenced by the recent experience at development period $j - 1$.

We shall return briefly to this matter in Section 10.2.4.

10.2.2 *Estimation*

There seems little need for any detailed discussion in this subsection. Since the problem has been set up as of the autoregression type (see (10.2.1.3) and the subsequent text), the estimation method used is the standard one for such problems. That is, the unknown coefficients in the linear function W are estimated by regression of $I_{red:k+1}$ on $I_{red:k}$, $I_{red:k-1}$, etc. The regression may be of the weighted type if this seems advisable.

10.2.3 *Projection of outstanding claims*

As in Section 10.2.2, little comment is needed. Once again the procedure to be followed is just as for autoregression problems.

Thus, if the experience period just completed at the valuation date is labelled b, then experience of the immediately ensuing period $b+1$ is forecast, following (10.2.1.3), as:

$$\hat{I}_{red:b+1} = W(I_{red:b}, I_{red:b-1}, \ldots), \qquad (10.2.3.1)$$

The experience of subsequent periods $b + 1$, $b + 2$, etc. is forecast using (10.2.3.1) recursively.

10.2.4 *Comment*

As the autoregressive model established by (10.2.1.1) and (10.2.1.2) can be viewed within the Kalman framework (see Section 10.3), most of our comment will be deferred until that more general background is considered.

However, it is pertinent to make one comment specifically in respect of the particular model used by Lemaire and quoted in connection with (10.2.1.4). This comment has wider applicability than to just that model.

The assumption was noted in Section 10.2.1 that:

(i) claim payments made in development period j are likely to undergo shifts from one period of experience to another;

(ii) the magnitude of such shifts is likely to be influenced by the recent experience at development period $j - 1$.

It is salutary perhaps to enquire into the rationale underlying (ii). The assumption may be considered in the context of the recommendations made in Section 8.2.4 of "a thorough exploration of the data ... to inform oneself about the subtleties of the data" and an "attempt at unravelling and comprehending the various interrelationships between factors". A corollary of these recommendations is that blind fitting of a model to data is taboo.

With this viewpoint in mind one can consider the possible mechanisms which might justify the tacit assumption (ii) involved in (10.2.1.4). There are, presumably, a number of possible such mechanisms. However, the one which comes to mind as most likely is that a retardation of the claim payment process has been occurring in recent times. This would have the effect, as illustrated in **Figs. 4** and **5** (Sections 7.3.2.4 and 7.3.3.1 respectively) (actually the illustration is of an acceleration rather than a retardation), of relocating some claim payments from development period $j - 1$ in experience period k to development period j in experience period $k + 1$.

This is precisely the type of dependence introduced by assumption (ii).

The consequences of this conjecture, if it is correct, for the predictive power of the autoregression model are interesting. In particular, what is the likelihood that this retardation will persist in the future? Note that the model predicts that it will continue forever. The result could be a very significant lengthening of the tail of the distribution of claim payment delays as this distribution is perceived some distance into the future.

It would be necessary to consider the realism of such a projection. Is the retardation of the payment process presumed to have been occurring likely to be a temporary phenomenon capable of reversal in the near future or a more persistent feature of the experience?

At the very least, the conjecture concerning the retardation should be examined (perhaps by reference to numbers of finalizations in the recent past) as to its apparent accuracy.

In the event of its accuracy, there is another consequence of the autoregression model (10.2.1.4) possibly even more serious than that discussed above. If the claim payments of a particular period of origin are in fact retarded relative to those of the preceding period of origin, this should manifest itself (other things equal) in an increase in payments in some development periods (of the later period of origin) and a decrease in others.

However, at the time of commencement of the retardation, or shortly thereafter, it is likely that claim payments of virtually **all** development periods (for the cross-section of periods of origin observed in a particular experience period) will contain an increased proportion of payments formerly associated with the preceding development period. The autoregression model will project this change into the future, again in **virtually all development periods.**

In this event, the total claim payments associated with successive periods of origin will be projected as steadily increasing even though (by the above assumption of "other things equal") the out-turn of experience will ultimately reveal them to be stationary.

None of the above commentary should be construed as general criticism of autoregressive models. As will be seen in Section 10.3 (into which framework the autoregressive models can be fitted), such models can perform an extremely useful function. However, the specific use of the autoregressive aspect of the models in tracking a signal generated by shifting parameters can be expected to be effective only if the details of the model upon which the autoregressive structure has been superposed are a reasonably accurate representation of reality.

10.3   Kalman filter

10.3.1 *Model*

The Kalman filter was introduced by Kalman (1960) in an engineering context. It has subsequently received publicity in the statistical context (e.g. Harrison and Stevens (1976)). Quite recently, in a series of papers, de Jong and Zehnwirth (1980, 1983a, b) and Zehnwirth (1983a, b) have suggested its use in the evaluation of outstanding claims.

The model is now described in its general setting, i.e. not in a context specific to claims reserving. Later it is adapted to the claims reserving context.

Consider a model of the form:

$$Y(t) = X(t)\beta(t) + u(t), \qquad (10.3.1.1)$$

where $Y(t)$ is a column n-vector of **observations** made at epoch t, $\beta(t)$ is a column p-vector of (unknown) **parameters** in force at epoch t, $X(t)$ is an $n \times p$ (known) **design matrix**, and $u(t)$ is a stochastic error term with expectation zero.

So far the model is just the standard multi-dimensional regression model. However, the Kalman filter now makes a significant departure from that regression model. Whereas the latter regards the parameters $\beta(t)$ as **fixed** (though unknown), the Kalman filter regards them as generated by another stochastic process. Consequently, if it is to be fully defined, the model must give details of this **hyperprocess** by which the $\beta(t)$ are generated. This is as follows.

$$\beta(t) = H(t)\beta(t-1) + v(t), \qquad (10.3.1.2)$$

where $H(t)$ is a known $p \times p$ **transition matrix** governing the development of the expected values of the random parameters, and $v(t)$ is another stochastic error term with zero expectation.

For fairly obvious reasons, (10.3.1.1) is referred to as the **observation equation**, and (10.3.1.2) as the **system equation**.

The covariance matrices, $U(t)$ and $V(t)$, of $u(t)$ and $v(t)$ respectively are assumed known, and the following null-covariance assumptions are made:

$$C[u(s), u(t)] = C[v(s), v(t)]$$
$$= C[u(s), v(t)]$$
$$= 0, \qquad (10.3.1.3)$$

for all $s \neq t$, and the last equality holds for $s = t$ also.

It is now necessary to explain the application of the Kalman filter to claims reserving. The vector $Y(t)$ represents claims experience of period t. This may be simply the claim payments, development period by development period, arranged in a vector. Alternatively, these payments might be subjected to some straightforward transformation before their arrangement in a vector, e.g. adjusted to constant money values, or transformed to payments per claim finalized (as defined in Section 7.3.2). It might also be possible to subject $Y(t)$ to a slightly more exotic transformation, e.g. logarithmic or inverse sine.

The vector $\beta(t)$ is interpreted as the vector of parameters governing the claims payment process during period t. Equation (10.3.1.1) then requires that the expectation of the (possibly transformed) data $Y(t)$ be expressible as a linear function of $\beta(t)$. It may be noted at this point that a logarithmic transformation of $Y(t)$, as mentioned above, is likely to be useful in the case in which $E[Y(t)]$ is a product of parameters (e.g. the separation method (Section 7.1.5)).

This linearity requirement is probably the most restrictive feature of the Kalman filter in the claims reserving context. Equation (10.3.1.2), it is true, also requires linearity. However, the dependence in the system equation of $\beta(t)$ on $\beta(t-1)$ will usually be so uncertain in practice that one is likely to be satisfied with a linear representation of it.

De Jong and Zehnwirth (1983a) have suggested that, even when the claims model is not naturally represented by a general linear model (10.3.1.1), it may be forced into this form by the use of a set of **basis functions**. The meaning of this is essentially as follows. Suppose that $E[Y(t)]$ takes the form $f(\Omega, \Theta, t)$ (c.f. (4.2.5)), where Ω denotes a set of parameters and Θ a set of observables. Then it is assumed that, to an adequate degree of approximation, $f(\Omega, \Theta, t)$ can be expressed in the form:

$$f(\Omega, \Theta, t) = \sum \beta_r(t) f_r(\Theta_r, t), \qquad (10.3.1.4)$$

where the summation runs over r, and the f_r are functions dependent on the Θ_r, subsets of Θ.

When the model is expressed in this form, (10.3.1.1) takes the form (10.3.1.4). The $\beta_j(t)$ make up the vector $\beta(t)$. The functions f_r, evaluated for the relevant arguments, make up the design matrix $X(t)$.

10.3.2 *Estimation*

Let Y_t denote the vector $\{Y(1),\ldots,Y(t)\}^T$, i.e. the totality of observations up to epoch t (assuming the first observation to relate to epoch 1).

Let $\beta(t/s)$ denote the minimum mean square error estimator of $\beta(t)$, conditional on $Y(s)$, $s \leq t$, which is linear in Y_s. Let $C(t/s)$ denote $\mathrm{Var}[\beta(t/s)]$. Assume that initial estimates $\beta(0/0)$ and $C(0/0)$ of $\beta(0)$ and $C(0)$ are available.

The Kalman algorithm, which produces $\beta(t/s)$, is stated in terms of the **Kalman gain matrix**:

$$K(t) = C(t/t - 1)X^T(t) \{X(t)C(t/t - 1)X^T(t) + U(t)\}^{-1}. \qquad (10.3.2.1)$$

Then the algorithm is stated as follows:

Parameter estimates:

$$\beta(t/t - 1) = H(t)\beta(t - 1/t - 1); \qquad (10.3.2.2)$$

$$\beta(t/t) = \beta(t/t - 1) + K(t)\{Y(t) - X(t)\beta(t/t - 1)\}; \qquad (10.3.2.3)$$

Covariance estimates:

$$C(t/t - 1) = H(t)C(t - 1/t - 1)H^T(t) + V(t); \qquad (10.3.2.4)$$

$$C(t/t) = \{I - K(t)X(t)\}C(t/t - 1). \qquad (10.3.2.5)$$

It is apparent from these two pairs of equations that the Kalman algorithm is operated recursively. One begins with the $\beta(0/0)$ and $C(0/0)$ assumed above to exist. From these, $\beta(1/0)$ and $C(1/0)$ are computed by means of (10.3.2.2) and (10.3.2.4). Next the gain matrix $K(1)$ is computed by means of (10.3.2.1). Finally, $\beta(1/1)$ and $C(1/1)$ are computed by means of (10.3.2.3) and (10.3.2.5).

This recursion has a very handy computational property. Because of it, data and estimates relating to most past epochs can be discarded. After the calculation of $\beta(t - 1/t - 1)$ and $C(t - 1/t - 1)$, all that need be stored for the calculation of $\beta(t/t)$ and $C(t/t)$ are:

(i) the estimates $\beta(t - 1/t - 1)$ and $C(t - 1/t - 1)$;

(ii) the structure constants $H(t)$, $X(t)$, $U(t)$ and $V(t)$;

(iii) the new data $Y(t)$.

Consider the case in which each $H(t)$ is equal to the identity matrix, i.e. the parameters are not subject to any secular drift but receive random shocks between epochs (see (10.3.1.2)). Then (10.3.2.3) can be cast in the form:

$$X(t)\beta(t/t) = [I - X(t)K(t)]X(t)\beta(t/t - 1) + X(t)K(t)Y(t). \qquad (10.3.2.6)$$

Thus $\beta(t/t)$ can be read as the matrix version of a convex combination of:

(i) the previous estimate of the transformed parameters $X\beta$;

(ii) the latest vector of data.

Expression of $X(t)\beta(t/t)$ in the form (10.3.2.6) emphasises the connection between the Kalman filter and other linear Bayesian methodology, a matter to which we shall return in Section 10.3.4.

It has also the advantage of indicating the manner in which the method may assign greater weight to more recent than older data. If $X(t)K(t)$ is contemplated as a scalar in (10.3.2.6) between 0 and 1, then that equation shows how the new data vector $Y(t)$ is given less than full weight. Weight $X(t)K(t)$ is assigned. At the next step in the recursion, the calculation of $X(t+1)\beta(t+1/t+1)$, data $Y(t+1)$ are assigned weight $X(t+1)K(t+1)$, and that part of $Y(t)$ included in $X(t+1)\beta(t/t)$ weight $1 - X(t+1)K(t+1)$. This latter assignement therefore weights $Y(t)$ by

$$[1 - X(t+1)K(t+1)]X(t)K(t)].$$

Thus $Y(t+1)$ is assigned rather larger weight than the older $Y(t)$. Older data vectors, $Y(t-1)$, $Y(t-2)$, etc. are assigned progressively decreasing weights. Such procedures were foreshadowed in Section 10.1.

10.3.3 *Projection of outstanding claims*

Since Section 10.3.1 required that the data vector $Y(t)$ be some transformation of the observed claim payments, future claim payments will be estimable from estimates of future $Y(t)$ provided that the transformation from one to the other is invertible. It is possible therefore to focus attention on estimation of $Y(t)$ for future values of t. These in turn depend, via (10.3.1.1), on estimates of $\beta(t)$ for future values of t.

In the notation of Section 10.3.2 what are required are the $\beta(t/b)$ for $t > b$, the valuation date. By (10.3.1.2),

$$\beta(t/b) = H(t)\beta(t-1/b), \qquad \text{for } t > b \qquad (10.3.3.1)$$

is an unbiased estimate of $\beta(t)$. By extension,

$$\beta(t/b) = H(t)H(t-1)\ldots H(b+1)\beta(b/b), \qquad \text{for } t > b \qquad (10.3.3.2)$$

is an unbiased estimate of $\beta(t)$. It then follows from (10.3.1.1) that

$$Y(t/b) = X(t)H(t)H(t-1)\ldots H(b+1)\beta(b/b), \qquad \text{for } t > b \qquad (10.3.3.3)$$

is the required unbiased estimator of $Y(t)$.

Similarly, the covariance matrix associated with $\beta(t/b)$ can be computed. By (10.3.1.2),

$$\dot{C}(t/b) = \ddot{H}(t)C(\dot{t}-1/b)\ddot{H}^T(t) + V(t) \qquad \text{for } t > \dot{b}. \qquad (10.3.3.4)$$

The corresponding covariance matrix of $Y(t)$, conditional upon Y_b, is by (10.3.1.1.):

$$X(t)C(t/b)X^T(t) + U(t) \qquad \text{for } t > b. \qquad (10.3.3.5)$$

Thus the program for the projection of outstanding claims at valuation date b consists of the following steps for each value of $t = b+1,\, b+2$, etc.:

(i) compute $Y(t/b)$ by means of (10.3.3.3);

(ii) compute recursively, $C(t/b)$ by means of (10.3.3.4);

(iii) use the last result to compute $\text{Cov}[Y(t)/Y_b]$ according to (10.3.3.5);

(iv) estimate claim payments for experience period t by application of the appropriate transformation to $Y(t/b)$;

(v) compute the associated covariance matrix by application of the appropriate transformation to $\text{Cov}[Y(t)/Y_b]$.

10.3.4 Comment

It is probably useful to present an example of the application of the Kalman filter to claims reserving. We treat briefly the example first given in this context (de Jong and Zehnwirth, 1983a). They treat $E[C_{ij}^*]$ as a function of just two arguments, j and $j+i$ (which, to be consistent with the notation used in Sections 10.3.1 to 10.3.3, we write as t). The observed values c_{ij}^* for fixed $t = i+j$ form the vector $Y(t)$.

In these circumstances (10.3.1.4) reduces to:

$$E[C_{ij}^*] = \sum \beta_r(t) f_r(j,t), \qquad (10.3.4.1)$$

where the summation runs ove r. In fact, de Jong and Zehnwirth (1983a) use:

$$E[C_{ij}^*] = \sum \beta_r(t) f_r(j), \qquad (10.3.4.2)$$

For $f_r(j)$ they adopt the form:

$$f_r(j) = (j+1)^r \exp(-r). \qquad (10.3.4.3)$$

Those authors also consider a specific form taken by the system equation. An autoregressive process on $\beta(t)$ is considered. For full details, which involve one or two complexities, the reader is referred to the original paper.

The reason for absence of treatment of the initialization problem here is that it may be of somewhat less significance than appears from the de Jong and Zehnwirth paper. It is necessary to recognise that most practical situations will include the availability of data of at least several experience periods. Because of the operation of the gain matrix, as demonstrated in Section 10.3.2, the adopted value of $\beta(0/0)$ will become of very little relevance after a certain number of periods. In broad terms, the larger $C(0/0)$, the larger $K(0)$ (see (10.3.2.1) and (10.3.2.4)), and so the more rapidly will the influence of $\beta(0)$ on subsequent $\beta(t)$ diminish, at least for small t. Within reasonably wide limits, therefore, the value of $\beta(0)$ adopted will not matter greatly.

As pointed out in Section 10.3.1, it is an essential part of the Kalman filter, as applied to claims analysis, to assume that $E[Y(t)]$ is a linear function of the parameters in force during period t. This may not always be convenient. If the parametric expression chosen for $E[Y(t)]$ is not naturally linear, difficulties may arise. Section 10.3.1 refers to the use of basis functions as a device to overcome these difficulties. The versatility of the Kalman filter thus depends on the extent to which useful models may be put in linear parametric form.

Consider the tractability of the invariant see-saw model in this respect. Equation (8.2.1.15) shows the parametric form of the model. It is:

$$E_i(t_i(j), f_i(j)) = \beta(t_i(j)) + \gamma/f_i(j). \qquad (10.3.4.4)$$

As pointed out in (8.2.1.17), the function $\beta(.)$ in (10.3.4.4) may be represented in linear parametric form usually without any great loss of accuracy.

Suppose now that one wishes to include superimposed inflation in the model. For the sake of simplicity, suppose that superimposed inflation is to be assumed to occur at a constant rate in the model. Any more general assumption than this will only increase the difficulties, elicited below, to which the Kalman filter is subject. In this case the model (10.3.4.4) will be modified to:

$$E_i(t_i(j), f_i(j)) = \lambda^{i+j}[\beta(t_i(j)) + \gamma/f_i(j)], \qquad (10.3.4.5)$$

where λ denotes the annual factor by which claims increase on account of superimposed inflation.

With λ included as an extra parameter in the model, the latter no longer appears in linear parametric form as it did in (10.3.4.4). The multiplicative term λ^{i+j} suggests a logarithmic transformation. However, such a transformation leads to the appearance of a term:

$$\log[\beta(t_i(j)) + \gamma/f_i(j)]. \qquad (10.3.4.6)$$

The parameters appearing in this term now do so non-linearly. It is here that the basis functions should come into play. But it is not clear whether there are in fact basis functions which will provide the required linear representation of (10.3.4.6) of sufficient generality. Of course, if it were known that (10.4.3.6) were dominated by one or other of the terms appearing inside the square bracket, it would be possible to use an asymptotic linear expansion of (10.3.4.6). However, such dominance may not occur in the real-life case.

None of these last comments should be read as decrying the Kalman filter. It appears that the great majority of models can be absorbed within its structure without serious distortion. Nevertheless, this observation should be tempered by two others:

(i) care may be required in fitting the more complex models into the Kalman filter framework, or even in assesing whether this is feasible;

(ii) empirical experience of the operation of the filter in the claims analysis context is as yet largely lacking, and to this extent the reliability of the technique may be regarded as unproven.

It was announced in Section 10.2.4 that the autoregressive methods dealt with in Section 10.2 could be interpreted within the Kalman filter set-up.

Now that we have the advantage of the pairs of equations (10.1.1) (10.1.2) and (10.3.1.1), (10.3.1.2), such interpretation is simple. Indeed (10.1.2) is a special case of (10.3.1.2), while (10.1.1) is a special case of (10.3.1.1) with identity design matrix.

Thus, the autoregressive methods of Section 10.2 can be regarded as akin to the Kalman filter, but possibly without complete modelling of the stochastic error terms involved in (10.3.1.1) and (10.3.1.2).

Finally, we mention some theoretical results brought to light by Zehnwirth (1983a,b). He reveals interesting and illuminating connections between the Kalman filter, credibility theory and classical (Gauss-Markov) regression theory (1983b). the main result is that the Kalman filter may be interpreted within either a Bayesian or classical context since both approaches lead to the same algorithm.

Zehnwirth (1983a) uses this result to generalize the Kalman filter in two directions:

(i) to deal with cases in which the covariance matrix $U(t)$ is itself a random variable;

(ii) the random variables u and v are non-normal.

11.   OUTSTANDING REINSURANCE RECOVERIES

In most circumstances in which an investigation of outstanding claims is necessary, interest will be focused on **net** outstandings. The difference between gross and net claims will usually consist of some combination of the following:

(i) proportional reinsurance;

(ii) non-proportional reinsurance;

(iii) statutory reinsurance (i.e. compulsory reinsurance with state-administered schemes).

The absence from the foregoing chapters of any comment on whether the methods of analysis and projection discussed in them should be applied to gross or net claims data constitutes a rather conspicuous omission. It is proposed to rectify this now, and in the process comment briefly on the estimation of future reinsurance recoveries.

It is obvious that, if only proportional reinsurance affected a portfolio, it would matter not a jot whether one analysed gross or net data; each is just a rescaled version of the other. Equally obviously, the same is not true of non-proportional reinsurance.

Consider, therefore, a portfolio affected by non-proportional reinsurance. Should analysis be based on gross or net claims data? The two possibilities are:

(i) analyse past and project future net claims experience, in which case the projection provides exactly what is required;

(ii) analyse past and project gross claims experience, in which case it is necessary to convert the projected gross experience to the corresponding net.

It is tempting to select the former option as the more direct. As will be seen, however, this is not the best course.

As an example of non-proportional reinsurance we shall consider **excess-of-loss** reinsurance. Such a consideration is not completely general, but will quite suffice to illustrate the points involved.

With excess-of-loss protection, a gross claim amount of x generates a liability to the direct insurer of $\min(x, R)$, where R is an amount which is independent of x and is called the **retention, deductible or excess point**. Clearly, the net claims experience of the direct insurer is a function of not only the gross experience but also the retention. The retention is of course likely to change from time to time. Therefore, it is quite possible for different periods of origin to be subject to identical gross experiences but for the corresponding net experiences to differ radically if associated with different retentions.

It follows that a model of net claims experience would need to incorporate a model of the corresponding gross experience plus the interaction with the excess-of-loss retention. Hence, gross claims experience is the more direct to model and the methods of analysis and projection discussed in preceding chapters should be applied to it.

The catch in doing this has been noted above. It is that a method of converting projected gross future experience to net is required. This is not a simple matter as the action of the excess-of-loss reinsurance on an individual claim is strikingly nonlinear, which is particularly awkward.

There appear to be two courses open for devising the required adjustment:

(i) obtain statistical estimates of individual claims and then apply the retention to them one by one according to the formula given above for the action of the retention;

(ii) obtain statistical estimates of gross outstanding claims **en masse**, obtain an estimate of the distribution of individual claim sizes, and use both of these items to estimate outstanding reinsurance recoveries in respect of gross outstanding claims.

The adjustment from gross to net is much simpler in case (i). However, the range of techniques available for the production of statistical estimates of gross outstandings in respect of individual claims is limited. This survey refers to only one such method (Section 9.3). It may also be noted that that method is quite demanding in terms of data; and it would appear to be in the nature of methods which produce statistical estimates in respect of individual claims that some input in respect of individual claims will need to be provided.

An outline of the procedure for (ii) is as follows. Consider a single period of occurrence, and let the distribution function of sizes of individual outstanding claims be denoted by $F(.)$. Then the amount of net outstanding claims is given by:

$$\int_0^\infty \min(x, R)dF(x) = \int_0^R xdF(x) + R[1 - F(R)]. \qquad (11.1)$$

There is no great difficulty in the application of (11.1). There may be considerable difficulty, probably due to lack of data, in obtaining an estimate of $F(.)$ in which much reliance can be placed. In practice the situation is likely to be further complicated by the effect of inflation on outstanding claims and the interaction of this with the retention.

It is worth emphasising that, in the case of adjustment of a bulk estimate of gross outstandings to the corresponding net figure, some calculation at least resembling (11.1) is necessary. A method sometimes used consists of adjusting the gross statistical estimates in the ratio:

$$\frac{\text{net physical estimates}}{\text{gross physical estimates.}} \qquad (11.2)$$

The circumstances under which (11.2) provides a correct adjustment would be rare. The reason for its inaccuracy can be seen by reference to a single claim. If the amount of the claim is above the retention, a change in its gross amount does not produce a proportionate change in the corresponding net amount.

The situation is investigated in some generality by Taylor (1982b). He shows that, if the ratio of true outstandings to physical estimates is the same for all claims, then (11.2):

(i) overstates net outstandings when physical estimates fall short of the corresponding actual outstandings;

(ii) understates net outstandings when physical estimates exceed the corresponding actual outstandings.

This can be stated briefly as:

> *Whatever adjustment is required (up or down) to bring gross physical estimates into line with the corresponding true outstandings, the proportionate adjustment to net physical estimates will be greater.*

Taylor (1982b) also gives a method for carrying this principle into practice. The method is based on the assumption stated above and the further assumption that claim size distribution comes from a particular family.

The family of available distributions is reasonably wide, and it seems unlikely that the accuracy of the method suffers greatly from the restriction on claim size distribution.

However, the earlier assumption of equal degrees of inaccuracy in all physical estimates can be troublesome. It is possible, and desirable, to deal with each period of origin separately. This results in the assumption in question being applied at least to claims of equal age and subject to the same retention. Nevertheless, it is quite conceivable that, on average, large physical estimates (which are associated with **recognised** large claims) are overstated while smaller physical estimates (some of which may be associated with **unrecognised** large claims) are understated; or at least overstated to a lesser degree than are large estimates.

Solution of this problem is difficult in the absence of further data. Taylor's method makes use of only:

(i) statistical estimates of gross outstandings;

(ii) gross and net physical estimates;

(iii) number of reported claims outstanding;

in respect of each period of origin. It is not surprising that a method based on such restricted data involves somewhat restrictive assumptions.

12.   ADDITIONAL GENERAL REMARKS
ON CLAIMS MODELLING

In a couple of interesting papers Albrecht (1983a, b) attempts to establish a body of mathematical statistical theory for a reasonably general risk model. This theory is then applied to a partial consideration of the claims reserving problem.

The consideration of the latter problem is limited in Albrecht (1983b). The only specific model with which it deals is that which underlies the separation method (Section 7.1.5). Nonetheless, many of the ideas expounded in the paper are adaptable to other models.

Albrecht's basic thrust is to represent risk models, wherever possible, by parametric regression models. He then develops the theory for such models. Within this context, he consider such matters as maximum likelihood estimation, likelihood ratio testing, residual analysis, and other such classical statistical methodology.

His final advice on claims modelling is contained in the following passage (Albrecht, 1983b):

> " *First try a parametric model because it allows the investigation of its goodness-of-fit to the data; if the statistical analysis shows that one cannot adequately describe the data with a parametric model, try the non-parametric. What then is lacking is a test , which helps to decide if the non-parametric model fits the data better than the parametric one.*"

We accept this as sensible advice. Indeed, the availability of devices for assessing goodness-of-fit is not useful in its own right, but is particularly useful in providing a rigorous basis on which statistically insignificant explanatory variables included in the model may be discarded, and greater parsimony of parameters achieved.

Comment on this matter has already appeared in Section 8.2.4 in connection with the see-saw model. It became apparent in that section that, when a parametric model of that sort is used, the number of parameters required by the model is likely to be less (often substantially so) than required by most or all of the usual non-parametric models, e.g. chain ladder (Section 7.1.1), separation (7.1.5), etc. Specific comparisons of models in this respect are found in Taylor (1982a).

It seems an inevitable conclusion of this line of reasoning that non-parametric models are highly likely to be inefficient forecasters. Because they incorporate no measures of goodness-of-fit nor significance testing of explanatory variables, they usually include more parameters than are necessary to model the particular aspect of the claims process under consideration. The result of this, as explained in Section 8.2.4, is the generation of large estimation errors, and hence inefficient forecasting.

It is perhaps worth mentioning here that de Vylder (1978) has proposed, in a particular context, the fitting of a model by least squares. Once again, the particular model considered perhaps contains less structure than is needed in practice. However, the essential idea of the paper is to encourage a recognition of the stochasticity of the claims process in model construction and fitting.

It is interesting to note that, independently of de Vylder's suggestions, the evolution of claims modelling appears to have proceeded along the path he recommends. One may observe that, among the various stochastic methods proposed, most do in fact use some version of least squares fitting. Witness, for example, the stochastic payments per unit of risk method (Section 8.1), see-saw method (Section 8.2), stochastic chain ladder (Section 9.1), stochastic separation method (Section 9.2), autoregressive methods (Section 10.2), and Kalman filter (Section 10.3).

13. ESTIMATION OF SECOND MOMENTS
OF OUTSTANDING CLAIMS

Section 1.3 argued strongly in favour of:

(i) a recognition in methodology of the fundamentally stochastic nature of the claims process;

(ii) the accompaniment, wherever possible, of an estimate of outstanding claims by an estimate of the degree of uncertainty involved in that estimate, i.e. the estimated second moment.

One needs to be quite clear as to precisely what this second moment is. It is in fact the **estimated variance of the estimated mean outstanding claims**, i.e. an estimate of the mean square deviation of the estimate of outstanding claims from the actual (unknown) amount.

The required recognition of stochasticity is built into the stochastic models of Chapters 8, 9 and 10. Those chapters provide little guidance as to the translation of the stochastic component of the model into an estimate of the second moment associated with an estimate of outstanding claims.

In this review we have adopted the stance that our purpose is to present the various methods available for obtaining the primary estimate (i.e. first moment) of outstanding claims. It is not intended that this approach should in any way be taken as a retreat from the assertion that an estimate of outstanding claims unaccompanied by a reasonably precise statement about the associated uncertainty constitutes incomplete advice. However, an already long review would have been made even longer by an attempt to include details of the computation of second moments.

In most of the cases of stochastic models dealt with earlier the computation of second moments is reasonably straightforward in concept though likely to require tedious and unattractive algebra. The interested reader will usually find most of the detail in the original references. For example, Taylor and Ashe (1983) give a fairly general outline of the calculations involved in connection with the invariant see-saw method, and trace through a numerical example to its conclusion.

Despite the relative straightforwardness in conceptual terms of the estimation of second moments, there are one or two points of slight subtlety which warrant mention here.

Firstly, there is the matter of the various types of error inherent in the forecast of outstanding claims (and indeed in the forecasts of many different kinds of model). These are classified by Bartholomew (1975) as:

(i) model specification error;

(ii) estimation error;

(iii) statistical error.

The first of these refers to the fact that the model chosen may not have the appropriate algebraic form. There is not a great deal that can be done in any formal way in order to make allowance for this in the estimated second moments. One might think in terms of some probability space of possible models, with a stochastic hyperprocess according to which the model actually used is selected from that space. However, lack of information about that hyperprocess will usually militate against much useful work along these lines towards the measurement of specification error.

Error (ii) refers to the fact that, by the stochastic nature of the claims process, there will be uncertainty associated with the estimates of model parameters even given that Error (i) is nil. Obviously, this uncertainty will generate uncertainty in the forecasts of outstanding claims.

Error (iii) refers to the inherently stochastic nature of the future claims process, even given its governing parameters. That is to say, even if Errors (i) and (ii) could be reduced to nil, there would still remain some uncertainty in estimates of outstanding claims.

Errors (ii) and (iii) are dealt with quantitatively by Seber (1977, pp.364-366). He shows that, as the number of parameters involved in a model (he considers linear models) increases, two things happen. Firstly, the goodness-of-fit of the model to the data improves. The interpretation of this (remember that there is assumed to be no specification error) is a reduction in the intrinsic variability of the claims process. This contributes to a diminution in the estimated uncertainty associated with the estimated outstanding claims. But secondly, because each parameter of the model must be estimated, and because there is uncertainty associated with each such estimate, the inclusion of each additional parameter in the model contributes to an increase in the total second moment.

There is therefore an optimum number of parameters for inclusion in the model such that the sum of the above two contributions to the total variance of estimated outstanding claims is minimized. This optimum may be achieved by the use of Mallow's C_p statistic (Seber, 1977).

One further point, perhaps obvious but worthy of mention nonetheless, is that the stochastic components included in the models of Sections 8, 9 and 10 allow for stochasticity in respect of only the claims process itself after considerations related to inflation, investment return and expenses have been eliminated. Thus when these stochastic components of the model are carried into estimation of variances, the latter measure the uncertainty in the estimates of outstanding claims as expressed **in real terms**.

When these estimates are converted into estimates of outstanding claims which include allowance for future claims escalation, investment return and expenses, the associated uncertainty is increased by the uncertainty inherent in the estimates of these additional parameters.

Strictly therefore, additional stochastic processes governing the development through time of these additional parameters need to be specified and investigated. However, there will usually be independence between these additional processes and the central one describing the claims process. Consequently, the problems of modelling, forecasting and estimating variances in respect of the two separate processes (claims process and additional parameters) can be decoupled and dealt with quite independently. The respective uncertainties of the two processes can be aggregated at the final stage.

For these reasons, the questions arising out of the modelling of future inflation, investment return and expenses have been regarded as outside the scope of this work.

14.   CHOICE OF FINAL ESTIMATES
OF OUTSTANDING CLAIMS

Chapters 7 to 10 presented various models of the claim process and the associated techniques of using those models to form estimates of outstanding claims. Often it will be possible to apply several of these methods to a single data set.

Various items of the literature recommend the use of several methods (e.g. Taylor and Matthews, 1977), the so-called "battery of methods". The intention is that one then examine the collection of different estimates obtained, and somehow select one's final adopted estimate as some sort of compromise between them. This raises two questions:

(i) precisely what is to be gained by such an approach?

(ii) how should the choice of final estimates of outstanding claims be made when all the results of the battery of methods have been surveyed?

As regards question (i) the possibility (indeed the near certainty) of specification error (see Chapter 13 for discussion) should be remembered. Each model is sensitive to particular factors and less sensitive to others. Usually, the investigator will not know in advance which is the correct model (or nearest thereto) to use. The reactions, or absence of them, of particular models to specific features of the data may provide some clues in this direction.

Naturally, the data themselves should be used as far as possible to screen out inappropriate models. It is for this reason, in the author's opinion, that examination of a large set of statistics derived from the raw data is an essential. Different statistics, like different models, will be sensitive to different features of the data. The greater the set of (essentially different) statistics tabulated and examined, the greater the chance that the particular features peculiar to the data set under consideration will be identified.

Thus, for example, tabulation of speeds of finalization (Section 7.3.2.1) will indicate whether any changes in these speeds have occurred. Tabulation of payments per claim finalized (Section 7.3.2.1) in cases where there have been changes in speed of finalization will indicate whether or not this statistic is robust against such changes. Tabulation of development factors (Section 7.2.3.1) will indicate any sudden or gradual change in the strength of physical estimates.

However, even after all apparently relevant tabulations have been carried out and examined, the situation may well be still far from clear as to the most appropriate model. It is possible, and perhaps useful, to view this situation in a framework expressed in terms of more formal concepts.

Chapter 13 introduced the idea of a stochastic hyperprocess according to which Nature selects the precise model followed by the claim process. One may think, in Bayesian terms, of a prior distribution on the hyperprocess. At the commencement of an investigation of outstanding claims this prior may reflect little more than total ignorance as to which model Nature will have selected in this case. The result of examination of tabulations of statistics will be to shift the prior by assigning, on the basis of the data, greater weight to some models and less weight to others.

However, it is unlikely in practice that the conclusion to be drawn from examining the data is so unequivocal as to lead to an assignment of unit probability to one particular model and zero probability to all others. In these circumstances, simple application of Bayes theorem shows that the posterior estimate of outstanding claims will be a probability-weighted blend of the models which have not been rejected totally.

We now turn to question (ii) raised above. In principle, this has already been answered in the preceding paragraph where the application of Bayes theorem is discussed. However, the use of this theorem requires an explicit statement of the prior. While the concept of a prior is useful in the argument given above, it is not especially edifying for the practical computations involved in forming the blend discussed there. In practice, one will usually still have only the most vaguely formed notion of one's prior as a result of an examination of statistics.

But carrying out projections on the basis of those models which have not been rejected outright can provide some useful information as to a reasonable prior. The reason for this is as follows.

If, instead of merely "examining" the statistics, one were to attempt a more formal assessment of the prior on the basis of the data, such assessment would need to involve tests of goodness-of-fit of the various models to the data. The better the goodness-of-fit, however "better" be defined, the greater might be thought the prior probability to be assigned to that model.

Now, as has been seen in the discussion of estimation error and statistical error (Chapter 13), simple goodness-of-fit will not necessarily provide a good test of the realism of a model. The reason is that it leaves estimation error out of account. But estimation error will be taken into account by the estimated variance associated with a projection of outstanding claims by the model in question.

Thus, we finally reach the conclusion that the prior description over the various available models might reasonably be chosen by reference to the estimated variances associated with the estimates of outstanding claims produced by those models. A practical, if somewhat crude, measure might be to adopt prior probabilities of the different models as inversely proportional to the estimated variances.

Such an approach represents no more than a particular formalization of the observation made in Section 1.3 that "Models which provide a truer representation of the actual process will tend to reduce the margin of uncertainty associated with the estimate".

It may not be necessary (or appropriate) to assume that the same blend of different models applies to all sections of the experience. For example, if the experience has been analysed, and outstanding claims estimated, according to the various periods of origin, then it may be appropriate to adopt a different prior (each one chosen in accordance with the principles described above) for each different period of origin.

It is easy to summon up practical circumstances in which such a procedure would be entirely in agreement with intuition. For example, suppose it were known from experience of a particular portfolio that physical estimates tended to be very reliable more than five years after the year of origin, but that they were quite unreliable at the end of the year of origin and the year following.

In these circumstances, the projected physical estimates method (Section 7.2.3) would seem intuitively the most superior for application to the old periods of origin, but quite unsuitable for the recent ones.

Such an intuitive choice would be supported by the more formal selection procedure outlined above. For the reliability of physical estimates in respect of old claims would manifest itself in a low dispersion of development factors, and hence in estimated outstanding claims; whereas the opposite would be true in respect of the recent periods of origin.

Two final points should be discussed in relation to the formalized procedure given above for blending the various estimates of outstanding claims. The following comments apply to any formal blending procedure which takes into account the estimated variances associated with the different estimates of outstanding claims. Their relevance is not limited to the particular case referred to above in which the weight assigned to a given estimate is proportional to the reciprocal of the associated variance.

Firstly, it must be realised that any such procedure is almost bound to be rough. As described, it takes no account of the correlations which undoubtedly exist between the results of distinct methods (conditional upon the model selected by Nature). There appears to be little hope of any accurate measurement of such correlations, so that the final selection procedure is likely to remain necessarily rough. Naturally though, this type of difficulty is not any sort of justification for a failure to adopt some means of blending results which is sensible in the light of the statistics which **are** available.

Secondly, there will usually be some constraints which need to be observed in the choice of final estimates and balanced against the guidance provided by the estimated variances of the different estimates as discussed above. For example, it would be most bewildering, and almost certainly unreasonable, if the final estimates for periods of origin i, $i + 1$, $i + 2$ and $i + 3$ were 75 per cent, 135 per cent, 60 per cent and 140 per cent respectively of the corresponding physical estimates. There would usually be no apparent reason for the physical estimates to show the excesses and shortfalls suggested by these results., Thus there is a constraint to be observed, roughly of the form that the ratio of physical estimates to final statistical estimates should be a relatively smooth function of period of origin. A second constraint might, for example, seek to limit in some way the variation in average claim size (in constant dollar values) with varying period of origin.

15.   STABILITY VERSUS SENSITIVITY
IN CLAIMS ESTIMATION PROCEDURES

Up to this point the problem of estimation of outstanding claims has been approached purely in the manner in which a professional statistician would normally approach a problem. That is to say, the problem has been treated as one requiring a "best" or "central" estimate.

Although it may sound peculiar, it is by no means self-evident to all non-life actuaries that such is a proper treatment of the problem.

For example, Benjamin (1976, pp.265-26) finds it appropriate **"to express a personal preference which is for the implicit method of setting a margin in the valuation basis rather than an explicit margin over and above a valuation basis set according to 'anticipated actual' [experience]"**. Various reasons are given for this view in the passage referred to and on pp.238-239. To a large extent the argument is roughly that the "anticipated actual" experience of the future will not be known with accuracy, and so an intended explicit margin of conservatism in estimated outstanding claims is likely to prove inaccurate also. It is suggested that the basis on which the outstanding claims are evaluated be chosen sufficiently conservatively that one can be certain that it contains a margin. No attempt is made to obtain a realistic estimate of the amount of outstanding claims, whereupon the margin of conservatism is an implicit one.

Similar sentiments can be found in Ryder (1976, p68):

> " *We cannot predict the future. What we do instead is to make a forecast of the future by extending observable trends on the recognized* **naive** *assumption that the future will be something like the past. And then we look for the inevitable forecasting errors. Possibly the most important area of actuarial expertise is the design of systems to modify the actuarial model of a process when these naive forecasts start their inevitable divergence from reality".*

This line of argument is typical of a theme which runs through the contributions made to the subject by Ryder in particular but also by other authors. A corollary of this type of argument is that, since one cannot expect to obtain accurate estimates of outstanding claims, one might as well take advantage of that fact and adopt a mechanism which produces smoothly changing "estimates" from period to period.

A similar conclusion is often reached on the basis of Benjamin's argument in favour of implicit margins. The conclusion is that, in claims estimation, stability of the estimates (i.e. a tendency for estimates to be self-consistent from period to period) should largely override considerations of sensitivity of estimation procedures to changes and trends in the data; and largely override considerations of accuracy of the estimates (which, admittedly, proponents of the stability philosophy usually claim to be unachievable in any case).

The difficulty with the implicit margin approach is, of course, that the recipient of actuarial advice based on it forms one of two views:

(i) due to a misunderstanding of the advice, he accepts the implicitly conservative estimates as accurate;

(ii) he understands the estimates to be conservative but, by the nature of the implicit conservatism, he has no advice as to what margin they contain.

Alternative (i) seems deplorably likely to occur in practice. However, with careful explanation it **should** be possible to eliminate this case. Alternative (ii) is much more problematic. The insurer has not in fact been given an unbiased estimate of his liabilities. He knows that the estimate he has been given is biased towards conservatism but not by how much. And the implicit margin approach does not permit his knowledge to progress beyond this point. For any attempt to quantify the degree of conservatism necessarily requires unbiased estimation of outstanding claims which immediately leads back to the explicit margin approach.

Ryder's argument is in a way a little more subtle. The argument is essentially that the entire concept of unbiased estimates of outstanding claims is a philosophical nonsense, and so perseverance in a quest for such estimates is futile and unjustified. The issues raised here lie at the very foundations of statistical theory, and it is not appropriate to go into them in a review such as this. Perhaps it suffices to say that there is a considerable body of opinion to the contrary, and leave readers to decide this fundamental issue for themselves. For our part, we proceed below (as indeed we have proceeded for a good deal of the above) on the assumption that the concept of unbiased estimates of outstanding claims is at least logically sensible even if difficult to obtain in practice.

It is a commonplace that the outstanding claims item in an insurer's balance sheet will often be of such magnitude that relatively small variations in it can alter a year's profit by a very large proportion. Consequently, it must be admitted that one of the desiderata to be observed in establishing a provision for outstanding claims is that the profit flowing from the estimates should be relatively stable from year to year. At this point, however, this is stated not as an absolute requirement but only as a desideratum to be balanced against the other main desideratum, that the amount of outstanding claims be determined as accurately as is possible. In order to decide how to strike a balance between these two, largely conflicting, objectives it is perhaps useful to consider exactly what penalties are suffered by managements which do not have access to accurate estimates of outstanding claims. There are three main areas which come to mind immediately as ones in which penalties will in fact accrue:

(i) rating of premiums;

(ii) disposition of assets;

(iii) consideration of dividend declaration.

We shall return shortly to a discussion of these three aspects of an insurance business. First, however, it may be suggested that, given that there exist **any** areas of an insurance operation likely to suffer from an inbuilt bias in actuarial estimates of outstanding claims, serious ethical problems could arise for professional actuaries in the giving of advice involving such estimates.

If such estimates are to be given to management, it is presumably necessary to explain the existence and nature of the inbuilt bias very carefully. Otherwise, it could easily be said that the advice proffered was misleading; that the actuary was asked to estimate one thing, and in fact estimated another without making that clear.

The fact that the estimates involved were thought to be conservative would not necessarily be a redeeming feature. Insurance companies can, in certain circumstances (some of which are mentioned briefly below), suffer from excessive conservatism just as they can from imprudence.

Let us return now to items (i), (ii) and (iii) above. As far as premium rating is concerned, it seems quite reckless for an insurer not to obtain the best available estimates of outstanding claims. The possible consequence of not doing so is ignorance of incipient trends in claim costs, with consequent estimation of premiums for new policies either at inadequate levels or at over-adequate levels which prevent effective competition. The fact is that circumstances do change from time to time, and the actuary should be alert to this fact and ready to respond, in premium rating, to such changes as they are identified.

As regards (ii), the insurer's investment policy may require that investments be chosen having regard to the profile of future cash flows. These will not be known with any accuracy if estimated by means of a conservative, but otherwise partly arbitrary model.

Consider (iii). Wrong decisions on this question, e.g. to pay a dividend when a true picture of solvency would militate against it, or not to pay a dividend because of a misguided notion that solvency is inadequate, represent perhaps the avenues of most immediate retribution of a malevolent Nature against management. It is clearly the case that ignorance of the true level of outstandings is likely to result in misstatement of the Company's liabilities and solvency margin, with the possible distortion of decisions as to dividend declaration of which the examples given above are the extreme ones.

In any event, from a legalistic viewpoint, there is probably little scope for departing from attempts at unbiased estimates. Accounting practice requires that accounts present "a true and fair view". It is difficult to argue that the balance sheet does this if outstanding claims are quantified at other than the most accurate estimates which can be obtained.

There is a partial reconciliation of the two objectives of accuracy and stability. If an insurer adopts a stable basis of estimation of outstanding claims from year to year which is sufficiently conservative, then, except in extreme circumstances, there need to be no concern about inadequacy of such estimates. Thus, an appropriate procedure might be to:

(i) obtain "best estimates" of outstandings at each balance date;

(ii) compare these estimates with estimates obtained on the "stable basis" to ensure adequacy of the latter;

(iii) show the results of the "stable basis" in the accounts;

(iv) for management accounting purposes, regard the outstandings as shown in the accounts as consisting of:

   (a) the real outstandings;

PLUS (b) some kind of equalization reserve.

The claims equalization reserve would be regarded as a hidden addition to the solvency margin.

The reason that this is only a partial reconciliation is that, strictly, claims equalization reserves are not exempt from tax as are outstanding claims provisions. However, in present Australian practice this point is rather academic. In practice, it is usually possible to proceed as described above and, in conformity with Step (iii), obtain full tax relief on the outstanding claims provision (including equalization reserve) shown in the accounts.

Of course, the disadvantage associated with the above procedure is that it leads to an understatement of the insurer's net tangible assets. This must be viewed as the price to be paid to ensure (relatively) stable emerging profit from year to year.

The procedure described above is one of **explicit margins** from a management accounting (though not a public accounting) viewpoint. That is, a conservative provision for outstanding claims is established, but the margin of conservatism is quantified as precisely as possible.

16.   IBNR CLAIMS

All of the models discussed in this review are framed in terms of "periods of origin". Although this terminology is rather non-committal as to its precise meaning, it has been implicitly assumed in places that "periods of origin" may be read as "periods of occurrence". This is indeed consistent with the most common practice, but by no means a logical necessity.

All of the methods discussed above are equally applicable to the case in which "periods of origin" means "periods of notification".

Although the period of occurrence and period of notification models are algebraically identical, there is an essential difference in their practical usage. This has already been touched upon in Section 9.3.4. The difference arises from the fact that when the latter type of model is used, and consequently outstandings are estimated notification period by notification period, it follows immediately that no estimates are obtained in respect of unreported (IBNR) claims. This requires that a separate estimate of the amount of IBNR claims be obtained.

Even when outstandings have been estimated by period of occurrence, so that the IBNR's of each period of occurrence are automatically included, an insurer may still wish to obtain estimates of the IBNR content of the estimates. This might be required, for example, in order that a valid comparison be made between the actuarial and physical estimates (the latter of which, by their nature, exclude IBNR's); or alternatively, it might be required in order that reasonable allowance be made for IBNR's in premium rating formulas based on physical estimates.

The separate evaluation of IBNR claims will normally consist of the following steps:

(i) estimate the number of IBNR claims,

(ii) estimate the average size of reported claims,

(iii) determine how the average size of IBNR's, relative to that of reported claims, varies according to the delay from date of occurrence to date of reporting,

(iv) combine (i), (ii) and (iii) to yield an estimate of the amount of IBNR claims.

It would be usual for the above steps to be carried out separately for individual periods of origin. An estimate of the IBNR claims associated with each period of origin is then obtained.

Because (ii) depends directly on the amount of claims incurred in the period of origin in question, the above steps are equivalent to the formula:

Amount of IBNR claims = Amount of claims incurred

×

IBNR factor

This approach is to be found in Skurnick (1973, p.36) who attribute it in turn to Bornhuetter and Ferguson (1972).

As remarked in Section 8.2.4, the estimation of the **number** of IBNR claims will not, in most cases (but with some notable exceptions), present great difficulty. Furthermore, step (ii) can be performed immediately in that:

EITHER a period of occurrence model will have been used, in which case estimated average claim sizes will be available in respect of the various periods of occurrence;

OR a period of notification model will have been used, in which case estimated average claim sizes will be available in respect of the various periods of notification;

This means that step (ii) can also be carried out without difficulty.

The problems arise at step (iii).   Since conclusions are required concerning differing delays between occurrence and notification, and are required separately in respect of different periods of origin (whichever definition of this is currently operating), it is apparent that what is required in principle is some sort of model of the claim payments $C_{.ikj..}$, i.e. according to periods of occurrence, notification and payment simultaneously.

It is not satisfactory, for example, to assume that average claim size is unaffected by the delay between occurrence and notification. It is perfectly possible that differences in this delay create fundamental differences in the conditions affecting different claims, which impinge in turn on the average sizes of those claims. For example, it is common in Employers Liability insurance to find that, whereas many claims notified after a very short delay involve only trivial claim amounts (a single medical consultation perhaps), the proportion of such cases is much smaller among those notified after a delay of say 2 years. Moreover, these later-reported claims tend to include a larger proportion of claims which were originally thought by the claimants to be unimportant but have subsequently deteriorated to a state of seriousness.

A contrary example is sometimes provided by Third Party bodily injury insurance. As such claims arise from motor vehicle accidents, it is sometimes possible for the insurer to establish arrangements with police and hospitals according to which those organisations notify the insurer of serious accidents virtually immediately. The result of such arrangements is the notification of the more serious claims to the insurer rather earlier than average. In this case average claim size tends to be decreasing function of delay from occurrence to notification.

While models of the $C_{.ikj..}$, as required above, are perfectly feasible, they are not to be found in the literature. The primary reason for this is probably that data are so seldom available in the form of the 3-way tabulation required by $C_{..ikj..}$.

In the case in which the $C_{..ikj..}$ are not avalilable, a hint as to the relation between delay in notification and average claim size may be obtained by an examination of the physical estimates. If, for example, newly-notified cases (i.e. cases notified in the last experience period) are recorded according to the delay in notification, then it will be possible to examine their average sizes on the assumption that their physical estimates all require adjustment by some common factor. The assumption of the common factor might be justified on the ground that the quality of physical estimates is a function of the time elapsed since notification, this latter being perceived as a proxy for the amount of information accumulated in respect of a claim as relevant to the physical assessment of its ultimate cost.

Such a procedure might be used in the absence of a better one based on the data available. It is, however, fraught with danger, since the assumption of the common factor may be totally wrong. It might well be the case, for example, that the mere lapse of time after the occurrence of an event generating a claim permits stabilization of the claimant's medical condition and so allows relatively accurate estimation of the cost of the claim immediately it is reported even though this might take place after a considerable delay. In this case, which is probably generally realistic, the quality of a physical estimate might be regarded as a random variable whose mean value is a function of both time elapsed since occurrence and time elapsed since notification of the claim.

APPENDIX A

It is necessary to obtain an approximate expression for the variance $V[X/Y]$ where X, Y are stochastically independent variates.

Now

$$V[X/Y] = V[X]V[1/Y] + V[X]E^2[1/Y] + E^2[X]V[1/Y]. \qquad (A.1)$$

Using a truncated Taylor series, we obtain:

$$E[f(Y)] \approx E[f(\mu_y) + (Y - \mu_y)f'(\mu_y) + \frac{1}{2}(y - \mu_y)^2 f''(\mu_y)]$$

$$= f(\mu_y) + \frac{1}{2}\sigma_y^2 f''(\mu_y), \qquad (A.2)$$

where

$$\mu_y = E[Y], \qquad \sigma_y^2 = V[Y].$$

Similarly,

$$V[f(Y)] = E[f(Y) - E[f(y)]]^2$$

$$= E[-\frac{1}{2}\sigma_y^2 f''(\mu_y) + (Y - \mu_y)f'(\mu_y) + \ldots]^2 \quad \text{(by (A.2))}$$

$$\approx \sigma_y^2 [f'(\mu_y)]^2 \qquad (A.3)$$

By (A.2) and (A.3),

$$E[1/Y] \approx \mu_y^{-1} + \sigma_y^2 \mu_y^{-3} = \mu_y^{-1}(1 + w_y), \qquad (A.4)$$

$$V[1/Y] \approx \sigma_y^{-2} \mu_y^{-4} = \mu_y^{-2} w_y, \qquad (A.5)$$

where $w_y = \sigma_y^2 / \mu_y^2$.

Substitution of (A.4) and (A.5) in (A.1) yields:

$$V[X/Y] = w_x w_y (\mu_x^2 / \mu_y^2) + w_x (1 + w_y)^2 (\mu_x^2 / \mu_y^2) + w_y^2 (\mu_x^2 / \mu_y^2). \qquad (A.6)$$

When

$$\mu_x = \mu_y = \mu, \qquad \text{and } \sigma_x^2 = K\sigma_y^2, \quad K \text{ const.}, \qquad (A.7)$$

then $w_x = Kw_y = Kw$ say, and so (A.6) becomes:

$$V[X/Y] = Kw^2 + Kw(1 + w)^2 + w. \qquad (A.8)$$

REFERENCES

GLOSSARY

AB Astin Bulletin

IAAGIS Institute of Actuaries of Australia General Insurance Seminar

JIA Journal of the Institute of Actuaries

PCAS Proceedings of the Casualty Actuarial Society

TIAA Transactions of the Institute of Actuaries of Australia

IME Insurance: Mathematics and Economics

Abbott,W.M., Clarke,T.G., Hey,G.B. and Treen,W.R. (1974). Some thoughts on technical reserves and statutory returns in general insurance. JIA, 101, 217-265.

Albrecht, P. (1983a). Parametric multiple regression risk models: theory and statistical analysis. Insurance: mathematics and economics, 2, 49-66. Paper presented to the 16th Astin Colloquium, Liege, Belgium, September 1982.

Albrecht, P. (1983b). Parametric multiple regression risk models: some connections with IBNR. Insurance: mathematics and economics, 2, 69-72. Paper presented to the 16th Astin Colloquium, Liege, Belgium, September 1982.

Anderssen,R.S. and de Hoog,F.R. (eds.). (1982). The application of mathematics in industry. Martinus Nijhoff Publishers.

Andrews,J.G. and McLone,R.R. (eds.) (1976). Mathematical modelling. Butterworths.

Ashe,F.R. (1982). A relationship between outstanding claims and speeds of finalization. IAAGIS,3, 140-154.

Baker, R.J. and Nelder, J.A. (1978). The GLIM system, Release 3. Generalized Linear Interactive Modelling. Numerical Algorithms Group, 7 Banbury Road, Oxford, U.K.

Bartholomew, D.J. (1975). Errors of prediction in Markov chains. Journal of the Royal Statistical Society, Series B, 37, 444-456.

Beard, R.E. (1974). Claims provisions for non-life insurance business — some historical, theoretical and practical aspects. Institute of mathematics and its Applications, Symposium Proceedings, 3,15.

Benjamin, S. (1976). Profit and other financial concepts in insurance. JIA, 103, 233-281.

Benktander,G. (1979). Inflation and Insurance. Appears in Kahane (1979).

Berquist,J.R. and Sherman, R.E. (1977). Loss reserve adequacy testing: a comprehensive systematic approach. PCAS, 64, 123-185.

Bibby,J. and Toutenburg,H.(1977). Prediction and improved estimation in linear models. John Wiley and Sons.

Bornhuetter, R.L. and Ferguson R.E. (1972). The actuary and IBNR. PCAS, 59, 181-195.

Brigstock,C.J. (1980). Rating the risks in a general insurance portfolio — a practical approach. IAAGIS 2, Broadbeach, November 1980, 190-206.

Brown, R.G. (1962). Smoothing, forecasting and prediction of discrete time series. Prentice-Hall, Inc.

Buchanan, R.A. and Lester,R.R. (1982). Workers' compensation ratemaking. Workers compensation underwriting seminar, Sydney, April 1982. Appears in same volume as IAAGIS, 3, 357-533.

Bühlmann, H. (1970). Mathematical methods in risk theory. Springer-Verlag.

Bühlmann,H.,Schnieper,R. and Straub,E. (1980). Claims reserves in casualty insurance based on a probabilistic model. Bulletin of the Association of Swiss Actuaries, 21-45.

Chalmers, A.F. (1976). What is this thing called science? University of Queensland Press.

Clarke, T.G. and Harland,N. (1974). A practical statistical method of estimating claims liability and claims cash flow. AB, 8, 26-37.

Craighead, D.H. (1979). Some aspects of the London reinsurance market in world-wide short-term business. JIA, 106, 227-277.

Craighead, D.H. (1980). Loss ratios on liability groups. Giro Bulletin, 29, 11-12.

Cumpston,J.R. (1976). Payments per unit of risk claims models. General Insurance Bulletin, 1, 8-11.

Cumpston,J.R. (1977). Discussion of Taylor and Matthews (1977). TIAA, 279-282.

Cumpston,J.R. (1979). Compulsory third party superimposed inflation. Unpublished.

Cumpston,J.R. (1980). Total payment follies. IAAGIS, 2, 335-347.

Cumpston,J.R. and Mack,D.J. (1978). Superimposed inflation. Australian Insurance Institute Journal, 1 (No.5), 17-20.

de Jong,P. and Zehnwirth,B. (1980). A random coefficients approach to claims reserving. Research Paper No. 219 in the series of occasional papers published by the School of Economic and Financial Studies, Macquarie University, North Ryde, NSW, 2113, Australia.

de Jong,P. and Zehnwirth,B. (1983a). Claims reserving state space models and the Kalman filter. JIA,110,157-181.

de Jong,P. and Zehnwirth,B. (1983b). Credibility theory and the Kalman filter. Insurance: mathematics and economics, 2, 281-286.

de Vylder, F. (1978). Estimation of IBNR claims by least squares. Bulletin of the Association of Swiss Actuaries, 78.

de Vylder,F. and Goovaerts, M.J. (eds.) (1979). Proceedings of the contact group "Actuarial Sciences". Mimeograph published by Instituut voor Actuariele Wetenschappen, Katholieke Universiteit te Leuven, Dekenstraat 2, B-3000 Leuven, Belgium.

Feller,W. (1950). An introduction to probability and its applications. John Wiley and Sons, Inc.

Finger, R.J. (1976). Modelling loss reserve developments. PCAS, 63, 90-106.

Fisher, W.H. and Lange, J.T. (1973). Loss reserve testing: a report year approach. PCAS, 60, 189-207.

Gelfand,I.M. and Fomin,S.V. (1963). Calculus of variations. Prentice-Hall, Inc.

Hachemeister, C.A. (1976). Breaking down the loss reserving process. Casualty Actuarial Society Loss Reserving Symposium, Chicago,

September 1976.

Hachemeister, C.A. (1978). A structural model for the analysis of loss reserves. Bulletin d'Association Royale des Actuaires Belges, 73, 17-27.

Hachemeister, C.A. (1980). A stochastic model for loss reserving. Transactions of the 21st International Congress of Actuaries, 1, 185-194.

Hachemeister,C.A. and Stanard, J.N. (1975). IBNR claims count estimation with static lag functions. Paper presented to the 12th Astin Colloquium, Portimao, Portugal; 1975.

Harnek, R.F. (1966). Formula loss reserves. Insurance Accounting and Statistical Association Proceedings.

Harrison, P.J. and Stevens, C.F. (1976). Bayesian forecasting. Journal of the Royal Statistical Society, Series B, 38, 205-247.

Homewood,C.J. (1968). Verification of technical reserves with particular reference to motor insurance. report by the Working Party on the verification of technical reserves, Insurance Committee, OECD, AS(68),1.

Huber, P.J. (1977). Robust statistical procedures. Society of Industrial and Applied Mathematics.

Johnson, R.L. (1980). A generalized statement of the claims runoff process. IAAGIS 2, 240-262.

Kahane, Y. (1979) (ed.) New frontiers in insurance: theory and practice. Erhard Center for Higher Studies and Research in Insurance, The Graduate School of Management, Tel Aviv University, Israel.

Kalman, R.E. (1960). A new approach to linear filtering and prediction problems. Journal of Basic Engineering, 82, 340-345.

Kemeny,J.G. and Snell,J.L. (1960). Finite Markov chains. D.Van Nostrand Company Inc.

Kimber, D.J. (1981). Presidential Address. TIAA, 479-512.

Kramreiter, H. and Straub,E. (1973). On the calculation of IBNR reserves II. Mitteilungen der Vereinigung Schweizerischer Versicherungsmathematiker, 73, 177-190.

Kremer,E. (1982). IBNR-claims and the two-way model of ANOVA. Scandinavian Actuarial Journal, 47-55.

Kuhn, T.S. (1970). The structure of scientific revolutions. University of Chicago Press.

Lemaire,J. (1982). Claim provisions in liability insurance. Journal of forecasting, 1, 303-318.

Linnemann,P. (1980). A multiplicative model of loss reserves: a stochastic process approach. University of Copenhagen, Laboratory of Actuarial Mathematics, Working Paper No. 32.

Linnemann,P. (1982). A multiplicative model of loss reserves: a stochastic process approach. Theory. A paper presented to the 16th Astin Colloquium, Liege, Belgium, September 1982.

Lundberg,F. (1909). Über die Theorie de Rückversicherung. Transactions of the 6-th International Congress of Actuaries, 1, 877-948.

Matthews,T.J. (1979). Discussion of Sawkins (1979).

Matthews,T.J. (1980). Some recent international developments of an actuarial nature in general insurance. IAAGIS 2, 371-408.

McLone,R.R. (1976). Mathematical modelling — the art of applying mathematics. Appears in Andrews and McLone (1976).

Mosteller,F. and Tukey,J.W. (1977). Data analysis and regression. Addison-Wesley Publishing Company.

Pollard,J.H. (1983). Outstanding claims provisions: a distribution-free statistical approach. JIA,109, 417-433. Also appears in IAAGIS, 3, 88-110.

Reid,D.H. (1978). Claim reserves in general insurance. JIA, 105, 211-296.

Reid,D.H. (1981). A method of estimating outstanding claims in motor insurance with applications to experience rating. Colloque: Les mathematiques en Sciences Actuarielles — 1981. Institut des Hautes Etudes de Belgique, Brussels, Belgium, 275-289.

Ryder,J.M. (1976). Subjectivism — a reply in defence of classical actuarial methods. JIA, 103, 59-91.

Sawkins,R.W. (1975). Some problems of long-term claims in general insurance. Transactions of the Institute of Actuaries of Australia and New Zealand, 336-387.

Sawkins, R.W. (1979). Methods of analysing claim payments in general insurance. TIAA, 435-519.

Seal, H.L. (1969). Stochastic theory of a risk business. John Wiley and Sons, Inc.

Seal,H.L. (1977). Approximations to risk theory's $F(x,t)$ by means of the gamma distribution. AB,9,211-218.

Seber, G.A.F. (1977). Linear regression analysis. John Wiley and Sons, Inc.

Skurnick,D. (1973). A survey of loss reserving methods. PCAS, 60, 16-62.

Taylor,G.C. (1977a).Separation of inflation and other effects from the distribution of non-life insurance claim delays. AB,9,217-230.

Taylor,G.C. (1977b). Some practical variations of the separation method. General Insurance Bulletin, 11, 9-16.

Taylor,G.C. (1979). Statistical testing of a non-life insurance model. Appears in de Vylder and Goovaerts (1979), 37-64.

Taylor,G.C. (1980). A Reduced Reid method of estimation of outstanding claims. IAAGIS, 2, 263-334.

Taylor,G.C. (1981a). A comparison of methods of estimation of third party motor outstanding claims. Colloque: Les mathematiques en Sciences Actuarielles — 1981. Institut des Hautes Etudes de Belgique, Brussels, Belgium, 291-320.

Taylor,G.C. (1981b). Speed of finalization and claims runoff analysis. AB, 12, 81-100.

Taylor,G.C. (1982a). Application of actuarial techniques in non-life insurance: establishment of provisions for outstanding claims. In Anderssen and de Hoog(1982). Proceedings of a seminar organised by the Division of Mathematics and Statistics, CSIRO and Pure and Applied Mathematics, The Faculties, Australian National University, Canberra, 3 December 1980.

Taylor,G.C. (1982b). Estimation of outstanding reinsurance recoveries on the basis of incomplete information. IME, 1, 3-11. Invited paper presented to a one-day seminar at the H.C.Oersted Institute, University of Copenhagen, Denmark, May 1981.

Taylor,G.C. (1983). An invariance principle for the analysis of non-life insurance claims. JIA,110,205-242.

Taylor,G.C. and Ashe,F.R. (1983). Second moments of estimates of outstanding claims. Journal of Econometrics, 23, 37-61. Paper presented to the 16th Astin Colloquium, Liege, Belgium, September 1982.

Taylor,G.C. and Matthews,T.J. (1977). Experimentation with the estimation of the provision for outstanding claims in non-life insurance. TIAA, 178-254.

Truckle,W.W. (1978). Estimating claims reserves in general insurance. GIRO Bulletin, 20, 3-17.

van Eeghen,J. (1981). Loss reserving methods. Volume No.1 in the series Surveys of actuarial studies, published by Nationale-Nederlanden N.V.

Verbeek,H.G. (1972). An approach to the analysis of claims experience in motor liability excess of loss reinsurance. AB, 6, 195-202.

Zehnwirth,B. (1981). Taylor's see-saw approach to claims reserving: a criticism. Insurance: mathematics and economics, 1, 99-103.

Zehnwirth,B. (1983a). A generalization of the Kalman filter based on either Gauss-Markov or linear Bayes theories. (forthcoming in Journal of the American Statistical Association).

Zehnwirth,B. (1983b). A connection between Gauss-Markov theory and linear Bayesian theory with applications to the latter. Research paper No. 244 in the series of occasional papers published by the School of Economic and Financial Studies, Macquarie University, North Ryde, NSW, 2113, Australia.

AUTHOR INDEX

SUBJECT INDEX